THE STORY OF THE 5TH BATTALION THE EAST YORKSHIRE REGIMENT, T.A.

L. M. Garwood, M.B.E.

Highgate of Beverley

Highgate Publications (Beverley) Limited
2002

Dedicated to
Major Thomas L. Ward, M.B.E., T.D.,
one of the first Officers of
The 5th Battalion, The East Yorkshire Regiment, T.A.,
who persuaded the author to write this story
and to
Lieut.-Colonel J. W. D. Forsyth, *p.s.c. East Yorkshire Regiment*
and
Prince of Wales's Own Regiment of Yorkshire,
a life-long friend
who first interested the author in the Regiment
and introduced him to many of the Officers.

Acknowledgements

Imperial War Museum, Information and Research Sevice (Janice I. Mullin, Mr. Christopher Hunt, Mr. David Parry, Dawn Baker) Lambeth Road, London, SE1 6HZ.
The author would like to acknowledge the courtesy and help given by Lieut.-Colonel (Retd) T. C. E. Vines of The Prince of Wales' Own Regiment of Yorkshire Museum, 3 Tower Street, York, YO1 1SB, for allowing access to the records of the East Yorkshire Regiment and permission to reproduce plates and maps;
Mr. Nigel de Lee, M.A. M.Phil., Department of War Studies, Royal Military College, Sandhurst, Camberley, GU15 4PQ.

British Library Cataloguing in Publication Data.
A catalogue record for this book is available from the British Library.

ISBN 1 902645 31 6

Published by

Highgate of Beverley

Highgate Publications (Beverley) Limited
4 Newbegin, Beverley, HU17 8EG. Telephone (01482) 886017

Printed by Highgate Print Limited
4 Newbegin, Beverley, HU17 8EG. Telephone (01482) 886017

THE REGIMENTAL BADGE

FOREWORD

The old county regiments of the line used to be the backbone of the British Army, renowned for their steadiness and reliability. This history gives an account of one battalion of one of these regiments. But it was a Territorial battalion which had an independent existence for only seven years, representing two other British military traditions, the voluntary principle, and resort to improvisation in times of emergency. The battalion was raised in 1939, and went to war in 1940, only partially trained. After escaping from the disaster on the Continent via Dunkirk, it went on to fight in the Western Desert, North Africa, Sicily, and North-west Europe. In these theatres it fought many hard actions and won many battle honours.

Much military history concerns 'the movement of large arrows on small maps'. This work does provide a general strategic background, but focuses on what was happening at the point of the arrow, in contact with the enemy. This makes it clear that it is the skills and qualities of the soldiers in battalions that win fights, and also that they can function decisively only in the context of action in cooperation with other units within the brigade and division.

This is the history of part of a regiment, but it is not a regimental history of the old-fashioned type. Triumphs are recorded and celebrated. But errors and bad behaviour and their unfortunate consequences are also mentioned, described and discussed. In order to be really useful and instructive military history needs to be honest in this way. This is a most useful work.

Nigel de Lee

INTRODUCTION

History continues, is never ending, and, since the life of the 5th Battalion, East Yorkshire Regiment, came to an end in 1947, this must be recorded as the story of a band of young men, from Hull and East Yorkshire, mostly in their late teens and early twenties, who, when, on the 1st April, 1939, Great Britain was faced with the likelihood of war and all Territorial units were duplicated, answered a call to enlist in the 5th Battalion, the East Yorkshire Regiment which was being raised by the Lord Lieutenant of the East Riding of Yorkshire, Colonel The Lord Middleton, M.C., who would be the first Commanding Officer.

It is hardly likely that many would have known that the Regiment was raised in June 1685 by Sir William Clifton, a Nottinghamshire baronet and first Colonel, when, following the accession of King James II and the rebellion led by the Duke of Monmouth (the illegitimate son of King Charles II and Lucy Walters, claiming to be the rightful Protestant heir to the throne), a spate of new regiments was formed. Few would know that H.M. King George VI was Colonel-in-Chief of the Regiment. More likely they would have knowledge of the Regiment from their fathers and other relations who had served during the First World War. Those living in Beverley would no doubt often have seen men from the Depot at Victoria Barracks marching to church on Sundays while those in Hull would have seen parades of the 4th Battalion T.A. in which older friends had served or were serving. They numbered around 450 and were joined by some 50 Officers, Warrant Officers and Non-Commissioned Officers from the Regular Army, Regular Army Reserve and the 4th Battalion T.A. who set to work on the 'recruits'.

The newly commissioned officers had no previous military experience and had to be given basic training in drill, marching, company and platoon formations, small arms and other weapons. Drill was conducted by the R.S.M., and other instruction by Warrant Officers and senior N.C.Os. There was rapid promotion of the new recruits to the ranks of N.C.Os. who had to be given training on 'Drill Nights' at week-ends and the summer training camp.

Although only partly trained, within a few months of the outbreak of war the Battalion embarked for Northern France, fought its way back to the French coast, experienced considerable hardship with a shortage of food and long days and nights of marching, until reaching Dunkirk, where, after being subjected to horrendous shelling and bombing, they embarked for England.

After a period of reorganisation, re-equipment and training, the Battalion sailed for the Middle East to begin a series of campaigns in Egypt, North Africa, Sicily, and North-West Europe: as hardened and experienced, officers and men they became soldiers who would bring renown to their Regiment.

When the war ended they were credited with gaining more Battle

Honours for the Regiment than any other battalion. They returned to their civilian employment. Did they suffer trauma as did those engaged in battle in the last part of the century? There was little sign of it. Were they subjected to a more bloody war? Many had been engaged in hand-to-hand fighting and 'gone in' with the bayonet. If there was shock they contained it. There were no counsellors to whom they could relate their tales and seek comfort!

General Montgomery decorates Pte. J. Bailey, 5th East Yorkshire, with the Military Medal, near Taormina, in Sicily.

Guarding against Ememy Raids on Messina.
The Bren gunner of the 5th East Yorkshires looks across the Strait of Messina to enemy-held territory on the Italian mainland.

CHAPTER I

BETWEEN THE WARS

THE TERRITORIAL ARMY BATTALIONS OF THE EAST YORKSHIRE REGIMENT (THE DUKE OF YORK'S OWN)

When at 1100 hours on the 11th November, 1918 peace was heralded, the Territorial Force Battalions of the East Yorkshire Regiment were widespread.

The 1st/4th, virtually wiped out at the Battle of the Aisne (27th May – 6th June, 1918), were, on the 15th July, 1918, reduced to a cadre strength of 7 officers and 34 other ranks, and collected at Cucq in France. On the 1st November orders were received to proceed with demobilisation. The other ranks were sent to 'F' Infantry Base Dept at Cucq and the Battalion was demobilised on the 6th November, 1918. The next day the officers were posted to other units. This brought to an end a Battalion formed on the 1st April, 1908, from the 1st Volunteer Battalion, The East Yorkshire Rifle Volunteers, which had been raised on the 21st May, 1859.

The 2nd/4th, formed in September, 1914, returned from Bermuda in 1919 for demobilisation after nearly three years of garrison duty in that country and was eventually disbanded in 1921.

The 3rd/4th Battalion had remained in England as a training unit in Bedlington and other places in Northumbria and Catterick, North Yorkshire, moving to Hornsea in East Yorkshire in July, 1917, where they remained until the Armistice, and then at a strength of 1,800 moved to Dalton Holme Camp, near Beverley to be gradually disbanded in April, 1919.

The 5th (Cyclist) Battalion, formed on the 1st April, 1908, spent the winter of 1914-1915 at Louth in Lincolnshire, patrolling large sections of the coast. In May, 1915, the Battalion was transferred to the East Yorkshire Coast with Headquarters at Withernsea, and subsequently Roos, to defend an area from Spurn Head to Bridlington. The Battalion was demobilised in early 1919.

The Peace Conference opened on the 1st January, 1919, at Versailles, and in June, 1919, the Peace Treaty with Germany was signed. The Allies having been victorious in 'the war to ends wars', governments, faced with the dire economic consequences of the war, set about reducing the cost of the armed forces. As there seemed no need for strong military forces, the strength of the Regular Army was reduced, and towards the end of 1919 the Territorial Force was disbanded.

But Winston Churchill, the Secretary of State for War, prevailed on the government to reconstitute a Territorial Force as the basis of a part-time organisation through which the British Army could expand in the event of war, rather than in the way that Lord Kitchener had proceeded in 1914 with the introduction of new armies of volunteers. The new force was to be known as the Territorial Army and was to come into being on the 1st February, 1920. On the 30th January, 1920, it was announced by the Secretary of State that recruiting would start at once.

The new terms of engagement were four years on the active list followed by one year on the Territorial Army Reserve, but, whereas the Territorial Force provided for service only on Home Defence, with the option of overseas service in the event of war, the new terms required an obligation for overseas service in the event of general mobilisation. Recruits were required to attend a minimum of forty drills during the first year of service, with twenty drills per annum thereafter, and attendance at the Annual Training Camp which lasted fifteen days. An annual bounty of £1.50 was paid to each soldier.

In the aftermath of war there was a reluctance to join the armed forces. Those who had seen war service were tired of war. They now wished to settle down in their homes and take up civilian employment. Both the Regular Army and the Territorial Army found difficulty in recruiting. Nevertheless, there were some who had valued the camaraderie of service life and felt a duty to rally round their old regiments.

The fourteen pre-1914 divisions were reconstituted as were Territorial Battalions forming part of the regiments of the Regular Army. The 4th Battalion, The East Yorkshire Regiment was re-formed and established its Headquarters at Londesborough Barracks in Hull, the site for which was obtained in 1863 from funds raised in 1863 by Lieut.-Colonel J. W. Pease, commanding the 1st (Consolidated) Battalion, The East Yorkshire Rifle Volunteers, and a committee.

The 5th (Cyclist) Battalion, having been demobilised in 1919, was disbanded in 1920, when all cyclist battalions were abolished, there being no place for them in the reconstituted Territorial Army.

The 50th (Northumbrian) Division, formed in 1908, was reconstituted as one of the fourteen Territorial Divisions formed at that time, with Headquarters at Newcastle, moving to Catterick Camp in 1921 and to Darlington in 1930. Major-General Sir Percival Wilkinson was appointed General Officer Commanding. The Division was made up of three brigades: the 149th (Northumberland) Infantry Brigade, the 150th (York and Durham) Infantry Brigade and the 151st (Durham) Infantry Brigade.

Headquarters of the 150th Brigade was established at Malton. It consisted of the 4th Battalion, The East Yorkshire Regiment, T.A., the 4th and 5th Battalions The Green Howards, T.A., and the 5th Battalion, Durham Light Infantry, T.A.

Colonel Arthur Easton, T.D., was appointed to command the 4th Battalion, The East Yorkshire Regiment, T.A., the effective date being the 15th February, 1920. He accepted the appointment on the understanding that it would be for only one year during which he would reconstruct the Battalion. He was succeeded on the 15th February, 1920, by the 2nd in command and O.C., H.Q. Company, Major Thomas J. Morrill, T.D., who had gone to France as a Company Commander in April, 1915, where he was wounded and sent home. He then became Adjutant and subsequently 2nd in command of the 2nd/4th Battalion and again went to France in 1917, where he was severely wounded and made a prisoner of war. On repatriation in late 1918 he became 2nd in command of the 2nd/4th Battalion, and in 1919 and 1920 served as 2nd in command of the 3rd (Special Reserve) Battalion and the 1st Battalion. In March 1920 his term of service cme to an end.

By the 11th February, 1921, the strength of the Battalion was 18 officers and 401 other ranks. The establishment was set at 636 all ranks. The Battalion was the largest in the 150th (York and Durham) Infantry Brigade.

At this time the officers were:

C.O. Colonel Arthur Easton, T.D.
2nd i/c and O.C., H.Q. Coy, Major T. J. Morrill, T.D.

O.C. 'A' Company	Major B. R. Sharp, M.C.	O.C. 'B' Company	Captain H. E. Jackson
	Captain H. Dales		2nd Lieut. A. E. Leach
O.C. 'C' Company	Captain M. Hurtley	O.C. 'D' Company	Captain T. S. Parker
	Lieut. B. V. Hildyard		Captain A. Good
	Lieut. W. M. Anderson		Lt. L. J. Chapman
Adjutant	Captain O. Philip	Assistant Adjutant	2nd Lieut. G. E. Sharp
Quartermaster	Captain C. E. Dromey	Transport Officer	Lieut. T. R. Buffey
Signalling Officer	Lieut. E. H. Hilken	O. i/c M.G. Platoon	2nd Lieut. E. C. Sharp

In 1919 the government had imposed a limit on defence expenditure on the assumption that there would be no war for ten years – 'The Ten Year Rule'. This policy gave control of expenditure to the Treasury and in consequence most of the money available went to the Royal Navy and the Royal Air Force. In consequence funding for the Army was restricted. There was no money to pay for new equipment: uniforms, equipment and weapons were provided from stocks left over from the First World War. The Territorial Army shared in this low funding.

In 1926, the year of the General Strike, the fifteen-day annual training camp was cancelled owing to the economic situation of the country and was not reintroduced until the early 1930s. During these years training was largely confined to drill, instruction in the use of weapons and visits at the weekends to the ranges for rifle practice, while in midweek use was made of the miniature rifle range. In the mid-1920s 'The Ten Year Rule' was extended annually. But in 1932, when the Chiefs of Staff requested that it be abandoned, the government agreed.

Then on the 30th January, 1933, Adolf Hitler took office as Chancellor of Germany and on the death of Field Marshal Paul von Hindenburg in July, 1934, became President while retaining the office of Chancellor. He embarked on an expansion and modernisation of the small army allowed under the Treaty of Versailles, 1922. This caused some anxiety to the British government.

In November, 1933, the government set up the Defence Requirements Committee composed of the Chiefs of Staff and representative of the Treasury and Foreign Office to report on the deficiencies of the three services and to draw up a programme to redress them. As a result the Air Defence of Great Britain was in 1936 entrusted to the Territorial Army, which was to benefit from increased funding.

In September, 1938, Herr Hitler laid territorial claims to the Sudetenland, part of Czechoslavakia. War with Germany seemed imminent, but the crisis passed when on Friday, 29th September, the British Prime Minister, Mr. Neville Chamberlain, together with M. Daladier of France and Senor Mussolini, the Italian Duce, visited Hitler at Munich and reached agreement on the transfer of the Sudetenland to Germany. Mr. Chamberlain returned to England with a promise of 'peace in our time,'

The Czech crisis aroused the people of Great Britain. There was a surge in recruiting. The British government resolved that steps must be taken to strengthen the armed forces of the nation with new and modern equipment, reorganisation, and an increase in personnel. The Prime Minister ordered Mr. Leslie Hore-Belisha, who had been made Secretary of State for War in 1937, to review the army and make the necessary changes in order to modernise and strengthen it.

At the end of 1938 a large number of Territorial Army infantry battalions were compulsorily converted into anti-aircraft units of the Royal Regiment of Artillery, necessitating the reduction of Territorial Army infantry brigades from four to three battalions. The reorganisation brought about the loss of one Territorial Army Division and several Territorial Army Infantry Brigades. Of the remaining thirteen, one became armoured, three motorised and nine remained as infantry brigades.

The 50th (Northumberland) Division was to be a 'Motorised' Division of two brigades, with its own transport for dismounted personnel to act in close support of armoured forces. With the 50th Division being reduced to two brigades, the 149th (Northumberland) Infantry Brigade was disbanded, resulting in the four battalions of the Royal Northumberland Fusiliers being allotted new roles. The 4th Battalion became a motor-cycle reconnaissance battalion of the divisional troops of the 50th (Northumbrian) Motorised Division; the 5th Battalion was reorganised and became the 5th Royal Northumberland Fusiliers (53rd Searchlight

Regiment); the 6th Battalion was converted to an armoured unit and became the 43rd (Northumberland) Battalion, The Royal Tank Regiment; the 7th Battalion retained its name but became a machine-gun battalion. The 5th Durham Light Infantry was transferred from the 150th Brigade to the 151st Infantry Brigade, which lost two battalions to anti-aircraft duties with the Royal Regiment of Artillery. Thus the 150th Brigade consisted of the 4th East Yorkshire Regiment and the 4th and 5th Green Howards.

Then in March, 1939, the Secretary of State for War, Mr. Leslie Hore-Belisha, authorised the doubling of the Territorial Army from 13 to 26 divisions. The 50th Division was duplicated by the 23rd Division and in consequence the 50th Division was renamed the 50th (1st Northumbrian) Motorised Division; the 23rd becoming the 23rd (2nd Northumbrian) Motorised Division.

The units of the Territorial Army were to be duplicated as soon as the original unit reached established strength. The 6th and 7th Battalions, The Green Howards were formed, duplicating the 4th and 5th, the 5th East Yorkshire Regiment duplicating the 4th. They formed a new infantry brigade, the 69th Infantry Brigade, which together with the 70th Brigade comprised the 23rd Division.

Within a few weeks it was announced that from July all men aged 20 would be conscripted for six months training with the Regular Army followed by three and a half years with the Territorial Army. They were given the ancient name *Militiamen,* a term from the Anglo-Saxon *fyrd*, to which all freemen were compulsorily recruited for short-term local service in time of war, but this time they were the first to be recruited for service in peacetime.

CHAPTER II

FORMATION, MOBILISATION, HOME DEFENCE DUTIES

With the announcement of the doubling of the size of the Territorial Army men came forward to enlist and potential officers submitted their names for consideration to be commissioned. Within a matter of weeks the 4th Battalion had been brought up to strength and the surplus numbers were available for a duplicate battalion. On the 1st April, 1939, Colonel The Lord Middleton, M.C., T.D., was commissioned to raise the 5th Battalion, The East Yorkshire Regiment, T.A., and early in June the Battalion came into being. Headquarters of the Battalion was established in East Hull with Companies placed in various parts of the East Riding The 2nd in command was Major (Brevet Lieutenant-Colonel) Curtis, ex-Indian Army, the Quartermaster, Lieutenant J. W. Scott. The first five officers to be commissioned on the 8th July were 2nd Lieutenants T. L. Ward, J. Fillingham, F. Durrant, A. Collingwood and G. Taylor.

The Battalion began its annual training camp at Halton, Lancs, on the 25th August, where wet and dull weather was experienced. Called back from camp, detachments were sent out to Catfoss, Paull Battery, Spurn and Kilnsea. General Mobilisation began on the 3rd September, with accommodation in East Hull.

Corps and divisions were formed, the Battalion being placed as below:

23rd (2nd Northumbrian) Division

Major-General A. E. Herbert, G.O.C.

69th Brigade – Brigadier The Viscount Downe
5th Battalion The East Yorkshire Regiment
6th and 7th Battalions The Green Howards

70th Brigade – Brigadier Philip Kirkup, T.A.
10th and 11th Battalions The Durham Light Infantry
12th Battalion The Durham Light Infantry renamed The 1st Battalion The Tyneside Scottish, The Black Watch

Divisional Troops

Royal Engineers,
233rd and 50th Field Companies; 508th Field Park Company

Infantry
8th Battalion The Royal Northumberland Fusiliers (motor cycle)
9th Battalion The Royal Northumberland Fusiliers (machine-gun)

In calling the Territorial Army to the Colours, His Majesty The King said:

'In all its long and glorious history, the British Army has never been called upon to take the field for a cause more just than that which is ours today. It has never entered on a campaign of which the issues were graver or more vital to the future of our race, and indeed to all civilisation.

I know well that you realise what is at stake and that, in the struggle which lies ahead, every man in my Armies will play his part with gallantry and devotion. It is my earnest prayer that God will have you in is His keeping and grant success to your arms.'

Within weeks the Battalion was brought up to strength with NCOs and men from the Regular and Territorial Army Reserve, and trained men from the Militia. With such a mix the War Office decided, to the grief of all Territorials, that the distinguishing 'T' was to be abolished from their uniform on the 27th September.

The first duties allotted were the guarding of strategic points in Hull and the East Riding, the training of Militia drafts from the Depot and newly enlisted volunteers.

When the 4th Battalion moved out of Londesborough barracks on the 23rd October, the 5th Battalion moved in. Although considerably under strength, the numbers were reduced at the end of November, when 100 men were sent to complete the establishment of the 4th Battalion at Stow-on-the-Wold in the Cotswolds. Limited training was carried out, the Battalion being short of equipment. Colonel William Henton Carver, M.P. for Howdenshire, who had taken a leading part in raising the Battalion, paid the Battalion a visit as did Brigadier The Lord Downe, commanding the 69th Infantry Brigade, and Major-General W. N. Herbert, G.O.C., 23rd Northern Division.

Militiamen arrived from the 15th Infantry Training Centre at Beverley, and there were changes in the detachments. Gradually, other troops from the 6th Home Service Battalion took over and by the middle of January the Battalion had reached a sufficient strength for overseas service, although not fully trained and equipped.

On the 1st February, 1940, all the detachments and companies assembled, at Bridlington. With them were the 6th Green Howards (from Middlesbrough) under Lieutenant Colonel M.R. Steel, and the 7th Battalion, the Green Howards, (from Bridlington) under Lieutenant Colonel Sir Charles F. Richmond-Brown, Bart. Shortly after arriving, Colonel The Lord Middleton relinquished command on being appointed to command the 6th Battalion, his place being taken by Lieutenant-Colonel D. J. Keating, M.C., from the 2nd Battalion in the B.E.F. where he had been 2nd-in-command

The Battalion was now able to start intensive training as a unit, hitherto not possible owing to its being split up in detachments. A party of two officers and six N.C.O.s were sent to the 2nd Battalion in the B.E.F. to gain experience, and large drafts arrived to bring the unit up to strength, including seven Regular N.C.O.s from the 1st Battalion in India.

Rumours of a move overseas became current in the unit towards the end of March, and those not fit for active service were posted elsewhere. The rest were given vaccinations and inoculations, the usual preliminary for overseas service, and embarkation leave was granted.

On the 6th April the Battalion's transport left for Southampton, and on the 23rd the Battalion, up to strength but poorly equipped, left by train for the port of embarkation. After embarking that day, Le Havre was reached the following morning, where they entrained for Yvetot in Normandy, south-west of the port.

The 23rd (2nd Northumbrian) Division was one of three Divisions (12th (Eastern) and 46th (North Midland and West Riding) sent to supply working parties on aerodrome construction and other pioneer work owing to the shortage of labour, it being intended that it should return to England after three months, to complete training. It was an incomplete division: there were no supporting arms, such as artillery; carriers; mortars; and signal equipment was practically non-existent. Many of the men had hardly fired a rifle and none had been given training with Bren guns or anti-tank rifles. There was only one Bren gun per platoon, when there should have been three, and one anti-tank rifle per Company, instead of three! There was no issue of revolvers, binocular or compasses to officers, but some had their own. They had not so much as been taught section drill at home; they had been wholly employed in guard duties.

*The Commander-in-Chief, Lord Gort, was horrified, but even more so with the 42nd (East Lancashire) Division. In a letter to General Ironside, the Chief of the Imperial General Staff, he wrote, 'I never believed it would be possible to see such a sight in the British Army. The men had no knives or forks and apparently lacked mugs. They were eating their meat with their fingers and placing it on the corrugated iron table tops.'

On another occasion Lord Gort, came upon men of General Thorne's 48th (Midland) Division at a dump. He went over and spoke to a Captain who obviously did not know who he was, and asked, 'How do you recognise the C-in-C's car?' He did not know, and, having expressed surprise, Lord Gort said, 'By the way, who is the C-in-C?' He said he did not know. As Lord Gort went away, the Captain said to Gort's personal assistant, Captain The Earl of Munster: 'Who is that major?'

On the 29th April the unit entrained at Yvetot for Bapaume, which was reached the following day, and marched to the small town of Grevillers, west of Bapaume, to a camp prepared for it by an advance party under Major C. C. Rice. It was to work on the construction of an airfield nearby. At 0430 hours on the 10th May, German aircraft swept over Arras and dropped bombs in the area of British G.H.Q. and neighbouring airfields at Doullens and Abbeville. The area around Grevillers was also bombed. It was fortunate that one of the first things done by the 5th Battalion on arriving was to dig slit trenches. They had no casualties but a neighbouring unit was not so lucky There were air raid warnings throughout the day but construction work on the airfield continued.

At dawn the Germans invaded Holland and Belgium in violation of the agreement to respect the neutrality of those countries. War in North-West Europe had begun, the Allied forces moving into Belgium. The 'phoney'

---

*J. R. Colville, *Man of Honour*.

war had in fact ended on the 9th April when German forces simultaneously attacked Norway and Denmark, the latter occupied in a single day.

On the 12th May a French 'plane crashed on the site at Grevillers where the 5th Battalion was still working on airfield construction. The work continued until the 15th May, when at 1630 hours orders were received to move by transport at 0700 hours next day. The Battalion packed up and waited, but it was not until 1130 hours that transport arrived; then it was split up into companies which were sent to various small places in the Bethune area in a defence role. Sgt. H. Nicholson and six men had been placed on guard at the aerodrome, but when the Battalion moved off they were overlooked. Four days later an officer of the Royal Engineers came upon them and ordered them to leave. They marched fifteen miles, seeing only a few sappers demolishing bridges. Eventually they rejoined the Battalion. An hour or two after they were ordered to move, the aerodrome was overrun.

On Sunday, 12th May, enemy forces advanced through the Ardennes and by night all the outposts of the French Ninth Army (General A. G. Corap) retired to the west of the Meuse. That night advanced parties of German troops crossed the Meuse in rubber dinghies and by the 13th had formed small bridgeheads on the western bank near Sedan and Dinant.

On the 14th May a German thrust with at least two armoured divisions developed on the French Ninth Army Sector. The next day German tanks swept in a continuous stream across pontoon bridges over the River Meuse, driving a gap between the B.E.F. and French First Army to the north of Namur, and the French Ninth and Second Armies to the south; thus Arras and the right flank of the B.E.F. was threatened.

This placed the French First Army, to the right of the B.E.F., in severe trouble; it lost ground and fell back On the 16th May the French General, Billotte, responsible for co-ordination of the Belgian, French and B.E.F. in the Northern sector, ordered a retreat from the Dyle to the Escaut.

By the 17th May the gap had become a corridor which ten armoured divisions had broken through on a front of some twenty miles south of the Foret de Mormal, their advanced guards of fast tanks and motor-cycles driving westward right across France, over the Meuse, across the Oise, along the Somme, straight for Abbeville and the coast. The way was now open for the Germans to cut the Allied force in half; the British Lines of Communication which ran south-westerly through Amiens, to Cherbourg, Brest and further south would be broken through and destroyed.

The British now had to extend their line and form a force to defend Arras. French G.Q.G. had placed Arras in the French zone, but, as they sent no troops for its defence, G.H.Q. at Arras organised a garrison under command of Lieut.-Colonel F. A. V. Copland-Griffiths, Welsh Guards, to provide the defence. The three divisions working on construction work and pioneer work in the rearward areas, the 12th, 23rd and 46th

Divisions, although ill-equipped and untrained, were brought forward and employed in a combatant role: the 12th Division to concentrate in the neighbourhood of Amiens; the 23rd Division (on an order from General George, Commander of the French Front of the north-east) to move to the Canal du Nord; and the 46th to move to Seclin. All administrative troops to be withdrawn towards the North.

At 0830 hours on the 17th May, the 23rd Division took up positions on the Canal du Nord from Ruyaulcourt (10 miles north of Peronne) to Arleux (6 miles south of Douai), a front of seventeen miles, divided into two sectors on each side of the Arras-Cambrai Road.

The 69th Brigade was given the sector north of the road with its left in touch with the French First Army at Arleux; the 70th Brigade to their right (with its right unprotected) at Ruyaulcourt, half-way between Douai and Peronne. The 5th East Yorkshires marched that day to Palluel on the Canal du Nord some 20 miles east of Arras, to take up a defensive position on the canal facing south-east. The Division was told it must live on half rations and what they could obtain from the country; in fact they received no further issue of supplies for fifteen days.

The 12th Division was covering Albert, Doullens, Amiens and Abbeville. These two Territorial divisions were alone in holding off any German armies from their course towards the sea.

On the Saturday the 18th, the troops in the Arras area, namely the Arras garrison, the 23rd Division and the 36th Brigade (Brigadier G. R. P. Roupell) from the 12th Division (Major-General R. L. Petre), were sent to strengthen the 23rd Division. The 36th Brigade, with four field guns, was to cover the north-western exits from further south. These troops were grouped under the command of Major-General Petre, and given the name 'Petreforce'.

Orders were received at 1000 hours on the 18th to blow up the eight bridges over the Canal du Nord between Ruyalcourt and the River Somme which had been previously mined. This was successfully accomplished, but the destruction of the main Arras-Cambrai bridge caused the death of many civilians, who followed up the patrol as soon as it withdrew after setting off the charges.

That evening the advanced troops of the German 1st Armoured Division reached the Canal du Nord and occupied Peronne, and the next day reached the Canal du Nord in force, crossed the canal and established bridgeheads in places. The line of the canal having been outflanked at Peronne, the 23rd Division was ordered to fall back: the 69th Brigade to withdraw and take up a position facing south along the River Scarpe, running east-west through Arras. The 70th Brigade to move to the west of Arras and cover the Arras-Doullens roads as far south as Saulty.

Just after midnight on the 19th the 69th Brigade began its move; the 6th Green Howards to take up defensive positions at Saudemont, the 7th Green Howards to the woods on Vimy Ridge near Thelus. At 0100 hours the 5th East Yorkshires at Palleul were ordered to prepare to move, as an enemy Armoured Division was reported advancing towards Bapaume some 16 miles south-west of Palluel. At 0400 hours orders were received to move to a position slightly in rear of the Canal, and by 0700 hours it was in place. During the morning the area was machine-gunned by enemy planes, but there were no casualties.

A further move back was ordered to be made at 1330 hours to a place just north of Arras to take up a defensive position along the canals running east-west near La Bassée some miles further north, but after some of the troops and baggage had left, further instructions were received that the baggage and the Battalion should remain for the night at Plouvain just north of the River Scarpe.

By 0630 hours on the 20th those who had gone to Le Bassee were back at Plouvain and the Battalion, less minor details, had been brought together.

Meanwhile at Saudemont the country was open and undulating with no natural obstacles for defence and ideal for an attack by armoured vehicles, but, with no attack forthcoming, at 2030 hours the 6th Green Howards set off to march to Thelus. Just after the last company had begun to move off Lieut.-Colonel M. R. Steel, the Commanding Officer, received orders to plug a gap on the north bank of the River Scarpe at Roueux. Positions were taken up just before dawn on the 20th; 'B', 'C' and 'D' Companies in the front line, 'A' and Headquarters Companies in reserve. Two companies of the 11th Durham Light Infantry were on the left flank of the 6th Green Howards, 5th East Yorkshires in Plouvain. To the right of the 5th East Yorkshires was a company of the 7th Green Howards; the remainder of the Battalion had gone on to Thelus and were too far away to be recalled. The bridges to the front were covered by French light tanks which were withdrawn at midday.

At daylight on the 20th it was found that the Germans were on the opposite bank of the river. At 0800 hours a German mortar on the other side of the Scarpe River opened fire on the lines of 'B' Company, 5th East Yorkshires, causing fourteen casualties, including two men who died of wounds. At 0900 hours French sappers blew up several bridges in the neighbourhood. The Battalion was then ordered to fortify the place. By 1000 hours this was done. During the afternoon, it was learned that German Infantry, mixing with a crowd of refugees, pushing handcarts, prams and bicycles and riding on farm carts carrying household belongings were streaming into the town, and selecting positions on the opposite side of the river. The Battalion established posts on the river bank to prevent this. Throughout the day, German mortars harassed the Battalion but failed to inflict further casualties.

On the night of the 19th/20th the 70th Brigade moved to the west of Arras to cover the Arras-Doullens road as far south as Saulty. The infantry had been marching during the previous two days, and, being tired, Brigadier Kirkup decided to ferry as many as possible in the transport which he had accumulated. The troops marched to Neuville

Vitasse where they rested until daybreak. Transport then began ferrying advance parties of the battalions to Salty and Beaumetz les Loges on the Arras-Doullens road, other troops marching until the transport returned to pick them up *en route.* With enemy aircraft active the troops marched in open formation with wide intervals. The transport met up with a battalion headquarters and a large body of troops from the Royal Army Ordnance Corps and some Auxiliary Military Pioneer Corps, mostly unarmed.

Just as they moved off they ran into the enemy, and about the same time the marching troops were attacked by tanks of the German 8th Armoured Division. The tanks fell on Brigade Headquarters and the bulk of the brigade was overrun and lost as a fighting formation. The survivors of the three battalions and some Royal Engineers who had joined them numbered only 14 officers and 219 other ranks. With the loss of the 70th Brigade, the 23rd (Northumbrian) Division at Seclin was in a depleted condition and the remnants of that brigade were used to join with the 69th Brigade.

German armoured divisions made considerable progress during this day. Following its destruction of the 70th Brigade, Major-General Erwin Rommel's 7th Armoured Division attacked Arras all day but was prevented from entering the town. During the evening the *S.S. Totenkopf* (Death's Head) Division came up on the left of the 8th Armoured Division and further encircled Arras. The 6th Armoured Division reached Doullens; the 2nd Armoured Division, Abbeville, then Amiens; the 1st Armoured Division, Albert. The whole of the country between the Scarpe and the Somme was theirs; the British lines of communication were cut, and the way to the Channel ports open.

* * * * *

At this point it might be well to leave the story of the 5th East Yorkshires and consider the overall situation which led up to the evacuation of Allied forces from Dunkirk.

With the German armoured divisions breaking towards the coast and capturing Amiens and Abbeville, the ports at Boulogne and Calais were threatened. The French First Army to the right of the B.E.F. was falling back on Douai and Cambrai.

On the night of the 18th May, Lord Gort met with General Billotte, responsible for co-ordinating the French and British Armies. After much discussion Gort was convinced that the French could not close the gap to the south, and in consequence the right flank of the B.E.F. would be exposed as would communications to the sea. G.H.Q. had drawn up a plan for this eventuality: the establishment of a defensive perimeter around the Channel ports of Ostend, Dunkirk, Calais and Boulogne so to fight it out, but, should it be necessary, embark as many as possible of the personnel of the B.E.F., abandoning stores and equipment.

Early in the afternoon of Sunday, 19th May, Lord Gort reported by telephone to the Secretary of State for War, Mr. Anthony Eden, and explained the situation. The War Cabinet met at four o'clock and sent the Chief of the Imperial Staff, Sir Edmund Ironside, to France to convey instructions to Lord Gort; para 1 of which read:

> 'The Cabinet decided that the C.I.G.S. was to direct the C-in-C. B.E.F. to move southwards upon Amiens, attacking all enemy forces encountered, and to take station on the left of the French Army.'

On delivering this at 0800 hours on the 20th May, Ironside was told by Lord Gort and his Chief of Staff, Lieut.-General Sir Henry Pownall, of the almost impossibility of such an operation. First he would have to disengage eight divisions from the Escaut front, fight a rearguard action all the way to the Somme and at the same time attack into an area at Amiens and along the Somme already strongly held by the enemy. Nevertheless, he was prepared to launch a southward attack with the 5th and 50th Divisions, his only available reserves, and he had in fact already planned an attack the next day in the neighbourhood of Arras; but he could only do this if he could get co-operation from the French. Ironside recognised the force of Gort's argument, accepted the plan, and set off for General Billotte's Headquarters at Lens where he secured the agreement from Billotte that two French divisions would be directed on Cambrai at the same time as the British divisions advanced on Arras.

On Monday, 20th May, the seventy-three-year-old French general, Maxime Weygand, who had been Chief of Staff to Marshal Foch in the First World War, was recalled from Syria and succeeded General Gamelin in Supreme Command of the Allied Forces.

At a meeting on the 21st May at Ypres, Weygand outlined plans for an offensive designed to close the gap in the south: two divisions of the B.E.F. and two of the French First Army would disengage and strike southwards towards Bapaume and Cambrai, while French troops assembling south of the River Somme, would strike Northwards to meet them. But this entailed the B.E.F. relieving some divisions in the line to form a reserve, the Belgians withdrawing to the River Lys; the B.E.F. leaving the Escaut line to assemble on the old positions on the French frontier between Maulde and Halluin; the Belgian Army to relieve one British division, the French First Army, two. But the relief could not begin before the 23rd/24th May, and the relieved divisions would not be ready to attack until the 26th. This was in effect the plan already made by the French general Billotte and was already in process.

Billotte, on his way back from Ypres, was fatally injured in a car crash and died two days later. His successor, General Blanchard, not having been at the meeting at Ypres, knew nothing of what had been decided.

The attack ordered by the British War Cabinet began on the 21st May, shortly before Weygand arrived in Ypres. The 5th and 50th (Northumbrian) divisions, each of only two brigades, were selected as the contribution of the B.E.F. together with the 1st Army Tank Brigade:

Major-General Harold E. Franklyin was placed in overall command. As stated earlier, the French had undertaken to co-operate in attack with two divisions of the French First Army but when the time came, the French, other than their 1st Light Mechanised Division, did not put in an appearance; however, the attack went in. Major-General G. le Q. Martel, commanding the 50th (1st Northumbrian) Division, took over responsibility for the attack with such forces as were available – the 1st Army Tank Brigade, the 151st Infantry Brigade of the 50th Division, and the 13th Brigade of the 5th Division. The French 1st Light Mechanised Division co-operated.

Franklyn's first objective was to secure the line of the Rivers Scarpe and Cojeul. The enemy was stronger than had been thought and, although the line was held and extended farther westward, the enemy was increasing pressure on the right, and also working round to the outskirts of Bethune. Without French support on the left, the force would be cut off. On the 23rd May, Lord Gort gave orders to withdraw to Seclin, (South of Lille) where the force would be suitably positioned to take part in any further counter-attacks.

The same day Gort met his three Corps Commanders, who reported increasing pressure from growing enemy forces on the Escaut line, and expressed the opinion that the existing line could not be held for more than twenty-four hours. It was considered necessary to retire to the defences of the Belgian frontier constructed during the previous winter. This would seriously affect the Belgians to the left of the B.E.F. whose own left flank would be in an exposed position.

Lord Gort decided that he could no longer carry out the instructions of the French Command and his own Government, and made what was perhaps his most fateful action of the campaign. Without waiting to ask authority of General Blanchard, at 1800 hours on Saturday the 25th he cancelled the orders for a break-out and ordered the 5th and 50th Divisions to abandon preparations for the attack southwards on the 26th and move at once to the threatening gap between the left of General Alan Brooke's II Corps and the right of the Belgian army.

Gort's decision was to have a far-reaching effect. When the Belgians capitulated on the 28th May, these divisions were instrumental in enabling the gap left by the Belgians between Menin and Ypres, to be closed. Earlier on the morning of Sunday the 26th, Lord Gort informed the Secretary of State for War of his actions and later in the day, he received the following personal message from Mr. Eden:

> 'I have had information all of which goes to show that French offensive from Somme cannot be made in sufficient strength to hold any prospect of junction with your armies in the North. Should this prove to be the case you will be faced with a situation in which safety of B.E.F. will be predominant consideration. In such conditions only course open to you may be to fight your way back to west where all beaches and ports east of Gravelines will be used for embarkation. Navy would provide fleet of ships and small boats and R.A.F. would give full support. As withdrawal may have to begin very early preliminary plans should be urgently prepared. You should also consider

urgently security of Ostend and Dunkirk to which latter port Canadian Bde group is being sent night 26th/27th. Prime Minister is seeing M. Reynard tomorrow afternoon when whole situation will be clarified.'

Returning to Sunday, 19th May, when Lord Gort reported his situation to the War Office and the Cabinet sent him instructions to attack to the south, further action was taken. War Office and Admiralty representatives met to consider plans for supplying the B.E.F. through the port of Dunkirk.

The next day Vice-Admiral Sir Bertram Ramsey, Flag Officer Commanding Dover, was appointed to plan and control evacuation should it be considered necessary. Lieut.-General Sir Douglas Brownrigg, Lord Gort's Adjutant-General, was instructed to arrange as soon as possible the evacuation of all non-fighting troops, from the ports of Dunkirk, Calais and Boulogne, possibly numbering forty-five thousand. Admiral Ramsey called for deep vessel ships, and a flotilla of small ships, boats and odd craft to assemble in the channel: the small craft to carry troops from the beaches to the deep water vessels which would lie off-shore, some of the larger vessels to collect troops from the Mole at Dunkirk. The R.A.F. would give the necessary air cover. By Thursday, 23rd May, the plans were well advanced and the operation was given the name 'Dynamo.' At this time it was intended that Dunkirk would be used as a port of supply from which a bridgehead could be held by Allied forces, and on the 24th May General Blanchard gave orders to organise a perimeter round Dunkirk. Unknown to the British, the French government was discussing an approach to the Germans for an armistice. Then on the 26th, with the situation deteriorating, the War Cabinet decided to evacuate. At 1900 hours on Sunday, 26th May, the Admiralty sent out the signal:

'Operation Dynamo is to commence.'

* * * * *

On the night of the 21st May the 5th East Yorkshires at Plouvain received orders to move to Thelus when relieved by another regiment. Proceeding by foot they reached their destination and rested in nearby woods, being disturbed by continual enemy bombing and machine-gunning. There were no casualties, but many fortunate escapes. Although tired, the morale of the men remained high.

On the 22nd May a continuous line of defences, some eighty-five miles long, was organised along the south-western front, based on the line of canals from the Escaut to La Bassee, Bethune and St. Omer to the North Sea. This formed a natural anti-tank barrier to prevent the German armoured divisions from driving into the rear of the B.E.F. facing east. It was divided into sectors from the sea at Gravelines to Millonfosse, each sector having a British commander. The troops on this eighty-five mile line did not exceed 10,000.

'Polforce', which had been formed to defend St. Pol and the canal from

Aire to Pont Maudit, was placed under command of Major-General H. O. Curtis, G.O.C. 46th Division, and took over the protection of the canal-line between Aire and Carvin. To his right, Brigadier C. M. Usher, commanding one of the Lines of Communication Sub-Areas, was given command of a group of troops to be named 'Usherforce,' to take over the right bank of the River Aa from Gravelines to St. Omer. Initially this force was made up of five batteries of heavy artillery used as infantry.

The German troops who had taken Abbeville had turned North and reached the North Sea at Gravelines, east of Calais, with others at St. Omer. Boulogne was captured on the night of the 22nd/23rd May. Calais, which had been defended by troops of the King's Royal Rifle Corps (60th Foot), the Queen Victoria Rifles (a Territorial Army battalion) and the Rifle Brigade, despatched from England on the 22nd May, was invested on the 26th.

* * * * *

The 23rd (2nd Northumbrian) Division, now with only one brigade – the 69th – had its Headquarters at Seclin and was placed under direct command of G.H.Q. B.E.F. Orders were received to withdraw some seventy miles to join 'Usherforce' on the River Aa, and take part in holding off a sustained German attack.

In *The Story of the Green Howards, 1939-45* by Captain W. A. T. Synge, it is recorded that 'Advance Divisional Headquarters, accordingly, with reconnaissance parties of Brigade Staff, Commanding Officers and Adjutants, set out at once for Gravelines where they arrived safely.' This does not seem to be completely correct.

A reconnaissance party of the 69th Brigade did in fact set off for Gravelines, as did the Commanding Officer 7th Battalion Green Howards, Lieut.-Colonel Sir Charles Richmond-Brown, and his Intelligence Officer, Lieut. Rupert Alec-Smith, but not the C.Os and Adjutants of the 5th East Yorkshires and 6th Green Howards. The order was subsequently cancelled, and from this time the Brigade Commander, The Viscount Downe, the Brigade Major, A. E. Brocklehurst, the Staff Captain A/Q. Richard Elwes, the Transport Officer, Captain Scrope, together with the Commanding Officer 7th Battalion Green Howards, Sir Charles Richmond-Brown, and the Battalion Intelligence Officer, Lieut. Rupert Alec-Smith, mysteriously disappeared from the scene of battle. It was later found that they had arrived back in England on the 27th May.

We must now try to discover what led to this, but first it is necessary to acquaint oneself with the positions of the battalions on that day.

At 0030 hours on the 22nd the 5th East Yorkshires embussed from Thelus for Wattignies, immediately south of Lille, and by 0530 hours had reached their destination except for a baggage party of three vehicles and 17 men who had got lost during the move. The officers were far from pleased as one of the vehicles carried the mess equipment and one batman. At 0900 hours the baggage party from Thelus arrived; the unit was complete, except for four men and two anti-tanks rifles taken over by the 4th Battalion. The 6th Green Howards ,who had moved to Roueux on the 20th, received orders the next day to move back to Farbus and in the afternoon reassembled in Vimy woods. On the 22nd they moved back to Gondecourt and joined with the 7th Battalion who had that morning left Vimy Ridge, near Thelus.

During the 22nd May, Lieutenant-Colonel M. R. Steel, commanding the 6th Green Howards, took over command of the 69th Brigade, and command of the Battalion devolved on Major G. R. Dixon. The circumstances under which command devolved on him are not recorded. Was he told to take command by H.Q. 23rd Division, or did he do no more than take command of the two Green Howards battalions when he found that Sir Charles Richmond-Brown had left. He could not have been ordered to take over command of the Brigade by Lord Downe for, as we shall see, he, too, was nowhere to be found. Added to this, Lieut.-Colonel Keating, commanding the 5th East Yorkshire was not aware of any change.

A pertinent and interesting account of the events from the 20th to the 23rd May was given to the author by Major Thomas L. Ward, M.B.E., T.D., then a 2nd. Lieut. and Brigade Intelligence Officer. Later this account was given in a tape recording of an Oral History Review for the Imperial War Museum. In making mention of telegrams sent by him to Headquarters 23rd Division between the 20th and 23rd May, Major Ward goes on to say that during these days he was duty officer at Brigade H.Q. without a break, as he was the only officer of Brigade H.Q. available. He had neither seen nor heard from any of the others during this time, and there had been no news of them at H.Q. 23rd Division. He could not believe that he, and some thirty other ranks, including 15 survivors from the battle of Arras had been abandoned, and wondered whether the rest of the Brigade had been captured when away from the Headquarters.

The enemy was close upon him and he felt that he should not remain where he was; H.Q., 23rd Division being on the move, lines of communications were disrupted. His nearest contact in the brigade was the 5th East Yorkshires, his own Battalion, commanded by Lieut.-Colonel D. J. Keating, and he made off to find him and seek advice and possibly instructions. Colonel Keating was astonished to hear that the Brigadier and the other officers of the Brigade were missing. He tried, as Major Ward had done to get news of them but without success. Colonel Keating said he understood that the three battalions of the Brigade were to fight a rearguard action and gradually withdraw to Dunkirk. He advised Major Ward to collect his troops and move quickly in the same direction.

As mentioned earlier, Advanced H.Q. 23rd Division, together with reconnaissance parties had been ordered to move to the Gravelines – St. Omer sector in support of 'Usherforce.' The 6th and 7th Green Howards set off immediately behind them. Reports came through that the enemy were in Hazebrouck, and across their route. The 7th Battalion turned back and returned to Gondecourt in the afternoon, but the 6th Green Howards got through safely to Gravelines with the reconnaissance parties. From this time on the 5th East Yorkshires and 7th Green Howards were to act independently. Having been separated from the 7th Battalion, Lieut.-Colonel Steel resumed command of the 6th Green Howards.

The 5th East Yorkshires at Wattignies on the 22nd May did not enjoy much rest. By midnight they moved off by transport for Holque but half way there were met by the G.O.C. 23rd Division, Major-General Herbert, and sent back to Wattignies which was reached at 0500 hours on the 23rd. However, the C.O., Lieut.-Colonel Keating, was missing. He had gone back to Holque, and was unable to get to them due to a break in communications. Major C. Cameron Rice 2 i/c assumed command of the battalion. The roads at Wattignies were machine-gunned by German planes throughout the day. One troop-carrying vehicle, with its load of men, failed to return after a night's run.

Having slept in the woods, the men were much refreshed, but one officer and 61 other ranks had become separated from the Battalion. Men of the Royal Northumberland Fusiliers, who had become separated from their battalion, joined up. Lord Gort had put the B.E.F. on half rations on the 23rd May but on the 24th the supply had been so reduced that the 5th East Yorkshires had to cut theirs down to one-third.

The Defence of Arras was now over. Allied forces, engaged against Germans greatly superior in number, had imposed an invaluable delay in the enemy advance. The Battle Honour **Defence of Arras** 19th - 25th May was gained for The East Yorkshire Regiment by the 5th Battalion

The withdrawal to Dunkirk began on the 25th, the 5th East Yorkshires moving at 1100 hours to Ligny, five miles west of Lille, where it lay up in woods. A French artillery regiment in action nearby brought an attack by enemy aircraft, which bombed and machine-gunned the woods, but there were no casualties.

The next day the Battalion marched ten miles from Ligny to Steenwerck, west of Armentières, where they bivouacked for the night. From Steenwercke they marched again on the morning of the 27th May, through Poperinghe, so damaged by enemy shelling that debris from fallen houses made marching extremely difficult; added to this were refugees with hand carts, bicycles, prams and farm carts which impeded the retreating armies.

Reaching some woods north-east of the town, the Battalion halted. Having been on one third rations for some time, advantage was taken of livestock abandoned by the owners, the butcher killing and cutting up pigs found in sties, and tied up cows, to supplement the rations. In some houses abandoned meals were found lying on tables. It was later found that the Battalion had shared the woods with part of the van of a Panzer formation thrusting west from St. Omer which had made its lager in the forest. Neither knew of the presence of the others.

At 0900 hours on the 28th the Battalion set off to march to Cronwerke where it bivouacked for the night. The Germans must have been relieved when the Battalion marched away. Soon afterwards a force was sent to mop it up.

* * * * *

During the day Lord Gort received a message from the Secretary of State for War which read:

> 'Your sole task is now to evacuate to England maximum of your forces possible.'

Gort set off for Dunkirk to see the French general Koeltz whose only orders had been to form a bridgehead there. General Koeltz told him that the King of the Belgians had asked for an armistice as from midnight 27th/28th May. This was the first intimation Gort had received of the King's intention. The B.E.F. was now left with a twenty-mile open gap on the eastern front between II Corps and the sea.

Meanwhile at Dunkirk on the 26th, the day evacuation started, German bombers set the harbour oil-tanks on fire and the next day ships in the harbour were sunk by bombing and incendiaries: only small ships could get in. Whilst these were suitable for evacuating men, they could not take off arms and equipment.

* * * * *

At 0900 hours on the 29th May the 5th East Yorkshires set off for Furnes, marching along bye roads to Killem Linde. Here they met up with the 7th Green Howards. That battalion had left Gondecourt on the 25th May, having returned there following the failure to reach Gravelines, and over the next four days had moved by way of Beaucamps, Le Petit Mortier, Steenwerke, and Peselmoek, north of Poperinghe. There is no available information as to who led and commanded them.

Just as the 5th East Yorkshires had finished the mid-day meal, orders were received to march once again. Before leaving, following the receipt of instructions, kit and equipment was dumped, transport destroyed by burning and rations for the following days handed out to each individual. The Battalion then continued its journey, crossed a mined canal bridge – blown up shortly afterwards – and marched without halt 17 miles to a mile short of Furnes on the perimeter defence line, which was reached at 0130 hours on the 30th May. Here, a Staff Officer of the 23rd Division stopped them. Two companies were sent to guard two bridges, entailing a five-mile march. Arriving there it was found that the bridges were already manned. They marched back to the Battalion, having on arrival marched thirty miles in the past 24 hours.

At 0700 hours the Battalion was ordered to patrol in front of the 50th Division, which was acting as rearguard to the B.E.F, despite the Battalion's lack of training. Having destroyed equipment the previous day, they had no arms other than rifles and bayonets. At 0900 hours they reported to the 4th Battalion on the canal at Houtem, and at 1430 hours took over that battalion's position, remaining there until evening, being heavily sniped and mortared by the enemy on the far side of the canal.

At 0200 hours on the 31st May, orders were received to move. Leaving one company with the 4th Battalion, the 5th East Yorkshires set of for Adinkerke, which was reached at 0600 hours, and from there marched to Bray Dunes on the coastline. Here they were met by Major-General Herbert, who had come to give moral support in their attempt to board ships to take them back to England.

For the past five days the Royal Navy had been dumping containers of water and crates of tinned food on the beaches, and at 0900 hours, for the first time in days, the men got a good meal. On finding that embarkation from the beaches was not possible, an attempt was made to construct a pier of abandoned vehicles so that embarkation could be made in small boats. Cigarettes found in the vehicles gave some comfort. A small number of troops got away, but it was time-consuming and unsatisfactory. The Battalion then formed up in column of companies and trudged seven miles along the beaches, covered with crude oil from sunken ships. The Mole at Dunkirk was reached some four hours later. Major C. Cameron Rice, the 2 i/c, had accidentally broken his foot a few days earlier. He endured the long slog without disclosing this to anyone.

On arriving in Dunkirk it was found that heavy shelling of the beaches and port had brought evacuation to a stop, but after fighter planes of the R.A.F. arrived the Luftwaffe was driven off and evacuation was restarted. The Battalion was called forward, made its way along the broken jetty, carrying their rifles and, as a disciplined body of troops, boarded the destroyer, *H.M.S. Harvester,* and sailed in the evening for Dover. It was the first of the battalions of the East Yorkshire Regiment to get away.

At Dover the troops were handed a picnic-meal in a paper bag and given a mug of tea. Chocolate and cigarettes were handed out. Members of the Women's Voluntary Service sent telegrams to individuals home addresses telling of safe arrival. Trains were boarded irrespective of corps or regiments; as each filled up it moved out to make room for another, then left for reception stations all over the country where, after being accommodated, fed, rested and partly refitted, they were sent to unit reassembly points, the units of the 69th Brigade to Launceston in Cornwall.

The story is told that when finally the Battalion was on board, the Adjutant, Captain A. R. Collingwood, found a place in the wardroom where he could sit. The steward brought him a cup of tea, and after taking two sips he fell to the floor asleep and remained there – oblivious to the dangerously overloaded condition of the vessel and German attacks upon it – until Dover was reached. Neither he nor Major Rice had had more than three hours sleep a night for the past fortnight, and for the last four days Major Rice had been in command of the Battalion.

There must have been a number of Officers who during the campaign conducted themselves in a manner over and above the normal course of duty, but special mention was made later of the conduct of the Quartermaster, Lieut. J. W. Scott, who despite all the difficulties never failed to keep the unit supplied.

Before leaving the events of Dunkirk, mention should be made of the 6th Green Howards and the remnants of the 69th Brigade Headquarters. The 6th Green Howards, whom we left at Gravelines on the 23rd May, stayed in the area until the 29th May, fighting a number of actions and displaying great gallantry. They then pulled out, marched nine miles to Bray Dunes, and then embarked at Dunkirk at 1800 hours on the 31st May for Folkestone.

2nd Lieut. Ward (himself an officer of the 5th Battalion), following the advice given by Lieut.-Colonel Keating, moved off for Dunkirk with what was left of H.Q. 69th Brigade He tells of his journey and events on reaching there:

> 'The roads were subjected to artillery and mortar fire and enemy aircraft machine-gunned the roads. Two miles out of Dunkirk we were stopped by Military Police and ordered to destroy kit and transport. All that was left was personal arms and field service rations. Leaving N.C.O.s and men to carry out these instructions, I set off with three men for Dunkirk to report to the Town Major. As we dodged explosions and falling buildings, an officer who was just passing was blown up and lost his head. Told by the Town Major to return and bring in my men I went back with the three others, again experiencing explosions along the roadside. On reaching the party I found that a meal had been prepared. Realising the risk of marching the party together into town, I split it into two groups each under an N.C.O and set off once more for the dunes at Dunkirk. The journey was uneventful, nc enemy bombers taking part in night raids. At the dunes we dug in and had a quiet night, but at first light enemy Stukas screamed down and bombed and strafed the beaches throughout the day, with heavy casualties all round but not to my party. During the intervals, to keep up spirits and maintain morale, discussion groups were formed. There were men from Hull, Leeds, Middlesbrough, Sunderland and Newcastle: Sunderland and Newcastle each outlining the merits of their respective football teams and players, of which there were two internationals serving in the Brigade, Wilf Mannion of Middlesbrough and Stephenson of Leeds. One man had a mouth organ with which he led singing.
>
> We were on the beach for two days. Eventually the duty Naval Officer called me in and told me to prepare for embarkation in two hours. Embarkation was to be from the wooden jetty which went well out to sea; many of the wooden cross pieces were missing but with difficulty the gaps were negotiated. The *m.v. Queen of the Channel* was waiting alongside, and the party boarded, and sailed. It was first light and the Stukas had resumed their daily attacks. After an hour at sea they dropped a bomb on the stern of the vessel, the ship began to list and it seemed obvious that it would sink. A small freighter came alongside and we were able to jump in. I spent the whole of the day sitting on an oil barrel, some others were equally fortunate, but most were sprawled on the deck or wherever space could be found. The freighter put in at Dover where we disembarked and proceeded to the railway station where the Salvation Army provided a cup of tea and a bun. We were then directed to enter a waiting train which, when full to capacity, moved off to a reception station at Yeovil in Somerset, where, after being fed and rested, we left for a short period of leave, before returning to duty.'

General, The Viscount Gort, Commander-in-Chief of the B.E.F., in his despatches made a special commendation of the three divisions sent to France to carry out military labour duties, the 12th, 23rd (which included the 5th East Yorkshires) and the 46th Division. Relating that these divisions had no artillery or administrative units, only skeleton armament and transport on a much reduced scale, the Commander-in-Chief goes on to say:

> 'Troops of these three divisions fought and marched continuously for a fortnight and proved, if proof were needed, that they were composed of soldiers, who despite their inexperience and lack of equipment, could hold their own with a better found and more numerous enemy.'

The Battle Honour **Dunkirk 1940** was awarded to those units which had taken part in the defence of the perimeter, but not to those who only passed through. It was gained by the actions of the 2nd and 4th Battalions, and, although one Company of the 5th Battalion had been co-opted by the 4th Battalion, the small numbers taking part did not qualify the 5th Battalion for the honour.

The presence of all three battalions in France and Belgium gained the Battle Honour **North West Europe 1940** for the East Yorkshire Regiment which was elected to be emblazoned on the Colours.

Major Thomas L. Ward, M.B.E., T.D.

CHAPTER III

IN DEFENCE OF ENGLAND

Arriving back in England, the 69th Brigade assembled on the 2nd June at Launceston in Cornwall. Morale was high. As a Territorial Battalion with help from only a few regulars, the Battalion had proved itself in battle, and was ready for any future call for action. After a day or two, personnel departed for a brief period of leave.

On returning from leave, 2nd Lieut. Ward found that the only officer at Brigade H.Q. was The Viscount Downe, who, following a brief greeting, left the room. The next morning it was found that the Brigadier had been posted elsewhere in the rank of Major. The other Staff Officers did not report back; they had all been sent to duties elsewhere: not surprisingly when one remembers that the Brigade Staff had been back in England a week before the units for which they were responsible.

The Viscount Downe, later promoted Lieut.-Colonel, went on to become Assistant Adjutant-General West Africa Command and appointed an O.B.E., and Deputy Lieutenant of the North Riding of Yorkshire. Captain Richard Elwes, the Staff Captain A/Q, a Territorial Army officer from the Northamptonshire Yeomanry, was promoted Major and appointed Deputy Assistant Adjutant-General, Home Counties Area. He went on to the War Office on promotion to Lieut.-Colonel and appointment as A.A.G. and was appointed an O.B.E. in 1944, remaining there until the end of the war. Returning to civilian life he was appointed a King's Counsel and a Judge of the High Court of Justice (Queen's Bench Division), and a Knight Bachelor. Major Arthur Evers Brocklehurst, the Brigade Major, a Regular Army officer, went on to become a Major-General in 1957, and was appointed C.B., and D.S.O.

* * * * *

Command of the 69th Brigade at Launceston passed to Brigadier John Anderson Barstow, M.C., formerly of the Black Watch, who had been holding an appointment at the War Office.

On the 14th June, Lieut.-General Claude Auchinleck returned from the campaign in Norway and was told that he was immediately to form V Corps in Southern Command. V Corps would be formed by the 4th Division, and the 50th (Northumbrian) Division with the 48th (South Midland) to come later.

On returning from France the 50th Division concentrated in camps around Knutsford in Cheshire, moving to Dorsetshire on the 21st June to take up a defensive role along the coast, from Lyme Regis to Christchurch. Its first task was laying mines on the beaches, digging fortifications and erecting barbed wire entanglements, in readiness for a likely invasion. Alongside were civilian contractors constructing pill-boxes, machine-gun posts and other fortifications in concrete.

The 69th Brigade concentrated at Launceston in Cornwall deployed its battalions on the 22nd June: the 5th East Yorkshires, once again under command of Lieut.-Colonel Keating, to Wimborne in Dorset, the 6th Green Howards to Admiral Hinton and the 7th Green Howards to Parkstone.

Following the return of the B.E.F. to England, the 23rd (2nd Northumbrian) Division was disbanded and in early July the 69th Brigade was allotted to 50th (1st Northumbrian) Division, renamed 50th (Northumbrian) Division. This Division had been formed in 1908 as one of twelve divisions forming the Territorial Force, its first G.O.C. being Lieut.-General Baden Powell, who in the same year had formed the Boy Scouts' Association.

Early in 1939 Mr. Leslie Hore-Belisha, the Secretary of State for War, authorised the grant of badges to all divisions both Regular and Territorial to be worn on uniforms and vehicles. The badge for the 50th Division was designed by Major Freeman Attwood, G.S.O. II, at Divisional Headquarters. It was that of two red T's on a black background which if turned on its side depicts an H for Humber, representative of the Division's recruiting area.

The other brigades were:

150th Brigade
Brigadier C. W. Haydon, D. S. O., M. C.
4th Battalion, The East Yorkshire Regiment
4th and 5th Battalions, The Green Howards

151st Brigade
6th, 8th and 9th Battalions The Durham Light Infantry

The G.O.C.-in-C was Major-General Gifford le Q Martel, D.S.O., M.C. Born in 1889, was commissioned into the Royal Engineers on the 23rd July, 1909. During 1916-1918 he served in the Tank Corps. In February, 1939, he took over command from Major-General W. N. Herbert who had completed his tenure of appointment. General Martel was a former Army and Inter-Services Welter-weight boxer both before and after World War I. A keen horseman, he had two horses transported to the Cotswolds when the 50th Division moved there in early 1940.

Early in July there was a further move of the 5th East Yorkshires to the coast at Swanage in Dorset, where in the Isle of Purbeck a defensive position was taken up. The Battalion was in close communication with the Armoured Column at West Lulworth, as well as with the Royal Navy, which was interested in the defence of the Isle of Portland.

Major R. J. Springhall arrived from a Staff appointment at the War Office to take over as 2 i/c from Major C. Cameron Rice who had joined the 7th Battalion on promotion to Lieutenant-Colonel. Two days later he was called away to another Staff appointment.

The Prime Minister, Mr. Winston Churchill, visited on the 17th July and went round to inspect the defences, and witnessed a demonstration of de-bussing and attack with tanks and aircraft. Shortly after, there was a visit from H.R.H. Prince Henry, Duke of Gloucester.

Lieut.-General Auchinleck's period of command of V Corps came to an end on the 19th July, on his being appointed G.O.C-in-C, Southern Command vide Lieut.-General Alan Brooke, who became C.-in-C. Home Forces. He was succeeded on the 21st July by Lieut.-General Bernard Law Montgomery, until now a Major-General commanding the 3rd Division in Eastern Command.

The defence works having been completed by the 31st July, limited training was carried out. There were frequent air-battles, a considerable amount of bombing and many alarms which called for the Battalion to man defences. When the code word 'Cromwell' was received on the 9th September 1940 indicating that an invasion was imminent, the Battalion 'stood to'.

Towards the end of September the 50th Division was told that it had been selected as the first Territorial Division to go to North Africa,

On the 27th September the 5th East Yorkshires were relieved of coast defence duties and moved to Poole in Dorset Here extensive training began, the Corps Commander, Lieutenant-General B. L. Montgomery having said:

> 'The 5th Corps must be able, by March 1941, to fight any enemy, anywhere and at any time. Battalions must be able to move sixty or eighty miles in Mechanical Transport, march twenty five miles, and fight a battle at the end of it.'

Very soon after this Brigadier Barstow died, and was replaced by Brigadier George Watkin Eban James Erskine, formerly of the King's Royal Rifle Corps.

In mid-November 1940, the 50th Division was ordered to move to Somerset, and on the 22nd November the 5th East Yorkshires left for Midsomer Norton, a few miles from Bath and Bristol. Two days later there was a heavy air raid on Bristol, and two companies were sent to assist the civil power in clearing the roads of debris. Further aid was given on several occasions.

Italy had entered the war on the 10th June 1940 as an ally of Germany, and the frontier between Egypt and Cyrenaica was threatened by a large force assembled near Bardia and Sollum. On the 12th June, a small British force took the offensive which started the war in the Western Desert.

The 50th Division came under orders for overseas on the 8th December, and on the 12th December there was a change in command, Major-General W. H. C. Ramsden, D.S.O., M.C., (a former officer of the East Yorkshire Regiment) taking over from Major-General G. Le Q. Martel, C.B., D.S.O., M.C., who had been appointed to command the Royal Armoured Corps.

Following the change in command, orders were received for mobilisation. Embarkation leave began around Christmas, but the departure for overseas was put off. Intensive training was stepped up, and equipment checked. At the beginning of January 1941, long route marches and tactical exercises in desert warfare were carried out on snow-covered Exmoor. One battalion of the Green Howards claim to have been inspected in tropical kit with snow on the ground. The training was realistic, strenuous and physically exhausting. There was loss of life.

Training came to an end in March; the Division finalised arrangements for embarkation and further embarkation leave was granted. In the first week of April all units were in inspected by His Majesty The King who wished them God Speed.

Major-General W. H. C. Ramsden, C.B., C.B.E., D.S.O., M.C. (Late of East Yorkshire Regiment).

CHAPTER IV

THE MEDITERRANEAN AND NORTH AFRICA

BRITAIN'S INTEREST IN EGYPT

In 1869 the Suez Canal was opened. Designed by a Frenchman, Francis de Lesseps and constructed with French capital, part of the shares became owned by the Egyptian ruler, Isma'il Pasha, Viceroy of Egypt for the Ottoman Empire. As a result of his reforms huge foreign debts were accumulated and in 1878, following secret negotiations, his shares were bought on behalf of Great Britain by the Prime Minister, Benjamin Disraeli. This gave Britain an interest in the operation of the Canal.

In 1879 Isma'il was deposed by the Ottomans. A rise of nationalism and anti-foreign feeling followed. In 1882, there was an uprising of the Egyptian Army under the Minister for War, Arabi Pasha,. Riots in Alexandria resulted in the massacre of Europeans.

Concern for the security of the Canal led to Britain dispatching a force under General Garnet Wolseley. In a short war the Egyptians were routed and order was restored. Britain decided that if the Canal was to remain safe for operations it would be necessary to maintain garrisons in the country. Although there was national Ottoman suzerainty, Britain was to dominate the country until the outbreak of World War I in 1914, when it became a protectorate, until independence under King Fu'ad I was granted in 1922. In 1936 his son, Farouk I, signed a Treaty of Alliance with Britain which retained rights to the British to maintain troops in Egypt for the defence of the Canal Zone, and also to guard Egypt's Western Frontier with Cyrenaica, which abutted the Italian Colony of Libya. The Treaty of Alliance gave the British the right to a road and railway from Alexandria to Mersa Matruh, 120 miles west of the frontier. A garrison had been maintained in Mersa Matruh even before the treaty, but, in anticipation of Italian hostility, the garrison was augmented.

During the 1930s Italy had developed Libya and built a road along the coast right up to the frontier, and with the likelihood of a future conflict with Great Britain had concentrated a large force based on the forts of Bardia and Sollum.

On the 10th June, 1940, Mussolini plunged the Italian nation into war, aligning herself with Germany in fulfilment of the pacts made in 1936 and 1939. Within twenty-four hours the 7th Armoured Division moved into action. The 11th Hussars – less one squadron left behind at Sidi Barrani – crossed the frontier and headed west. Fort Capuzzo and Maddalena fell on the 14th June. During the last part of June and most of July the small British force in the Western Desert remained on the offensive. This was not to last. The Italians brought forward two divisions towards the frontier and on the 10th August attacked. Fort Capuzzo, which had been destroyed after its capture, was occupied by the Italians. General Wavell, the Commander-in-Chief in the Middle East, mounted a few cross-border operations from his forward base at Mersa Matruh and awaited an Italian invasion,

Mussolini, keen for a victory, pressed Marshal Graziani, the Italian C-in-C, to attack but Graziani deferred the attack claiming, legitimately, that his forces were not ready. On the 7th September, Mussolini issued a peremptory order: Graziani must begin his advance in two days' time. Graziani gave way and the long-awaited attack began on the 13th September. The Italian Army advanced fifty miles and stopped at Sidi Barrani where a chain of fortified camps was built. Here they stayed until the 8th December when Wavell launched Operation 'Compass' by the Western Desert Force under command of Lieut-General Richard O'Connnor. O'Connor had only the 7th Armoured and 4th Indian Divisions to oppose the Italian Tenth Army of eight divisions. The British attack, well supported by tanks and artillery, drove the Italians out of Sidi Barrani in three days, – five Italian divisions being annihilated – back to El Agheila on the Tripolitanian frontier where they halted. At the same time as the assault on Sidi Barrani, an attack was launched at Mersa Matruh and armoured units entered Buq Buq. O'Connor pursued the remainder, driving them out of Bardia which fell on the 5th January, 1941; Tobruk was captured on the 22nd January. The advance continued along the coast; Benghazi was taken by the 6th Australian Division which had replaced the 4th Indian Division (withdrawn after Sidi Barrani for the campaign in East Africa), while the 7th Armoured Division headed inland for the town of Beda Fomm, fifty miles south of Benghazi where a large enemy column was surprised, and on the 8th February the Italians surrendered. In two months, XIII Corps (Western Desert Force had been renamed in mid-January) had advanced over 400 miles and at a strength of 30,000, and, for the loss of only 500 men killed, had routed the Italian Tenth Army and taken 125,000 prisoners, more than 1,000 guns and destroyed or put out of action 400 tanks. Here the advance was held up in order to build up supplies for the intended drive to Tripoli, while 7th Armoured Division and 6th Australian Divisions were withdrawn to re-equip. Meanwhile, on the 7th February, O'Connor had ordered a small armoured force southward to Agedabia and El Agheila, the latter being reached the following evening. The enemy showed no resistance.

With a clear passage through El Agheila, O'Connor was prepared to drive forward to Tripoli. This was not to be. On the 11th February Wavell received a telegram from the Chief of the Imperial General Staff that no serious operation was to be undertaken beyond Benghazi; only a minimum force was to be left to hold Cyrenaica as a large force was to be sent to Greece (see page 30).

On the 12th February the German General Erwin Rommel arrived in Tripoli to take command of the *Deutsches Afrika Korps,* and on the 24th

March attacked and captured El Agheila. Having reorganised and strengthened, the Axis forces advanced, and on the 7th April were on the outskirts of Tobruk which Wavell decided to fortify and hold even if it was by-passed. By early June the XIII Corps was back on the Egyptian frontier at Sollum. From then on until the battle of El Alamein on the 23rd October, 1942, the opposing forces see-sawed across North Africa.

THE 50th DIVISION SAIL FOR THE MIDDLE EAST

Advanced Divisional Headquarters of the 50th Division, together with 150th and 151st Brigade, sailed from Liverpool on the 23rd April 1941, to join their convoy in the Clyde, leaving the 69th Brigade to continue training in Somerset, until the 30th May when it entrained for Gourock.

On the 1st June the 69th Brigade embarked on *H.M.T. Mooltan,* sailing in convoy on the 3rd June for Egypt. The route through the Mediterranean was closed to shipping, other than for special convoys to Malta, resulting in a long and tedious voyage round the Cape of Good Hope and through the Red Sea.

The troops were to experience a great deal of discomfort. The ship was one of a number of the Cunard liners, hastily converted into troopships. Before the war they had plied the North Atlantic routes, had little ventilation, and had not been designed for the heat of the tropics. Throughout the journey 'black-out' was strictly observed: the port holes firmly closed. The passenger accommodation was crammed to capacity. For officers, living in cabins, the voyage was comfortable and pleasant, but not so for the men who slept below deck in hammocks slung closely together. The holds carried warlike stores. The convoy was escorted by ships of the Royal Navy, cruisers, destroyers and at times larger ships, including an aircraft carrier.

On leaving Gourock a westward course was set, far into the Atlantic, then south for some days, then due East. There was little for the troops to do. The cramped conditions restricted training other than Physical Training which was carried out on the decks. To avoid boredom during the day, lectures were given on military training, and talks and discussions based on pamphlets of the Army Bureau of Current Affairs. In the evenings there were concerts and sing-songs, card schools and darts tournaments.

Stopping at Freetown, the capital of Sierra Leone, from the 16th-20th June for the ships to 'coal' and take on provisions – the troops were not allowed ashore – the convoy rounded the Cape of Good Hope reaching Durban on the 4th July. Here the troops disembarked and were accommodated in Clairwood Camp, six miles from the town.

The stay in Durban allowed relaxation in perfect weather, there was no 'black-out,' no food rationing and supplies of food were plentiful: a great change from England and on the ship. The South African people were generous, kind-hearted and hospitable and many friendships were made.

Embarking on the 11th July on *H.M.S. Mauretania,* another ship of the Cunard Line, the journey continued up the east coast of Africa, and through the Red Sea, reaching Port Tewfik on the Suez Canal on the 21st July, where the troops disembarked, entraining for El Quassassin, a large tented military encampment in the desert on the banks of the Canal between Ismailia and Cairo.

* * * * *

Meanwhile two disasters had occurred. Before dawn on the 28th October, 1940, the Italian army in Albania crossed the frontier with Greece at various points.

After the Italian occupation of Albania on the 7th April, 1939 (Good Friday), Greece and Roumania were threatened. The British Prime Minister, Mr. Neville Chamberlain, gave an undertaking in the House of Commons on the 13th April guaranteeing support to Greece in the event of an attack by the Axis powers, and, although the treaty was invoked on the day of the invasion, it was not until the 6th April, 1941, when the Germans invaded the country that it was possible to send a force to give assistance. Most of this force was to come from the Western Desert, and with the halting of operations there on the 7th February units were withdrawn.

The force sent, named the Anzac Corps (reminiscent of World War I), consisted of the 6th Australian Division, the New Zealand division and 1st British Armoured Brigade. Although the force was predominantly ANZAC, command was given to a British Officer, General Henry Maitland Wilson. After a series of short and bitter battles, by the 20th April the Imperial force was overrun. Most of the troops evacuated were sent directly to Crete, a base for the Royal Navy from which warships could protect convoys *en route* to Malta; its strategic position required that it should be held.

On the 20th May the Germans launched a massive air attack on Crete with dive-bombers, parachute and glider-borne troops. After a gallant defence in which a heavy toll was taken of the Germans, the exhausted troops, outnumbered, were evacuated and on the 1st June the island fell.

A decision was now made by the Prime Minister to change command in the Middle East, General Sir Archibald Wavell going to India to take over as Commander-in-Chief from General Sir Claude Auchinleck, who on the 30th June arrived in Cairo to take command of the Western Desert Force from Wavell.

The force in the Western Desert consisted of only one corps, the XIII. When it was joined by XXX Corps on the 26th September it was formed into an Army and designated the Eighth Army; command was given to General Sir Alan Cunningham, who had led the successful invasion of Italian Somaliland and Ethiopia.

IN DEFENCE OF CYPRUS

With the Germans in Crete, Cyprus seemed to be another base from which the Axis might advance through the Middle East. The island had been conquered by the Turks in 1571 but came under British administration in 1878, and became a Crown colony in 1925. It was vital that it should be put into a state of defence. The task was given to the 50th Division, the directive from the G.O.C.-in-C., Middle East, to Major-General Ramsden being short and very much to the point: 'Hold the island for His Majesty's Government.'

* * * * *

After only a few days in Quassassin, the 50th Division (less the 150th Brigade), which had been sent to the Egyptian/Libyan border on the 23rd June, left for Port Said *en route* for Cyprus. Embarking on destroyers at Port Said, on the night of the 7th August (the Royal Navy had suffered severe losses during the evacuation of Crete and would only sail at night so that the ships could be clear of the island by daylight), the Division landed the next day at Famagusta in Cyprus. Instead of systematically unloading the equipment and stores the naval ratings, anxious to get away, rolled everything down the gangway; some items going into the sea had to be retrieved later.

The 5th East Yorkshires went to Ktima in the west of the island and the 6th and 7th Green Howards to Limassol. During the voyage the ship carrying the transport was torpedoed and the whole of the transport lost.

On the 15th August, the 150th Brigade (4th East Yorkshires and 4th and 5th Green Howards), which had been detached to Bagush on the 23rd June to defend aerodromes in the rear of the forward areas of the Western Desert, arrived to rejoin the 50th Division. The 4th East Yorkshires went to Candia (Heraklion); the 4th Green Howards were stationed at Ailaskya, the 5th Green Howards at Larnaca.

This was to be one of the most pleasant countries in which the Division would be stationed. There was bathing in the clear, warm sea, food was in abundance, wine and fruit available at reasonable prices. The Cypriots gave the men a warm welcome, and resulting friendships were continued after the war when some returned to the island as tourists and holiday-makers. In the weeks to come, officers and men were able to avail themselves of the opportunity to exchange visits. The stay of the 4th East Yorkshires was unfortunately marred by an outbreak of diphtheria which claimed some casualties

The task of preparing the island for defence was immense: time was of the essence as almost any day a landing by airborne troops from Crete or the Dodacanese islands was expected. Immediately on landing trenches systems were dug, pill-boxes and other defensive systems for three brigades were put in hand and positions taken up. Then followed the construction of roads and aerodromes. The 69th Brigade had experience of this kind of work when as part of the 23rd Division in France in April 1940 it had been engaged on similar work. Supplies of food, water and petrol for ninety-one days were brought in and stores sufficient for an expected thirty-one thousand army and air force personnel. The Prime Minister had asked to be kept fully informed as to progress and to be told when the first pillbox was completed.

The G.O.C.-in-C., Middle East, General Sir Claude Auchinleck, together with the Minister Resident in the Middle East, Mr. Oliver Lyttleton, and Air Marshal Sir Arthur Tedder, A.O.C.-in-C. Middle East, toured the island at the end of August, inspected the defences, and expressed satisfaction with what they saw.

The defence works having been completed, training began. There were long marches in the blazing sun, and tactical exercises in the central plain which gave the 69th and 151st Brigades an idea of the desert they would soon experience.

Then on the 31st October orders were received for the 50th Division to move to Palestine. It had been thought that it would take six months to put the defences of the island in a satisfactory state of defence. It had been achieved in three. Before the Division departed the Pioneer Corps had set up Civil Labour Control Teams which eventually employed twenty-three thousand civilian labourers.

At the beginning of November the 5th Indian Division arrived from Haifa to relieve the 50th Division. The defence of the island was to be handed over to the 5th Indian Division, together with all stores, equipment and divisional transport.

The 50th Division withdrew on the night of the 5th November for Palestine, crowded on the decks of destroyers of the Royal Navy, and on the 7th November arrived at Haifa, the 69th Brigade going on to a camp at Acre, the 5th East Yorkshires at Jalama Camp on Mount Carmel. At Haifa the Division took over all stores, equipment and transport left behind by 5th Indian Division. It was a poor exchange. The 5th Indian Division had campaigned in Abyssinia, Eritrea, North Africa and Iraq. The equipment taken over was in poor condition and most of the transport was worn out; in fact, almost nine hundred vehicles were completely unserviceable.

PROTECTION OF THE PERSIAN OIL WELLS

With the Russians entering the war in August, 1941, supplies of munitions were required by them, and with the Arctic sea route being uncertain a route through Iran was essential. At this time the Germans were advancing along the North coast of the Black Sea with a threat to the Caucasus, and there was every likelihood of their breaking through into the Persian Gulf and advancing to India. A right of passage through Persia was demanded by the Russians and British together with the expulsion of the German mission in Teheran, which had a considerable influence on the government of Persia, and the three thousand Germans, thinly disguised as diplomats, technical advisers, engineers and businessmen. The approach was ill received and a combined Anglo-Russian invasion was decided upon.

The British element comprised the 5th and 10th Indian Division and the 2nd and 9th British Armoured Divisions under command of Major-General William Slim. The invasion of Persia began on the 25th August, Abadan was occupied and the force advanced on Kurmanshah. Quickly the Russians and British occupied all Persia with the exception of Teheran and the district round it. The Persian Prime Minister promised to close the German and Italian legations, send home their diplomats and hand over to the Allies all other Germans and Italians in Persia. Eventually the legations were closed, but no attempts were made to stop the activities of the Germans and Italians who remained. A joint Anglo-Russian ultimatum demanding the surrender of all Germans and Italians within forty-eight hours was delivered on the 10th September. By the 13th about one-third of the Germans were sent by train into the British zone but there was no indication that the others would follow. The British and Russian Governments ordered Teheran to be occupied by their joint forces on the 17th September.

Realising that his capital would fall, on the 16th September, Riza Shah Pahlavi, who had started life as a stable hand and by cunning and guile and the leading of a *coup* in 1921, deposed Ahmad Shah Qajar, abdicated in favour of his son, Mohammed Reza Pahlavi.

The German threat to the Persian oil wells remained; ten German divisions were poised to attack south-East into Persia through the corridor to the East of the Caspian sea. The 50th Division was placed under orders to move to Iraq to protect the oil fields and hold off any invading force.

* * * * *

General Auchinleck, having launched 'Operation Crusader' on the 18th November, aimed at destroying the enemy along the coast and relieving the garrison in Tobruk which had been under siege since the 8th April, 1941. The 150th Brigade was taken out of 50th Division and placed in G.H.Q. reserve. Leaving Haifa on the 30th November *en route* for Egypt, the Brigade reached Amiriya, ten miles west of Alexandria, on the 1st December. From there it went by rail to Sidi Haneish, west of Bagbush in the Western Desert, to re-equip and carry out further training in desert warfare, mobile brigade exercises and movement through minefields. Before the brigade left it was stripped of most of its transport and stores in order to make the 69th and 151st Brigades mobile.

The 50th Division, now with only two brigades, left Haifa on the 29th November for the seven hundred mile journey to Iraq. Proceeding in single file in the part-worn transport recently acquired (which constantly broke down), and lorries of the Royal Army Service Corps, a route was taken, south of Lake Tiberias, across the River Jordan, into TransJordania on a fairly good road (the surface being mostly hard gravel sand), and then keeping near to the pipeline, across the desert. This was the Division's first experience of desert driving.

The column was headed by the 69th Brigade, and lead by Lieut. T. L. Ward, the Brigade Intelligence Officer. He had a difficult task as no maps were available. Halting for two days at the R.A.F. Station at Habbaniya, the Commanding Officer of the 5th East Yorkshires, Lieutenant-Colonel J. T. Thornhill, and the Adjutant, Captain A. W. Edgar, were entertained by Captain Harry Piers Chadwick, who had been commissioned into the Regiment on the 29th August, 1935, and was at that time seconded to the Iraq Levies.

Proceeding via Baghdad the 69th Brigade arrived at Kirkuk in the Iraq oil fields on Sunday the 7th December, the 151st Brigade at Two Rivers. A dug-in tented camp was made; the floors were clay, as slippery as ice. Having driven 100 miles a day in poor transport, the drivers and maintenance staff were to be congratulated. The weather was extremely bad: dust, torrents of rain, intense cold at night with 10-12 degrees of frost (18 one night). There was snow and ice. It was said to be the worst conditions experienced by the 69th Brigade during the war. Rations were fairly good. Cooking arrangements were primitive with home -made stoves fuelled by crude oil. There was a nightly rum ration which did much to raise morale!

On this day, following the attack by the Japanese on Pearl Harbour, the United States of America was at war with Japan. The British War Cabinet authorised the immediate declaration of war upon Japan, this being communicated to the Japanese Ambassador in London the next day. On the 10th December Germany declared war on the United States.

When the weather permitted, training was carried out in desert and mountain warfare. Christmas was celebrated with turkey and plum pudding. The Divisional concert party put on a pantomime in a wet marquee with lighting by oil lamps

As the threat to the oil fields did not materialise, the Russians holding their line and the Germans retiring, the British Force was withdrawn from Iraq, the 50th Division being ordered back to Palestine. The 151st Brigade remained, moving on to the Eski Kelle to dig defences on the crossings of the Great Zab and Kazir rivers: they would follow a week later.

On the 12th January 1942 the 69th Brigade moved off. The 5th East Yorkshires left behind ten of the lorries which were unserviceable. The 69th Brigade returned over the same route, reaching Roshpinna in Palestine on the 21st January, 1942. A week later the Brigade moved further North via Damascus to the Ras Baalbeck area in Northern Syria to relieve the 6th Australian Division in the Baalbeck area. The 6th Green

Howards and 5th East Yorkshires relieved the 2nd/4th Australian Infantry Battalion in El Aine camp, the 7th Green Howards, the 2nd/11th Australian Infantry Battalion at Djeideide. The Australians were off to defend Singapore, the Japanese already advancing through Malaya.

In anticipation of an attack by the Germans southwards through Syria, and the possibility of a further rising of hostile elements in Syria, following the war there against French Vichy forces which had gone on from the 7th June until the 12th July, 1941, the 69th Brigade laboured to construct defences, building pillboxes, digging anti-tank ditches and laying wire. During the short stay there the troops were able to visit Beirut and the famous ruined temples of the ancient city of Baalbeck.

However, while the 50th Division had been on its journeys to and from Iraq, the Eighth Army had, on the 10th December, 1941, relieved Tobruk; rapidly pursued the retreating Axis forces to Gazala, from where Rommel withdrew on the 15th December; Benghazi was entered on the 24th December, and on the 6th January, 1942, the pursuit was halted at El Agheila. If more tanks had been available to General Ritchie he might have destroyed Rommel's army, but unfortunately 200 Crusader tanks were under repair in the XIII Corps workshops.

Then on the 21st January, Rommel made a reconnaissance in force, and, finding little opposition, advanced, breaking through the light forces at Agedabia on the 22nd, Saunnu on the 23rd and Msus on the 25th; Benghazi fell on the 29th. Two other moves eastward were made, one along the coastal area to Derna, then southward to Tmimi, the other through Charruba and El Mechili. Both sides had reached the practicable limit for the line of their communications, the Germans at Tmimi and the British at Gazala. Between the two lines lay twenty-five miles of flat desert which became a 'No-Man's Land'. Auchinleck ordered General Neil Ritchie commanding the Eighth Army to form a line of defence from Gazala to Bir Hacheim, fifty miles to the south, and dig in. Until this time neither the Germans nor the British had attempted to form any sort of continuous 'line'. In fact this was impossible with the number of troops available.

CHAPTER V

THE CAMPAIGN OF THE 50th DIVISION

EGYPT AND LIBYA

On the 12th February, 1942, the 50th Division was ordered to the Western Desert of Egypt.

Still without the 151st Brigade, the Division set off. The route was via east of Beirut and Haifa, Beersheba, Gaza, over the Sinai Desert, across the Suez Canal near Ismailia, and on to Wadi El Natrun Camp near Alexandria which was reached on the 16th February. The next day it left for the Western Desert via Mersa Matruh, Sidi Barrani, Sollum, then crossing into Cyrenaica to Fort Capuzzo, and on the 20th February arrived at a camp near Acroma some fifteen miles south-west of Tobruk. They had covered the long road journey, some 1,000 miles, in eight days.

The next day the 50th Division was called forward to take over from the 4th Indian Division. To the North around Gazala on the coast was the 1st South African Division with the 1st Free French Brigade fifty miles to the south at Bir Hacheim. The 50th Division in the centre had a frontage of twenty-five miles to cover. The 150th Brigade, already part of the line and under command of the 4th Indian Division, had taken over positions from the 1st Free French Brigade between Bir El Naghia and Alem Hamza. It now reverted to the command of the 50th Division. On the 22nd the 151st Brigade took up a position a few miles south of Alem Hamza, forming a continuation of the left flank of the 150th Brigade, with the 69th Brigade to the rear forming part of the Divisional Mobile Reserve with tanks of the 42nd and 44th Battalions, Royal Tank Regiment.

The first task was to strengthen the defensive works which had been under construction by the Indian Brigade. The defences were consolidated, with digging, the laying of minefields and the erection of barbed wire entanglements; observation posts, ammunition dumps and ration stores were constructed, and the site camouflaged. Much hard work was put into this.

The weather was at this time of the year glorious, warm and sunny days, cool and dry by night; morale was high and the men were fit and well. When this work had reached a satisfactory point, training was carried out in mobile and desert warfare, and defensive patrolling was carried out at night around the Brigade area searching for enemy reconnaissance groups.

In early March there was offensive patrolling by 'Jock Columns' (formations originated by Brigadier Jock Campbell, V.C., D.S.O., M.C.), small, self-supporting and highly mobile strike forces of all arms, designed to go out on long range into the desert, keep watch on enemy movement, gather information and strike and raid specific objectives. On occasions these patrols were out for a stretch of several days.

One such took part on the 20th March and succeeding days. It was the first major desert action of the 50th Division, which at this time was the only British infantry division in contact with the enemy in any part of the world. Given the name, 'Operation Fullsize', two self-supporting columns of all arms, one from each brigade of the 50th Division, were to conduct fairly large-scale attacks to harass enemy landing grounds at Tmimi and nearby Martuba with the object of drawing off enemy air forces based on these airfields for a sufficiently long time to enable the Royal Navy to get a vital relief sea-convoy through to the relief of Malta. A third column composed of a squadron of Matilda infantry tanks together with infantry, artillery, carriers and anti-tank guns, was to move to Bir Temrad to cover the assembly of the Timimi column and cover the withdrawal of both columns. The combined operation was placed under Brigadier J. S. (Crasher) Nichols, commander of the 151st Brigade.

The columns moved off on the night of the 20th/21st March. The column from the 150th Brigade to attack Martuba was from the 4th East Yorkshires and commanded by Lieut.-Colonel Dudley Stewart Norman, a former officer of the Royal Dublin Fusiliers who had joined the East Yorkshires in 1922 on the disbandment of the regiment. It consisted of 'C' Company of that battalion and the unit's carriers together with the 5th East Yorkshires from the 69th Brigade in support. The column also included mortars, 25-pounder and anti-tank guns, Bofors, engineers and a field ambulance.

The first move was made when Captain Dennis E. Field set off with a small force to seize an enemy observation post at Ras el Eleba and secure the right flank of the column. This was successfully carried out after sharp fighting. Brigadier C. W. Haydon, commanding the 150th Brigade, arrived at the scene of the fighting and got a bullet through his forage cap.

The next morning in daylight the column got to within two miles of Martuba aerodrome and opened fire. Enemy aircraft took to the skies and dive-bombed and machine-gunned the column. Ammunition for Bofors guns was blown up early in the attacks, reducing the anti-aircraft defences. At midnight on the 21st the column withdrew. Forty vehicles had been lost and casualties had been suffered.

The second column under the direct command of Brigadier J. S. Nichols comprised the 7th Green Howards of the 69th Brigade under command of Lieut. Colonel F. E. A. Macdonnell and infantry from the Durham Light Infantry of 151st Brigade, supported by tanks, artillery, medium machine-guns of the 2nd Cheshire Regiment, and anti-tank guns, forming the Tmimi column. Its first task was to capture an enemy outpost on a ridge in sight of and within artillery range of Gabr el Aleima known as 'The Pimple'. The ridge was taken and held for two days, and on the third morning the Durham Light Infantry, supported by tanks, artillery, medium machine-guns and anti-tanks units, attacked Gabr el Aleima under cover of a smoke screen. After a hard fight Gabr el Aleima was captured. The enemy reacted strongly with Stuka dive bombers in support. The columns suffered some losses, but, considering the amount of dive-bombing, the casualties were not high. Over one hundred and fifty prisoners were taken. The Durham Light Infantry went on to Tmimi and harassed the enemy. The 7th Green Howards dug in at Gabr el Aleima. On the afternoon of the 24th March the Durham Light Infantry broke off its engagement and retired through the 7th Green Howards. Meanwhile German Artillery fire had been brought down on The Pimple which lasted until almost dark. Two hours later the 7th Green Howards received orders to retire and return to the Gazala line. The combined raids yielded more than two hundred prisoners and five 76mm guns. Operation 'Fullzise' proved a success, in that the convoy safely reached Malta.

On the 6th April the enemy advanced in force across No-Man's Land and took up positions from where the columns of the 50th Division had been manoeuvring: Bir Temrad, Sidi Bregisc and Rotunda Segnali.

Aware that the enemy would be in a position to attack before the Eighth Army was ready, General Auchinleck the C-in-C, ordered Lieut.-General Neil Ritchie, C.B.E,, D.S.O., M.C., to set about forming a defensive front: the establishing of fortified points, known as 'boxes' at strategic points, with a covering network of minefields between 'boxes'. Each 'box' was a large area, roughly a mile square, extended to minimise damage by air attack, protected by its own minefield, defended by an infantry brigade with its own artillery, engineer and transport support, and stocked with sufficient supplies of water, food, petrol and ammunition to enable the box to hold out for several days, even if outflanked. These 'boxes' were to be designed for all-round defence, with barbed-wire entanglements.

The line would stretch fifty miles from the coast at Gazala southwards to the isolated French fortress at Bir Hacheim. It was broken to the north by the old desert track of Trigh Capuzzo which ran from Rotunda Mteifel el Chebir through Knightsbridge to El Adem immediately to the south of Tobruk. It was also broken to the south by the Trigh el Abd running from Rotunda Mteifelt el Chebir to Got el Ualeb, Barrel and Bir El Hammet. This track would allow freedom of manoeuvre to the east for armoured formations. To the south of Bir Hacheim the country was open.

The 50th Division was given orders to fight a defensive battle to the last man and steps were taken to prepare the defences. Narrow slit trenches were to be dug flush with the ground without parapet, making them difficult to see. Vehicle pits were also dug as were dugouts where men could sleep. These were some four-foot deep and six-foot square covered by sheets camouflaged with nets. Field guns were to be sited in anti-tank positions as were salvaged Italian guns, mostly 47-mm., although useless against German Mark III and IV tanks. Only the 69th and 151st Brigade had 2-pdr anti-tank guns, twelve to each brigade. Additional minefields were to be laid.

There being a shortage of pneumatic drills and other mechanical devices, digging proved extremely difficult, as solid rock was found twelve inches below the sand. Owing to the extremes of temperature, work began immediately after early morning breakfast and ceased at around 0900hours and recommenced in the late afternoon as the day cooled off. During the day there were dust storms and nights were extremely cold with thick damp mists. There was insufficient wire to cover the forward infantry posts and, although additional minefield had been laid, the defences did not completely cover the boxes. The length of the front was such that it was necessary to use many of the troops for patrolling purposes, and in addition standing patrols had to be placed in the Rotunda Mteeifel area to look out for enemy reconnaissance units.

On the 20th April, the 150th Brigade, standing on the Bir El Jeff – El Hamza position, was relieved by a brigade of the 2nd South African Division, and moved south to take up a position around Got el Ualeb south of the Trigh Capuzzo, from the 200th Guards Brigade (later renumbered 201st Guards Brigade), the latter being withdrawn to the area known as Knightsbridge.

Eighth Army's dispositions from North to south were:

> The 1st South African Division, from Bir El Jeff north to the sea.
> A brigade of the 2nd South African Division continued the line from Bir El Jef to Alem Hamza, with the 200th (later renumbered 201st) Guards Brigade twenty miles to the east of the South Africans in reserve in a 'box' in the neighbourhood of Knightsbridge. Just behind them was the 1st Armoured Division (2nd and 22nd Armoured Brigades and a support group).

The 'box' to the south of Alem Hamza with its southern flank resting on the Trigh El Abd was given to the 151st Brigade (West) and 69th Brigade (East) to hold.

Behind the line, in reserve, was the 7th Armoured Division (4th Armoured Brigade and a support group).

A further gap of six miles carried down to the 'box' of the 150th Brigade at Gott El Ualeb.

There was a further gap of ten miles before the isolated Bir Hacheim position was reached. This was held by the 1st Free French Brigade under General Pierre Koenig.

A minefield had been laid from the sea as far as Alem Hamza, covering the front of the Army, but further south, mines had been laid in irregular belts to allow freedom of movement to the armour.

> The 50th Division had as its mobile reserve:
> Headquarters, 1st Army Tank Brigade (Brigadier O'Carroll), consisting of the 44th Battalion, Royal Tank Regiment and a squadron of the 42nd Battalion, Royal Tank Regiment.

One Squadron, South African Armoured Cars.
287th Battery, 124th Field Regiment, Royal Artillery (Major Ian Bransom).
6th Bn. The Green Howards (Lieut.-Colonel E. C. Cooke-Collis).
One Machine-gun company. The 2nd Cheshire Regiment.

The 1st South African Division with a brigade of the 2nd South African Division had a Mobile Reserve consisting of the 32nd Army Tank Brigade, (7th and 42nd Battalions, Royal Tank Regiment.

The 8th Battalion Royal Tank Regiment covered the coastal strip between Gazala and Tobruk.
The 4th Battalion Royal Tank Regiment was in the town of Tobruk, as was the 2nd South African Division, which had no transport as this had been allocated to the divisions in the line.
Tobruk was to fall to Rommel on the 21st June.

THE BATTLE OF GAZALA

It was Rommel's intention to move south with two German and one Italian armoured division, round Bir Hacheim, turn north, outflank the British positions from the rear, then capture Tobruk and advance towards the Egyptian frontier.

At 2200 hours on the 26th May in the moonlight, Rommel opened his attack from Rotunda Mteifel el Chebir advancing in the North between Gazala and Sidi Muftah with infantry of the Trento and Sabrata Divisions of the XXI Italian Corps under the command of the German, Lieut.-General Ludwig Cruwell. Part of the attack, unsupported by tanks, fell on the whole front of the 151st and the 69th Brigades (the 5th East Yorkshires, now commanded by Lieutenant-Colonel T. W. G. Stansfield, an officer of the Green Howards, who had succeeded Lieut.-Colonel J. T. Thornhill on the latter's posting to command the 4th Battalion). This attack intended as a diversion was held up on the line of outposts on the front of the 151st Brigade. On the 69th Brigade front a heavy toll was taken of the Italians by rifle and light automatic guns as they advanced in a solid line; the Brigade having the advantage of being in prepared positions, drove them off.

The southern advance across the front of the 150th Brigade drove in the standing patrol of the 4th East Yorkshires two miles east of the town of Rotunda Mteifel el Chebir on the morning of the 27th and headed along the Trigh el Abd for the minefield at Got El Ualeb to attack the 150th Brigade.

The main striking force of *Afrika Korps* (90th Light. and 15th and 21st Panzer Divisions – together with the Italian Ariete Armoured Division), moved round Bir Hacheim, the Eighth Army's southern flank, and then north with the intention of outflanking the British positions, engage and defeat the British armoured forces with an attack by tanks from east of the line combined with an infantry attack from the west, then head for Acroma and El Adem, with all the Axis forces the object being the capture of Tobruk which was expected to fall by the 30th May. An attack by the Italian Ariete Division with support from some tanks from 21st Panzer Divisions resulted in the Free French Brigade at Bir Hacheim holding on tenaciously.

By early morning of the 27th May the Germans had turned the open flank south of Bir Hacheim swept round the rear of the 150th Brigade and moved northwards where they met stiff resistance from the British armoured divisions in the general area of Bir el Harmat and Knightsbridge and were halted. But a tremendous battle was to rage round the 'box' of the 1st Armoured Division for several days until a stalemate ensued.

The enemy made little progress on the 'box' of the 69th and 151st Brigades on the 27th May and during this time a series of defended localities were constructed to the east of the 69th Brigade with Acroma, to cover communications with Tobruk, and to keep the enemy away with patrolling and aggressive action outside the 'box'.

On the morning of the 28th May the enemy began infiltrating through the minefields at the southern centre of 150th Brigade 'box' and by 1900 hours tanks had got through further south, attacking a standing patrol of the 5th Green Howards under command of Captain H. I'A. Dennis which was forced to withdraw. By 2300 hours the enemy had got into the gap between the box of the 150th Brigade and that of the 69th/151st Brigades to the north, and had broken through the defences at Got El Ualeb to the south; ammunition was running short. There was little that Brigadier Haydon commanding the 150th Brigade could do other than hope that a promised armoured column would come to his assistance.

During the 28th, a German Fiesler Storch reconnaissance 'plane was shot down over the 150th Brigade 'box'; the pilot was killed but General Ludwig Cruewell, G.O.C. *Afrika Korps,* under Rommel, was captured and made a prisoner of war.

At 1030 hours the next day the enemy advanced on the southern front of the 'box' and on both the fronts to the north and south there was heavy shelling, mortar and small arms fire. This continued throughout the day. On the western and eastern sides the enemy was well established and by dawn on the 30th the 150th Brigade was surrounded.

The Axis forces to the east of the 'boxes' were beginning to run short of petrol, oil, water and stores and on the 30th May Rommel ordered his engineers to cut gaps through the minefield at Trigh el Abd between Bir Hacheim and the 150th Brigade, thus allowing his well-stretched forces to be more quickly supplied. By lifting the minefield between the 69th Brigade and the 150th Brigade, Rommel was able to shorten his lines of communication and establish a direct route east and west along the unoccupied Trigh Capuzzo to an area of land to the east of the 151st Brigade which was given the name 'The Cauldron'. The 150th Brigade was now cut off from the rest of the Division.

There were continuous attacks throughout the 30th May, and in one instance tanks got through a minefield and captured the whole 232nd Field Company, Royal Engineers.

The Division had by this time been under heavy fire for four days, the shortage of water had meant no washing or shaving, and the desert winds had driven sand into clothes; there was hair and stubble on faces; eyes and ears were crusted, lips flaked. All were exhausted. Meals of bully beef, biscuits and a limited show of water showed in the men's physical condition, but despite this they remained in good heart and exhibited *esprit de corps.*

At 0830 hours on the 31st May there was heavy shelling from the south, east and west, and at 1030 hours an attack was launched against 'B' Company of the 4th East Yorkshires and 'F' Troop 286th Battery, R.A. in the north-east corner of the 'box'. They put up a gallant defence, refusing a German offer of surrender, but by 1600 hours the company and troop were virtually wiped out. The company commander, Captain C. A. Good, C.S.M. W. Robinson and the commander of 'F' Troop were killed.

At midday another attack was launched where 'A' Company of the 4th East Yorkshires joined with the 5th Green Howards. There was no minefield before them. The enemy advanced in armoured carriers and to hold the position all available men from headquarters of the battalions were rushed to the point and the situation saved. The battle went on all day and by nightfall a serious situation had developed; only twelve of the twenty-four guns of the 72nd Field Regiment R.A. were serviceable ,with only a hundred rounds available to the regiment; the 286th Medium Battery was down to six guns with twenty rounds per gun; 2-pdr ammunition and ammunition for machine-guns and rifles had virtually run out. There were only thirteen tanks serviceable and few vehicles left.

On the morning of the 1st June an attack was launched on all fronts with tanks shielding infantry in 3-ton lorries, whose advance on debussing was covered by intense fire from machine guns and mobile artillery: dive bombers swooped down. The main attack began in the north and by 0900 hours the position was overrun. In the south the attack opened with a heavy barrage of artillery fire along the whole two miles of the front followed by infantry under cover of machine-gun fire. The Brigade fought on in a continuously contracting area, company positions were overrun, most of the 2-pdr. anti-tank guns were knocked out. The infantry battalions had virtually run out of 2 pdr. machine-gun and rifle ammunition. The thirteen remaining tanks were put out of action, as were the twelve 25-pdrs. Many officers and senior N.C.O.s had been killed and wounded, casualties were high, the wounded lying in the sand were repeatedly wounded, and by 1400 hours, with ammunition expended and a shortage of water, the 'box' was overrun and the battle over.

This was the final battle of the 150th (Northumbrian) Brigade. A few escaped, but others who survived became prisoners of war. The 4th East Yorkshires ceased to exist as a fighting formation and went into suspense, as did the 72nd Field Regiment R.A.

There were many acts of gallantry. Two of those of the East Yorkshire Regiment are recorded. Pte H. (Nobby) Clarke, an officer's batman, entirely regarding his own safety, went out with drinks of water for the wounded under intense shell-fire. His bravery resulted in the award of the Military Medal.

Private Harold Robinson was awarded the Military Medal for saving the lives of many wounded. In one case, with only scissors and clasp knives, he amputated and tended the arm of one man who would certainly have died had he not received this prompt attention.

The Medical Officer of the 4th East Yorkshires, Captain A. Thompson, R.A.M.C., and all the medical staff were wounded, but continued to administer to the wounded, not only throughout the battle, but afterwards as prisoners of war.

One last word on the 150th Brigade. Brigadier Haydon, who had skilfully and gallantly commanded the Brigade in France and the desert, had been given orders to get away should the situation so deteriorate that a collapse seemed certain, and seeing the fall of the position in the north at 0900 hours on the 1st June, handed over to Lieut.-Colonel L.C. Cooper, commanding the 4th Green Howards, and left in an armoured car. On the way he met with two tanks making for the same point to which he was going. Halting to speak to their commander, he got out of the armoured car and was killed outright by a shell. Field Marshal Rommel appeared at the scene of the battle and asked for the Brigadier in command. Sadly his request could not be met.

Meanwhile, Rommel launched a full attack on Bir Hacheim on the 1st June. The French garrison under its commander, General Pierre Koenig, fought gallantly, but completely cut off and, short of food and water, was forced to retire on the 10th June. The supply line to the east of Gazala was now secure. The withdrawal from Bir Hacheim left the desert to the south of the 69th Brigade in possession of the Germans.

With the loss of the 150th Brigade the enemy had become established in the very centre of the British positions in the Gazala line. The 69th and 151st Brigades remained in their respective 'boxes' and in the next few days carried out aggressive operations and patrolling outside their own positions.

Having secured the supply line along the Trigh Capuzzo to the forces east of Gazala, Rommel drove north on the 5th June and broke through the British positions to form a laager which later was aptly named 'The Cauldron'.

General Ritchie ordered a counter-attack in order to rescue the beleaguered troops, and re-establish the Gazala line. This was to be made by armoured units, and, after they had broken through, the infantry from the 'boxes' would follow.

In moonlight on the night of the 4th/5th June 1942 the tanks set off, to be met by artillery fire and the armour of the *Afrika Corps*. Very soon the 7th Armoured Division was overrun, many tanks were put out of action, and others turned away with holes in their sides from armour-piercing shells. British tank strength was reduced from 400 to 170. The attack proved a failure.

On the 11th June, Rommel turned eastward and the next day, in a pincer movement by the 15th and 21st Panzer Divisions, trapped the 2nd and 4th Armoured Brigades deployed in front of the Knightsbridge 'box,' a defensive position south of Acroma, held by the 22nd Guards Brigade. On the night of the 13th Rommel turned northward, turning his full force on the Knightsbridge 'box,' and by nightfall had destroyed much of the British armour and was in possession of the battlefield.

The Gazala line was cut off. All that remained were the 1st South African Division, the brigade of the 2nd South African Division and the 69th and the 151st Brigades forming the 50th Division. They were isolated. The 69th and 151st Brigades were surrounded on three sides, the 90th German Light Division to the south, the 15th and 21st Panzer Divisions to the east, and the Italian Brescia and Pavia Divisions to the west.

The Army Commander gave orders to abandon what was left of the Gazala-Bir Hacheim line, each 'box' to take whatever course it thought best and fight its way out, at the same time reinforcing Tobruk. The South Africans, covered by the 50th Division, opted for the coast road to Tobruk, which was not wide enough to take more than one division. Here in 1941 the Australians had held out in a four-month siege.

The South Africans hoped to do the same. The 50th Division was ordered not to move until the South Africans were clear of their positions. As this would take twelve hours any element of surprise was lost.

Major-General Ramsden decided on a risky plan to break-out, not to the east which would have brought the Division into territory overrun by German armour, but through the German and Italian defensive ring in the west, before the Italians could react.

Two bridgeheads were to be established, one based on the 69th Brigade, the other on the 151st Brigade, through which the remainder of the Division in two Brigade columns would pass, and once through the bridgehead turn south, push forward some thirty miles across enemy lines of communications, round Bir Hacheim, then turn east towards the gap in the wire at Fort Maddalena and Sheferzen on the Egyptian frontier two hundred miles away, beyond which the whole of Eighth Army had withdrawn.

A shortage of three-ton lorries meant that all surplus stores, equipment, mines and explosives that could not be carried were to be concentrated in dumps, buried or demolished. Destruction by fire was not possible as this would alert the enemy to what was going on.

All surplus stores were destroyed on the 14th June, rations and water were allocated for only three days, the men were to wear cardigans and carry only light equipment. Sufficient petrol for a three-hundred-mile journey was allotted.

The operation began on the night of the 14th/15th June. 'Sortie' gaps in the main minefield had been cut in readiness. Fortunately owing to a sandstorm the enemy was unable to observe either from the ground or from the air that transport was being brought up and portable stores loaded. There was no time for reconnaissance, little was known about the enemy minefields.

Orders were given to Lieut.-Colonel T. W. G. Stansfield commanding the 5th East Yorkshires, to form No.1 Group, move out and make a gap in the enemy position, establish a bridgehead and hold it until the 69th Brigade had passed through. The Brigade would then form small 'commando' type groups of all arms which would fight independently and make their own way to the Egyptian frontier. To the right, Lieutenant-Colonel M. L. P. Jackson, of the Green Howards in command of the 8th Battalion the Durham Light Infantry would form No. 2 Group and do the same for the 151st Brigade.

No. 1 Group was the first to move off. The 5th East Yorkshires, with 16 Valentine tanks and artillery in support were given the task of spearheading the breakthrough. This was one of the few occasions when tanks were used in the dark. As dusk fell they embussed and moved forward.

At 2000 hours, having debussed, the attack was launched in two waves, hitting the Italians as they slept, catching them entirely by surprise. It is related that one platoon advanced in step towards the astonished Italians singing 'Rule Britannia', and it was not until they were within ten yards of the enemy that they adopted the 'on guard' position. Then with bayonet, tommy-gun, pistol and grenade they put paid to any dug-out showing signs of life. Dumps seized and set on fire, vehicles ambushed and looted. In the *melée* Italians fired on Italians. Two companies were held up for a time but, when they were joined by a third, the enemy's resistance was broken down. Four of the tanks went up in flames from mines or direct hits.

By 0300 hours on the 15th June, having successfully formed a bridgehead round the gap that had been forced, the 6th and 7th Green Howards, 69th Brigade Headquarters and an Ordnance company passed through the area illuminated by the flames of burning vehicles and streaks of tracer. Shells were falling all round the vehicles, but slit trenches and dug-outs took a far greater toll of these than the ill-judged fire of the Italians. As the lorries passed through, many Italians tried to give themselves up as prisoners, clambering on to the vehicles, and having their knuckles rapped in order to stop them clinging on.

From the opening of the enemy's offensive until the date of the fighting withdrawal there were countless deeds of courage under great difficulties and stress. Some of these deeds have been recorded, but there are many which will never be known.

Private Albert Robinson's company of the 5th East Yorkshires took part in an attack on a strongly held position, the object being to cover the closing of a gap in a minefield. There was very little cover and throughout the action the attack was subjected to heavy artillery, Breda and motorised machine-gun fire. On his own initiative, Robinson crawled two hundred yards in front of his platoon headquarters, between two enemy machine-gun posts, neither of which could fire without hitting the other. Settling himself comfortably he proceeded to pick off the crews of the posts with great deliberation. Private Robinson was awarded the Military Medal.

Company Sergeant Major Thomas Mattock went out accompanied by a private soldier and attacked and destroyed the whole crew of an enemy machine-gun post which had been holding up his company's advance. He was awarded the Distinguished Conduct Medal.

There is one odd story about events which took place just before dark on the evening of the 14th June. Major Paul Parbury, in command of a battery of field artillery operating with the 5th East Yorkshires, was approached by a subaltern of the battalion, who, thinking that the Major's carrier was one of the battalion's, ordered Major Parbury to 'damned well' go and silence a machine-gun that was holding up the advance of his platoon. Without hesitation Major Parbury charged the post in his carrier. Having silenced the gun he returned to the subaltern and said, 'I've done that.' Still not recognising him, the subaltern told him to 'damn well' silence another post, and again Major Parbury, in spite of artillery and machine-gun fire, charged the post and silenced the gun. Major Parbury was later awarded the Military Cross for gallantry.

Lieut.-Colonel Stansfield gave an account of how the gap was made:

> 'We really knew very little about the enemy minefields, namely, which were live and which were dummy ones. There was no time for reconnaissance. My orders were to move out at 8 p.m., make a gap of three thousand yards in the enemy position and hold it until 3 a.m., by which time the whole Brigade should have passed through. Lt.-Col M. L .P. Jackson, also of the Green Howards, commanding a battalion of the Durham Light Infantry, was to do the same thing on my right for the 151st Brigade. In the ensuing action, Lt.-Col Jackson won the Distinguished Service Order. I was given six tanks, all that were left in the Division after the Knightsbridge battle, and, having set out at 8 p.m., soon reached the enemy lines. I saw four of my tanks go up in flames from mines or direct hits, one very gallant crew continuing to fire their gun, although the tank was on fire, and eventually burnt out. It was now nearly dark, but the whole area was lit up by tracers, shells, mortar bombs and burning vehicles. We could have taken masses of prisoners. The Italians thought that we were making a "push" for Benghazi. One of my officers captured an Italian General in his silk dressing gown. At 3 a.m., the 6th and 7th Green Howards having passed through, we turned south and made for Bir Hacheim.'

The Group, having embussed, set off to follow the rest of 50th Division. Although some of the columns became split up and lost their direction, while others ran into a minefield, the Group fared well on the whole,

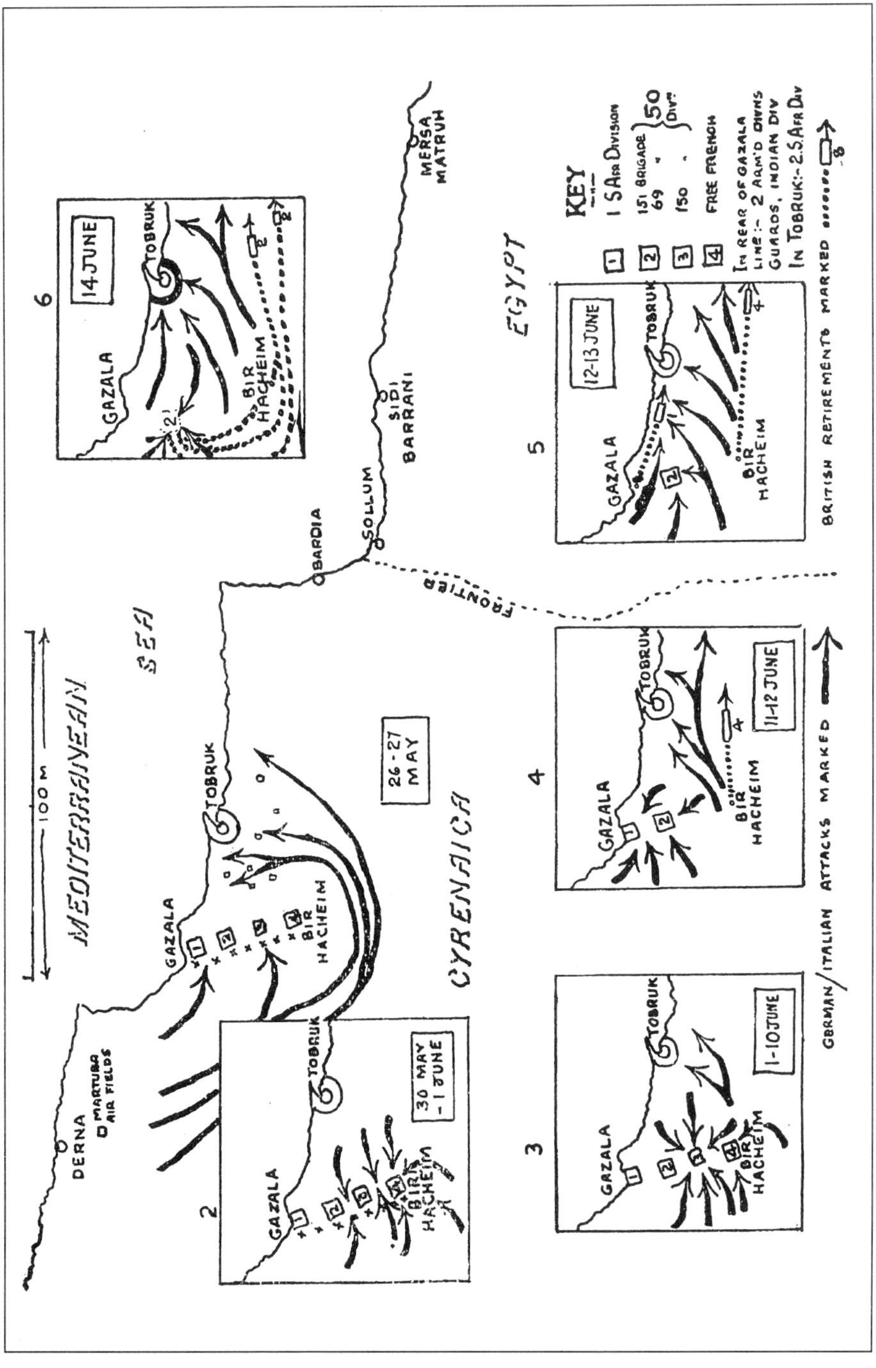
MEDITERRANEAN
SEA
100 M
DERNA
MARTUBA AIR FIELDS
GAZALA
TOBRUK
BIR HACHEIM
26-27 MAY
CYRENAICA
BARDIA
SOLLUM
SIDI BARRANI
MERSA MATRUH
EGYPT
FRONTIER
2
30 MAY -1 JUNE
3
1-10 JUNE
4
11-12 JUNE
5
12-13 JUNE
6
14 JUNE
KEY
1 S Afr Division
2 151 Brigade
69 "
3 150 "
50 Divn
4 Free French
In rear of Gazala line:- 2 Arm'd Divns, Guards, Indian Div
In Tobruk:- 2 S Afr Div
British retirements marked
German/Italian attacks marked

passing through several protected encampments unmolested.

The Germans sent up reconnaissance planes, but they flew in the wrong directions, and, by the time the mistake was discovered, the survivors of the 50th Division were on course, south to skirt Bir Hacheim, and then east.

The 4th and 5th Battalions, The East Yorkshire Regiment are credited with gaining the Battle Honour **Gazala** (26th May – 21st June) for the Regiment, which was elected to be carried on the Colours.

* * * * *

The 2nd South African Division (Lieutenant-General Klopper) at Tobruk, together with a Guards Brigade and an Indian Infantry Brigade, were ordered to defend the port as long as possible after evacuation of the other forces, but they were insufficient in numbers to hold the very long perimeter. Rommel attacked with dive-bombers and almost all his armour. The garrison fought with great gallantry, but with food and ammunition running low, further fighting could only lead to heavy casualties. On the 21st June, 1942, Lieutenant-General Klopper, commanding the garrison, surrendered. Some 33,000 men, mostly South Africans, became prisoners of war. Major-General Ramsden's decision proved right. Had he gone along the coast road, the 50th Division might well have been caught up in the Tobruk perimeter.

* * * * *

The 69th Brigade, having battled to hold the enemy while the rest of the Division moved away, had little to do other than follow up. After a journey of 200 miles they halted at Scherferzenon a few miles west of the Libyan-Egyptian border, Here they enjoyed a welcome rest, stretching legs after being cramped up in lorries and the usual 'brew-up' of tea, going on to Bir Thalatha where on the 21st June the scattered forces of the Division assembled.

The Division was considerably weakened by loss of vehicles, kit, equipment, reserve ammunition and weapons. Most important was the loss of signal stores and wireless trucks. The weather was extremely hot, there was a shortage of water and the troops were exposed to the sun; there being no shade many suffered from heat exhaustion.

The Commander-in-Chief had decided that the frontier could not be held. The 50th Division was ordered to retire in conformity with the general plan to a prepared 'box' twenty-five miles south of Mersa Matruh and dig in and reorganise.

Orders were then received for the Division to take up a line from Mersa Matruh to Buq Buq and act as rearguard for the whole army; hold off the enemy and let through the retiring columns.

On the 21st June, a column formed mainly from the 69th Brigade and all the divisional artillery took up positions around Buq Buq to cover the withdrawal of 10th Indian Division, which was at that time holding Sollum, and then act as rear-guard back to Mersa Matruh. The 10th Indian Division began to withdraw that morning, passing through the brigade column on the night of the 22nd/23rd June. The column withdrew to Sidi Barrani on the 24th and, after destroying dumps of food and stores retired the next day, reaching Mersa Matruh in the early hours of the 26th, where the whole of the 50th Division assembled. Here the Eighth Army was preparing to make a stand. A defensive position was taken up south-east of the town with the 10th Indian Division garrisoning the port.

On the 26th June, General Auchinleck relieved Lieutenant-General Neil Ritchie of command of Eighth Army, and personally took command. Having decided not to hold Mersa Matruh but to withdraw to El Alamein, at 1800 hours he ordered the 50th Division to take up a rearguard position some two miles east of Mersah Matruh to cover the withdrawal of other formations including the 10th Indian Division and the 10th Corps H.Q.

On the same day, the Commander of the 69th Brigade, Brigadier L. L. Hassell, D.S.O., M.C., was evacuated sick, command going to Lieutenant-Colonel E. C. Cooke-Collis of 6th Green Howards. Lieut.-Colonel Cooke-Collis had effectively commanded the Brigade for much of the fighting in Libya, owing to the ill-health of Brigadier Hassell. Although wounded at an early stage in the retreat from the Gazala line, Cooke-Collis had refused to be evacuated and was to be found wherever there was action. For his leadership and bravery in the actions around Bir Aslagh from the 27th/29th May, and during the rearguard operation from Buq Buq to Mersa Matruh Brigadier Cooke-Collis was awarded the Distinguished Service Order. He was subsequently awarded a bar for the part he played at Mareth, which will later be related.

At 2000 hours on the 26th June, just as the 69th Brigade began to move off to new positions they were attacked by a large force of Stuka dive-bombers. They dug themselves in and all was quiet until the afternoon of the 27th June when an enemy column of some two thousand vehicles crossed the Siwa Road, to the south-east of Mersa Matruh. The 10th Indian Division in the port and the 50th Division around it were isolated.

At 1700 hours orders were issued for an attack by the 50th Division with the 69th Brigade to the left and the 151st Brigade on its right, on the enemy's supply lines, to destroy transport, disorganise supplies and to delay the advance. Having completed the operation, units would return to the positions to the east of Mersa Matruh.

The 69th Brigade in troop-carrying transport, supported by light tanks, crossed the starting line at 2100 hours the 5th East Yorkshires to the left, the 6th Green Howards to their right, the 7th Green Howards in reserve behind 5th East Yorkshires.

As the 5th East Yorkshires advanced they came upon a nullah crossing their front. As soon as they went over the crest they came under artillery fire, the enemy gunners, owing to the bright moonlight reflected on the windscreens, having noticed the vehicles from two miles off. The shelling set fire to a number of trucks and casualties were caused to both sides. The advance continued until the leading troops ran into an enemy column and came under attack from a vastly superior force. With casualties mounting and the loss of vehicles, Brigadier Cooke-Collis ordered a withdrawal. By dawn on the 28th June the 50th Division had completed a difficult night march and was back to its original position east of Mersa Matruh.

During the day, a German motorised division with supporting tanks and 88-mm guns closed round and attacked; the whole of the divisional positions were subjected to a heavy bombardment by artillery and Stuka dive-bombers.

At midday, orders were received from H.Q. X Corps to break out, and head for Fuka. It was a grim undertaking. The troops had been fighting all the previous night, shelled all day, and were tired and exhausted. There was a shortage of weapons and of serviceable transport. The going would not be easy, as this time in place of 'soft' Italians the Division would be up against considerable large forces of the stubborn *Afrika Korps* between the divisional positions and Fuka.

In order to escape unnoticed Major-General Ramsden decided to break out south during what might have been hours of darkness, but instead there was a full moon. These orders were passed to Brigade Commanders and given out to the Battalion Commanders of the 69th Brigade by the Brigade Commander at 1730 hours.

During the evening the Division was divided into a number of small columns of all arms with about thirty vehicles, each being given a different rendezvous, and starting time. They were to make their way south through the enemy positions across ravines, on to the plain, then eastwards to rejoin the main part of the Eighth Army.

At 2100 hours, just as the columns formed up in preparation for the break-out, Brigadier Cooke-Collis came upon Lieut.-General Sir William G. Holmes, commanding X Corps, whose car had broken down, who informed him that Fuka had been in enemy hands since 1600 hours that afternoon. As it seemed that the enemy attack would not be on a full scale General Ramsden decided that the original orders for a break-out should be carried through.

The enemy was holding the escarpment in strength, and it was necessary to make a gap in the enemy position. As at Gazala, the 5th East Yorkshires were given the task of covering the passage out of the 'box' of the 69th Brigade column which included General Ramsden and Divisional H.Q. In order to make the gap they had to advance in single file along a narrow track to get to the top of the escarpment before light.

As they made their way through the twisting wadis to the gap, they encountered soft sand and slit trenches making it difficult for vehicles to negotiate. Some stuck fast in wadis, and had to be manhandled on to firmer ground. Every vehicle so held up halted the whole column. Roads had to be made with tarpaulins from the vehicles, covered by brushwood, over which even heavy vehicles were able to pass. At 0300 hours on the 29th, two hours before dawn, vehicles were still climbing prodigious slopes over small loose rocks. Parties of men posted on either side of a chosen path were organised to push forward each of the smaller vehicles. Jeeps with four-wheel drive and engines that could develop 60 h.p. hauled up the 3-ton lorries with men pushing behind them.

After a storming attack against enormous odds in a confused and slightly disorganised night battle the summit was reached and secured and the gap made. The escarpment was crossed under heavy artillery and machine-gun fire. There were considerable casualties. The column, covered by what was left of the 5th East Yorkshires, got clear. What was left of the Battalion then disengaged, re-embussed and followed on. The part played by the Battalion was recognised by the immediate award of the Distinguished Service Order to the commanding officer, Lieutenant-Colonel Thomas Stansfield.

There followed a nightmare journey east across country in an area quite unknown to the troops, in pitch darkness, and full of enemy troops. The column became split up into small sections as in the dark it was almost impossible to follow the man in front. Groups ran head on into enemy lines – sometimes right through them; some were badly shot up; some ran clean over precipices; others broke down and had to be towed or abandoned ; some went completely astray in the desert; some were blown up on minefields. With Fuka, the original rendezvous, in enemy hands, the columns went on to reach the stop-line at El Alamein-Ruweisat, on the 30th June.

At dusk the 6th Green Howards were attacked but held on until 2100 hours when they formed four columns and made their way up the narrow track created by the 5th East Yorkshires. On reaching the summit it was decided that vehicles should individually cross the escarpment with utmost speed and then re-assemble. As they crossed the three miles of escarpment they came under heavy machine-gun and anti-tank gun fire A burning tank lit up the sky. Only ten vehicles reached the re-assembly area. Moving on a short distance they came upon minefields in front, and a ravine about two-hundred-feet deep on the right. They could not turn east as the area was occupied by a stronger force of the enemy. 'Every man for himself' was ordered and men set off to walk by crossing the ravine and into the desert, and in two days had reached the Alamein-Ruweisat line, from where they were sent back to Mareopolis, arriving there on the 2nd July.

The 7th Green Howards had received orders to cover the withdrawal of the rest of the Brigade and at 2315 hours follow on, but in the event of an enemy attack they were to stand fast and fight it out. As night fell the positions were heavily machine-gunned and shelled, and about 2030 hours German infantry, unsupported by other arms, advanced in solid formation. With the assistance of the carrier platoon of the 5th East Yorkshires they were driven off. Intense artillery and mortar fire was brought down on the position, causing many casualties. Unsure as to whether the Brigade column had got safely away, Lieut.-Colonel Macdonnell decided to fight to a finish, but first decided to send 'B' Echelon transport, the artillery and the machine-gun platoon, which was running short of ammunition, to join the brigade column. As soon as the enemy heard the transport starting up they increased their fire. Shortly afterwards, enemy tanks broke through and overran the forward positions. The Battalion had for six hours held off a much larger force of the German 90th Light Division, inflicting heavy casualties, and thus enabling the 50th Division to escape.

What was left of the Battalion got away and, after marching across about a hundred miles of desert, with only the food and water with which they started off, rejoined the Brigade.

The Division was now considerably depleted. Casualties had been heavier than in the Gazala break-out. Of the original 800 men of 5th East Yorkshires who had set out to defend their 'box' at the Gazala line, only 170 were left, All the 'B' Echelon transport had been lost at Mersa Matruh. The 7th Green Howards, having lost its commanding officer, its second-in-command, and most of the men, had temporarily ceased to exist.

Casualties in the Division since the opening battle at Gazala on 26th May numbered 8,875, including the loss of the 150th Brigade. The average strength of battalions in the 69th and the 151st Brigades was only 300 men, and most of the transport lost.

In the words of General Ramsden it had been a 'rough party.'

The 5th Battalion was credited with the award to the Regiment of the Battle Honour **Mersa Matruh** (26th – 30th June, 1942).

RUWEISAT RIDGE
1st-29th JULY

Rommel's forces had been halted. The Eighth Army, much reduced after the losses of Gazala, Tobruk and Mersa Matruh, and, with its armoured forces severely weakened, took up a new defensive line between El Alamein close to the sea in the north down to the Qattara Depression, a large impassable salt-marsh, forty miles to the south.

Auchinleck fixed the right of his line at El Alamein, down to the Ruweisat Ridge eight miles south. This was to be manned by Lieut.-General Willoughby Norrie's XXX Corps. The line from the Ruweisat Ridge southwards to the Qattara Depression was to be held by Lieut.-General W.H.E. 'Strafer' Gott's XIII Corps.

X Corps (Lieut.-General William G. Holmes), which had suffered heavily in the previous week, was sent back to the rear to refit, regroup and be brought up to strength.

At dawn on the 1st July, Rommel launched his attack. The 50th Division was given no rest and went back into the line along the Ruweisat Ridge. Three Battle Groups (strong mobile columns made up of a small number of infantry and many guns) were formed from the 69th Brigade (the 151st Brigade had gone back to Mareopolis) to hold the key position on the Ruweisat Ridge. The enemy attacked fiercely and for four days the battle edged back and forth. When the fighting died down on the 4th July they were relieved by the 9th Australian Division and with the rest of X Corps withdrew to Mareopolis, the 50th Division to re-form with only two brigades (the 69th and 151st), there being no replacement for the lost 150th Brigade.

On the 7th July, Major-General Ramsden was promoted Lieut.-General and took command of XXX Corps from Lieut.-General Willoughby Norrie; Major-General J. S. (Crasher) Nichols, M.C., a former officer of the Border Regiment, assumed command of the 50th Division on the 11th.

At Mareopolis the task of re-forming and re-organising the Division began. The field artillery had lost a large number of guns and some thirty per cent of its strength as had all other arms and services.

The 5th East Yorkshires received reinforcements, from 'the reserves' of the 5th Battalion (purposely left out of the battles) and survivors of the 4th Battalion from Gazala. The 6th Green Howards were reinforced by drawing on the depleted 7th Battalion and, on the 14th July, Lieut.-Colonel G. W. Eden was appointed to command. Even so, the infantry battalions had only been increased in strength to around four hundred and fifty. Training began but this was to be cut short.

Auchinleck, having held Rommel in the north, but failed to drive him off, now switched his attack from the Alamein area to Ruweisat Ridge, at the same time moving his Headquarters to the Ruweisat Ridge to be in closer control of the battle and in tune with the conditions of the troops.

On the 12th July the 69th Brigade received orders to move to a position immediately east of the Ruweisat Ridge to construct defence lines. By the 18th July, the major part of the defences having been completed, the Brigade was placed under command of the 5th Indian Division with orders to send a brigade group to take up a position on the Ruweisat Ridge by dawn the next day, and hold off any enemy break through.

There was a hasty reorganisation. The 5th East Yorkshires and 6th Green Howards were brought up to full strength, the latter by drawing on the 7th Green Howards. The two battalions of 69th Brigade were far from the highly organised and disciplined battalions they had been in the earlier battles; there had been no time to train as complete units and in many cases the reinforcements were unknown to Company and Platoon commanders. The brigade group moved off with the machine-guns of 'B' Company, 2nd Cheshire Regiment and 233rd Field Company R.E.

On the 20th July the 69th Brigade was ordered to head twenty miles to the south to come under the command of the 7th Armoured Division. Brigadier Cooke-Collis was given orders to attack strong enemy positions in the southern sector of the 7th Armoured Divisions lines. A composite battalion of the 201st Guards Brigade was placed under his command for this operation, which was to be carried out in three phases on the night of the 21st/22nd July. The first phase was the capture of Taqa Plateau; the second Jebel Kalakh. Phase 3, dependent upon the success of the first two, was for the 4th Armoured Brigade of the 7th Armoured Division to pass through and work behind the enemy lines in the hope that they would be forced to withdraw.

There was little information available to the Brigade Commander about the area occupied by the enemy, and reconnaissance of the Taqa Plateau and Jebel Kalakh could not be made during daylight as it was under direct enemy observation and surprise on the night would be lost.

Brigadier Cooke-Collis viewed the whole operation with misapprehension. The composite Guards battalion was very much under strength and its troops tired from weeks of continuous fighting; the 69th Brigade, a composite force designed for a limited operation, the 4th Armoured Brigade had only small Stuart tanks and armoured cars.

The composite battalion of the Guards Brigade was ordered to attack and capture the eastern end of the Taqa Plateau and Naqb el Khadin and on the successful completion of the action the 5th East Yorkshires and 6th Green Howards to attack the Taqa Plateau from the south.

In the afternoon of the 21st, the 5th East Yorkshires and 6th Green Howards (roughly two and a half companies strong – the others being kept back under Brigade Control as support companies) moved forward in transports from the Ruweisat Ridge to the forming-up position some three miles east of Garet El Himeimat: Four hours later the position was reached. This was as far as they could go unobserved in daylight. When darkness fell they advanced to a point about six miles south of the Taqa Plateau where they debussed. The going had been hazardous; soft sand in places compelled the men to jump out of the vehicles, push them and dig them out while others had to be towed, but both battalions were formed up by 0100 hours. Meanwhile the Guards composite battalion had been successful in carrying out its task and reached its objectives by 2300 hours.

At 0130 hours the 5th East Yorkshires on the left, and the 6th Green Howards on the right, moved forward, and, when daylight came, had reached the southern edge of the plateau, without encountering the enemy, but as soon as it became daylight they came under heavy machine-gun fire. By 0830 hours, the two-and-a-half companies of the 6th Green Howards were firmly established on the plateau but, coming under heavy mortar and machine-gun fire, could make no further progress. On the left the 5th East Yorkshires had not been able to get further than the southern edge. Both battalions had suffered casualties. During the morning the companies of the 6th Green Howards were withdrawn to conform with the 5th East Yorkshires, in order to consolidate the position against counter-attack which the enemy was preparing.

Throughout the day they were subjected to continuous artillery and mortar fire which caused a considerable number of casualties while many of the men suffered severely from heat exhaustion. Lieut. Colonel G.W. Eden commanding the 6th Green Howards was wounded.

The shelling was followed at 1600 hours by a counter-attack on both battalions with armoured car and tank support. A hard battle was fought, with heavy casualties, and the enemy driven off by artillery and mortar fire but patrols sent out that night found the enemy being reinforced in strength for further action

On the 23rd, there was more shelling and considerable mortar fire, the enemy attempting to dislodge the troops from the plateau. The heat was intense and the water ration was reduced to less than half a water-bottle per man. As it seemed to the Brigade Commander that there was no hope of further progress, and the force had suffered heavy losses, he asked for permission to withdraw. This was granted and at 2100 hours the force began to retire under cover of darkness. The departure was unnoticed by the enemy, and Garet El Himeimat was reached at midday on the 24th July.

Having endured the appalling heat of the plateau, the lack of food and water, and the exertion of pushing their vehicles through patches of soft sand during the long drive back through the night, all were looking forward to a good night's sleep. Then in the evening orders were received for the 69th Brigade to move north again to Alam El Dakar to take part in an attack through the enemy's minefields near Alamein station.

To make up for the losses sustained during the previous three days a composite battalion of one company from each of the battalions of the Durham Light Infantry switched from the 151st Brigade to the 69th Brigade, and one from the 5th East Yorkshires, all under command of Lieut.-Colonel S. Battiscombe of the Durham Light Infantry. A battalion of the 9th Australian Division was ordered to co-operate with them.

The 69th Brigade moved off and made its way over heavy going. When darkness fell orders were received to halt and rest. The march was resumed at first light and Alam El Dakar reached at 1000 hours on the 25th. Here they dug in and rested for thirty-six hours before going into the attack..

At 2200 hours on the 26th the 6th Green Howards advanced through the composite battalion of the 5th East Yorkshires and the Durham Light Infantry to the gap in the enemy minefield. Heavy artillery fire fell on them as they progressed. The company from the 5th East Yorkshires lost direction and one company of the D.L.I. lost touch with both the others. The remaining two companies found difficulty in keeping in touch. In the moonlight they advanced five thousand yards; the Germans let them pass and then cut off the line of retreat and communications. At first light the 6th Green Howards arrived at their destination outside the gap which was only wide enough for the passage of infantry and light vehicles. Steps were taken to widen the gap for the passage of tanks, but the only tanks to use the gap were those of the enemy. At midday British tanks arrived but owing to some misunderstanding they did not pass through the gap but settled down and waited. This resulted in the area being subjected to dive bombing and artillery fire.

In the early evening, enemy tanks appeared in force, outnumbering and outgunning the British tanks. A tank battle took place and the British tanks withdrew, putting down a thick smoke-screen which blew to the west and enabled the enemy tanks to move forward unseen. Orders were received to withdraw on the night of the 27th July.

The Composite Battalion was isolated and after a vigorous resistance the survivors of the Durham Light Infantry, including the commanding officer, were captured, as were most of the 5th East Yorkshires and Australians. The 69th Brigade arrived back at Mareopolis on the 29th July to join the rest of the 50th Division.

The Division was given the task of defending the Northern Delta, and, although remaining in the Eighth Army Order of Battle, came under command of the G.O.C. British Forces in Egypt. The area to defend stretched from the sea to a point fifty miles south of Alexandria and included all the Delta area. This needed far more troops than those in the Division and in consequence seven additional brigades were brought into command.

During the first week in August, three or four days' leave was granted to all ranks in either Cairo or Alexandria. For many it was their first leave since arrival in the Middle East. The battalions were re-equipped, reinforced and carried out training, at the same time enjoying some well earned rest and enjoyed bathing in the sea. On the 25th July, Auchinleck had issued a Special Order of the Day:

> 'You have done well. You have turned a retreat into a firm stand, and stopped the enemy on the threshold of Egypt. You have done more. You have wrenched the initiative from him by sheer guts and hard fighting and put HIM on the defensive in these last weeks. He has lost heavily, and is short of men, ammunition and petrol. You have borne much, but I ask you for more. You must not slacken. If we can stick it, we will break him. STICK TO IT.'

A War Office communique issued later singled out the 50th Division for special commendation at this juncture:

> 'Their toughness and discipline saved more than themselves. At Alamein they helped to halt the German and Italian Divisions who were pushing on, flushed with success and expecting an easy conquest of Egypt. During those weeks, from late June, a few tired formations saved the world from disaster . . . for many days (these formations) . . . alone barred the way to the Nile. In each phase of the struggle, the 50th enhanced their reputation as dashing and determined fighters.'

An overall Battle Honour, **Defence of Alamein Line,** covering the 1st to the 27th June, 1942, was granted and gained for the East Yorkshire Regiment by the 5th Battalion.

* * * * *

Auchinleck had accomplished the almost impossible. He had halted Rommel on the Alamein line, sixty miles from Alexandria. The Axis hopes of reaching the Nile Delta and taking Cairo were over.

It was obvious, that with his desperately tired army and armour reduced in numbers, no further progress could be made. The Alamein line must be held until the arrival of reinforcements, the 44th (Home Counties) Division had arrived in mid-July and were in the Delta, the 51ast (Highland) and 8th Armoured Divisions were on their way. For the moment, the Eighth Army must go on the defensive.

In 'Personal History. The Story of the Highland Light Infantry,' Vol. IV it is remarked:

> 'Sir Claude Auchinleck frustrated the enemy at the eleventh hour, and sowed the seeds for victory.'

After the fighting of the 26th July, Rommel said in his despatches:

> 'The British had again suffered heavy casualties – a thousand prisoners and 32 tanks – and their command now lost all taste for further attacks. The German Italian Front had shown itself to be no longer penetrable by forces of the size they were committing. It was certain that we could continue to hold our front, and that, after the crisis we had been through, was at last something. Although the British losses in this Alamein fighting had been higher than ours, yet the price to Auchinleck had not been excessive, for the thing that mattered to him was to halt our advance, and that, unfortunately, he had done.'

On Saturday the 1st August, the Prime Minister, Winston Churchill left Lyneham airport en route via Gibralter for Cairo, and after a day at Gibralter arrived in Cairo on the 3rd August. The Chief of the Imperial General Staff, General Sir Alan Brooke, had arrived earlier, as had Field Marshal Jan Christian Smuts, Prime Minister of the Union of South Africa and overall commander of the Union's forces. Smuts was a member of the British cabinet, a long time friend and colleague of the Prime Minister, whose views and advice had been sought on many occasions and in whom Churchill placed great trust. Field Marshal Sir Archibald Wavell, Commander-in-Chief in India, and Auchinleck's predecessor had also been called to the conference.

Auchinleck was not there to meet them, being in his desert H.Q. behind the Ruweisat Ridge. After placing Lieut.-General Ramsden in command of the Eighth Army, he left to meet those assembled who were to decide the future command in the Middle East.

At a conference on the 6th it was decided that Lieut.-General, The Honourable Harold R. L. G. Alexander, D.S.O., M.C., should be appointed Commander-in-Chief, Middle East Command, replacing General Sir Claude Auchinleck, and on the 10th the Prime Minister sent him the following directions. (See opposite, page 57).

At the same conference there was a discussion as to who should be appointed to command the Eighth Army. Churchill favoured the appointment of Lieut.-General William Gott, G.O.C. XIII Corps, (who had been in the Western Desert from the beginning) to command the Eighth Army. But on the afternoon of 7th August, the 'plane on which he was travelling on leave was shot down soon after taking off on the Burg el Arab-Heliopolis route to Cairo: a route which the Prime Minister had used only a few days before. Gott had got clear, but, realising others were

Most Secret

BRITISH EMBASSY,
CAIRO.

Direction to General Alexander

Commander in Chief in the Middle East

1. Yr prime & main duty will be to take or destroy at the earliest opportunity the German-Italian Army commanded by Field Marshal Rommel together with all its supplies & establishments in Egypt & Libya.

2. You will discharge or cause to be discharged such other duties as pertain to yr Command without prejudice to the task described in paragraph 1, which must be considered paramount in His Majesty's interests.

WSC
10. Aug. 42

A.F.B.
CIGS.
10.8.42

in the wrecked plane, returned to help to rescue them. The plane blew up, resulting in his death.

The choice was now Lieut.-General Bernard Montgomery, D.S.O., presently commanding the South-Eastern Army in England, and G.O.C-in-C designate of the First Army for the landings under General Eisenhower in North Africa on the 8th November. This appointment had been held by General Alexander until on the 6th August he was appointed to succeed Auchinleck.

Informed of the appointment on the 8th August, Montgomery left by air on the 10th, arriving in Cairo early on the morning of the 12th August. The change of command was to be effected on the 15th August. Auchinleck told Montgomery, 'that he, (Montgomery) was to go down to H.Q. Eight Army in the desert the next day and spend two days "getting into the picture".' He was, himself, still commanding the Eighth Army, and had ordered Ramsden to act for him. Furthermore Montgomery would not be taking over command of the Eighth Army until the 15th August, that being the day that he would hand over as C.-in-C Middle East to General Alexander.

In the afternoon the Deputy Chief of the General Staff, Major-General John Harding, was called to the office of the C-in-C Middle East to find Montgomery sitting in the C-in-Cs chair, while Alexander was sitting on the desk. He was asked to tell Montgomery about all the commanders at present in the desert down to brigade level – 'those who are good and those who are not good'. Major-General Ramsden fell into the category 'not good' with great emphasis.

The next morning, having said nothing to the contrary, Montgomery left Cairo to drive to Tac. H.Q. Eighth Army H.Q., just behind Ruweisat Ridge. Just outside Alexandria he was met by Brigadier Francis (Freddie) de Guingand, Brigadier General Staff, Eighth Army, who had been told to accompany him. In the car, on the way up to meet Ramsden, de Guingand, was, like Harding asked to give 'a run down' not only on the commanders, but on the operational situation, Intelligence of the enemy, and on his own views. de Guingand expressed his opinion of Ramsden as 'bloody useless'. reinforcing the opinion of Harding, and saying it was shared by most officers at Eighth Army Headquarters. Was this being said since it was sensed that this was what Montgomery wanted to hear? Did not Harding and de Guingand acknowledge the bold and imaginative stroke which had got the 50th Division away from the Gazala Line?

Arriving at G.H.Q., Montgomery told General Ramsden *to return to

---

*With Major-General Nichols having been appointed G.O.C. 50th Division, there was no place for Ramsden. He was sent back to the United Kingdom and given command of the 3rd British (Iron) Division, destined to be one of the three British Divisions to assault the coast of Normandy in 1944. When Montgomery returned to England in January 1943 to take command of the 21st Army Group he disposed of a large number of major-generals and other senior officers whom he described as 'mostly quite useless – the B.G.S. Intelligence was no good at all, the Major-General Administration, a bit of a dud.' Major-

XXX Corps and, without waiting until the appointed date, took over command of the Army, and from there sent a signal to G.H.Q. in Cairo:

'. . . Lt.-Gen Montgomery assumed command of Eighth Army at 1400 hrs today.'

In some quarters it was thought to be an act of calculated insolence – reminiscent of his take-over of V Corps from Auchinleck in July, 1940. Montgomery then went on to address officers from all branches of Eighth Army's staff, operational, artillery, engineers, administration, intelligence, plans, signals and staff duties. The sixty officers stood to attention and saluted. Returning the salute, he stood on the steps of Auchinleck's caravan and told them to sit in the sand. He told them that his orders were to make a stand – to end the cycle of British defeat. He was not impressed by Eighth Army.

'I do not like the general atmosphere I find here. It is an atmosphere of doubt, of looking back to select the next place to which to withdraw, of loss of confidence in our ability to defeat Rommel, of desperate defence measures by reserves in preparing positions in Cairo and the Delta.

All that must cease.

Let us have a new atmosphere.

The defence of Egypt lies here at Alamein and on the Ruweisat Ridge. What is the use of digging trenches in the Delta. It is quite useless; if we lose this position we lose Egypt; all the fighting troops now in the Delta must come here at once, and will.

Here we will stand and fight; there will be no further withdrawal. I have ordered that all plans and instructions dealing with further withdrawals are to be burnt, and at once. We will stand and fight here. if we can't stand here alive, then let us stay here dead.'

Montgomery at once set about reorganising the Eighth Army. His first priority was to appoint three Corps Commanders in whom he could have confidence. Major-General Brian Horrocks was sent out from England, arriving on 28th August to take command of XIII Corps, no appointment having been made on the death of Gott. Major-General Sir Oliver Leese, Bart., who was commanding the Guards Armoured Division in England was flown out to replace Major-General Ramsden* at XXX Corps; Major-General Herbert Lumsden who had long been commanding the 1st Armoured Division in the desert succeeded Lieut.-General William G. Holmes at X Corps; and Brigadier John Harding, Deputy Chief of the General Staff at GHQ Cairo, took command of the 7th Armoured Division.

The strength of the Eighth Army was built up. Reinforcements were arriving and would soon outnumber the Germans by just under four to one and the combined Axis forces by two to one. The tanks destroyed in earlier battles were replaced and additional ones arrived, all of improved

---

General Ramsden was also relieved of command. The Regimental Journal of the East Yorkshire Regiment, 'The Snapper', says 'Major-General W. H. C. Ramsden having completed the recognised three years as a Field Force Commander, was appointed to command the Soudan Defence Force and British Troops Soudan and Eritrea.' Certainly he had completed three years service as a Major-General having been appointed to command 50th (Northumbrian) Division in November, 1940, but could not Monty's opinion have played some part in his leaving?

pattern and equal to those of the Germans. There were five British tanks to one Axis. Increased supplies of stores and ammunition were arriving: self-propelled guns; anti-tank guns of more power than hitherto; 'planes and equipment in great quantities. But before these could be assembled for any great attack, Rommel was to make his last play for Egypt.

THE BATTLE OF ALAM HALFA

On the night of the 30th August, Rommel launched an attack to the south by the *Afrika Korps* between the Alum Nayil Ridge and the Qattara Depression, hoping to surprise the Eighth Army by a dawn raid to the rear after a drive eastwards, but the *Afrika Korps* got bogged down in a minefield and was halted by attacks by the R.A.F. a few miles beyond it. Rommel then turned north towards the coast and made a very heavy attack on the Alam Halfa Ridge. This was to be Montgomery's first battle with Eighth Army.

Lieut.-General Brian Horrocks, who had arrived from England three days earlier and had taken over XIII Corps, was to play the major role in the battle. The 44th (Home Counties) Division was called forward, to hold

Group Captain Lewis, commanding Bomber Wing Forward Headquarters Desert Airforce, plots pinpoints of target given by Major T. L. Ward, 8th Army Liaison Officer.

the position on the ridge. The 15th and 21st Panzer Divisions attacked the positions but were pinned down by perpetual bombing and accurate artillery fire. The 7th Armoured Division deployed to the south to strike at the flank of the advancing armour and on the 2nd September Rommel began a gradual withdrawal.

On the 4th September the 151st Brigade was sent into the Alamein line to come under command of the New Zealand Division, and take over part of the line in the New Zealand sector, just south of Ruweisat Ridge. Two of the battalions of the Durham Light Infantry were brought up to strength with two rifle companies of the 5th East Yorkshires and two from the 6th Green Howards; a machine-gun company of the 2nd Cheshire Regiment, and 505th Field Company, R.E.

The Brigade sent out many highly successful patrols, gaining information which proved of great value later at the Battle of Alamein. They dominated 'No-Man's-Land' and clashed with the Italian Folgore Division of parachutists. One task was the recovery of derelict carriers and other vehicles which the New Zealanders had abandoned when earlier moving back. Covering parties went out at night in front of the minefield, while breakdown parties brought in the abandoned vehicles.

Having halted, Rommel positioned his forces to invite a counterattack, but when this did not materialise, he moved forward again. Now the Desert Air Force attacked, and the artillery found the massed enemy forces a perfect target. After a few days the enemy losses in tanks and soft-skinned vehicles were severe, and many tanks were stuck in the soft sand. The bombing of Tobruk by Wellington aircraft of Air Marshal Coningham's Desert Air Force prevented petrol and supplies getting through, and on the 7th September Rommel withdrew. This battle was probably the turning point of the desert war, and possibly more significant than the forthcoming battle of El Alamein.

* * * * *

THE 50TH DIVISION PREPARES FOR THE BATTLE OF EL ALAMEIN

At the end of September the 151st Brigade passed to the command of the 44th (Home Counties) Division but went up into the line..

The 69th Brigade, having completed its well-earned rest, carried out intensive training, but also had the role of defending Alexandria in case of attack by parachute or glider forces. An organisation was set up to train infantry reinforcements for the whole Division, and, although these reinforcements did not arrive until the 12th September, such was their keenness and enthusiasm that by the end of the month they were ready to take their places in the battalions.

On the 1st October the remainder of the 50th Division began to move up to the allotted XIII Corps area in the south where it continued in reserve. The 69th Brigade moved up on the 3rd October to an area behind the front for training, but on arrival was ordered to move next day into the New Zealand box to dig defensive positions, and, on the 6th, the two detached companies of the 5th East Yorkshires and 6th Green Howards returned from duty with the 151st Brigade, and training was begun.

On the night of the 9th/10th October the 69th Brigade relieved the 132nd Brigade of the 44th (Home Counties) Division in the Munassib Depression and on the 10th the 151st Brigade rejoined the 50th Division. The 1st Greek Brigade under Colonel Katsotos which had been with the 44th Division also joined the Division.

The 50th Division had once again taken its position in the front of the Eighth Army and was holding a sector of the line from just south of the Ruweisat Ridge in the north up to and including the Munassib Depression in the south.

The three brigades were in the line as follows:

Right: 1st Greek Brigade with supporting arms
Centre: 151st Brigade – then a considerable gap covered by minefieldsdown to:
Left: 69th Brigade.

The gap would later be filled by the 132nd Brigade of 44th Division which would come under 50th Division for a short time.

* * * * *

Between the 10th and 23rd October training was carried out behind the lines, At the same time wiring and mine laying was carried out, but units of the 69th Brigade went into action.

At 1900 hours on the 13th October, the 5th East Yorkshires, followed by the 6th Green Howards, moved off in column and arrived at their dispersal point at about 2200 hours and from there marched to their forward positions. By 0300 hours the next morning they were established in defensive positions some fifteen hundred yards from the enemy, which was holding two formidable hill features on the southern side of the Munassib Depression known as the 'The Moor' and the 'The Cape', the 7th Green Howards, now up to strength, but still short of equipment, moving into positions overlooking the Munassib position from the north. Opposing them was the Italian Folgore Division of volunteer parachutists.

Patrols went out, making contact with enemy working parties behind strongly wired defensive positions some three hundred yards east of Pt. 94 on the Moor, the enemy putting up considerable resistance. During the next ten days fighting and reconnaissance patrols went out by night harassing the enemy and gaining information about the defences in front of the enemy's forward localities, such as wire obstacles, booby traps on the wire, anti-tank and anti-personnel wire, and ground over which the Brigade would fight when the Battle of Alamein began. While this was going on, orders were received for an attack on the 'Moor' commencing at 1105 hours on the 25th October.

CHAPTER VI

THE BATTLE OF ALAMEIN

CODE NAME – OPERATION LIGHTFOOT

The Prime Minister, having seen the British Army continually defeated since the start of the war, was anxious for an early attack, and urged that it should take place at the beginning of September, but Montgomery was not prepared to start until troops had been brought up and trained and all supplies and stocks of ammunition were in position. It was also considered important to launch the attack at the time of a full moon so that the troops could see the minefields.

The battle of Alam Halfa had caused delay, and preparations were not ready for the September moon. The next full moon was on the 24th October, and plans were made for the attack to take place on the 23rd October.

On the 6th October the British and Axis forces were facing each other on a line of forty miles from the sea to El Alamein and down to the salt marsh of the Quattara Depression, with XXX Corps to the north of the line from the sea to the Ruweisat Ridge, XIII Corps from there to the Qattara Depression, and X Armoured Corps in reserve astride Cairo-Alexandria road. The composition of these Corps were:

X Corps	*XIII Corps*	*XXX Corps*
1st Armd Div.	7th Armd Div.	9th Australian Div.
8th Armd Div.	44th (Home Counties) Div.	51st (Highland) Div.*
10th Armd Div.	50th (Northumbrian) Div.	2nd New Zealand Div.
		1st South African Div.
		4th (Indian) Div.

Other Formations
1st Greek Brigade
1st Free French Brigade
2nd Fighting French Brigade
Fighting French Flying Column
9th Armoured Brigade
23rd Armoured Brigade (Valentine Tanks)

The German and Italian forces had, after Alam Halfa, established themselves in fortified positions behind minefields and anti-tank defences five miles deep. Their Order of Battle had the 164th,Trieste, 90th Light, 15th Panzer and Littoria Armoured Divisions in the north; the centre weakly held by the Italian Bologna Division, the German 21st Panzer and

*Re-created after having been lost at St. Valery in June, 1940

Italian Ariete (Motorised) Division; three German Infantry Divisions, and the Italian Brescia, Folgore and Pavia Divisions in the south.

Montgomery's plan was for an attack along the whole line so that the enemy could not perceive where the main attack would fall, but with a sufficiently strong attack in the south with XIII Corps to draw off the enemy from the centre, while to the north the 1st and 10th Armoured Divisions launched an attack against the strongest held part of the line, to drive two corridors through the line and minefields and let X Armoured Corps pass through and break out into the open country.

Meanwhile, to deceive the enemy as to the point of attack, these divisions were kept back behind XXX Corps. The 50th Division, having been under command of the G.O.C. British Forces Egypt since 29th July, whilst remaining in the Eighth Army 'Order of Battle,' had returned to XIII Corps, and was deployed at the southern end of the British line.

In order to elude the German Commander, General von Stumme, into expecting the main attack to take place in XIII Corps area, mocked up tanks, dummy lorries, guns made of wood, dumps with empty tin cans, and a dummy pipeline some twenty miles in length had been laid out. Thus the enemy expected the Eighth Army to attack the weakly held centre near the Ruweisat Ridge: Rommel could then direct his powerful force in an overwhelming flank attack.

The plan for the XIII Division was an attack to the south by the 44th (Home Counties) Division between Himeimat and the Munassib Depression to create a gap through which the 7th Armoured Division in position behind XIII Corps, would make a diversionary attack and then switch to the north at the last possible moment. The night after the attack by the 44th Division, but not until the 7th Armoured Division had got through the gap, the 50th Division would make a frontal attack on two hill features, a strongly defended 'island' in the Depression code-named 'The Moor,' and an isolated strong-point on the plateau on the south side of the Munassib Depression code-named 'The Cape.' Having achieved the first objective a move would be made to capture a line of defences three hundred yards behind the hill features. Support for the main attack would be given by the divisional artillery of both the 50th and 44th Divisions and the 7th Armoured Divisions.

The G.O.C 50th Division gave responsibility for the main attack to the 69th Brigade; the 5th East Yorkshires on 'The Cape' to the left, the 6th Green Howards on 'The Moor' to the right; the 151st Brigade to assist on the right, while the 1st Greek Brigade further to the north was to make a diversionary raid. Holding these strong positions was a young fascist battalion of the Italian Folgore Division.

The 151st Brigade was ordered to silently push forward one battalion of the Durham Light Infantry during the night to take up positions on the plateau north of the Depression and dominate the position at daybreak. A second was to be ready at first light to mop up the enemy position in co-operation with the 69th Brigade.

All was now ready for the great battle: commanders of Corps, Divisions, Brigades, Battalions and units knew the details of the plan. Montgomery briefed the press during the morning of the 23rd and then issued his Order of the Day. (Opposite).

At 2140 hours on Friday the 23rd October, a tremendous artillery barrage of 1,000 guns on a front of over six miles, with one British gun every twenty-three yards, poured a tornado of fire upon the deep zone of enemy defences. This was the signal for the opening of the Battle of El Alamein. The barrage raged at its height for twenty minutes.

A brilliant moonlight night had been chosen, and at 2200 hours the infantry advanced. By 0530 hours the next morning they were on a line six miles long, four miles west of the enemy's advanced minefields, and by 0800 hours the two corridors in the north had been completely opened to allow the tanks of X Corps to convert the break-in, to break-through, but further minefields to the west prevented any general advance. It was not until 1800 hours that the armoured brigade of the 1st Armoured Division in the northern corridor got through. It was then attacked by the 15th Panzer Division. The 10th Armoured Division in the southern corridor in the XXX Corps sector made little progress. and it was not until 0800 hours on the 25th that the division was out in the open, where it should have been twenty-four hours earlier. Rommel's Panzer Divisions then drew to a position opposite the northern corridor, and for the time being X Corps was put into reserve.

In the south on XIII Corps' front the attack of the 44th Division failed to secure a bridgehead through the minefields . Many casualties were suffered, and so, on the morning of the 25th October, 50th Division ordered the 69th Brigade supported by the 4th Armoured Brigade to attack 'The Cape' and 'The Moor' and give support on the front of the 44th Division.

During the day the artillery of the 44th and 50th Divisions laid down a barrage, following this up at 2230 hours with a smoke screen. Under cover of this screen the 5th East Yorkshires and 6th Green Howards moved to the starting line which was crossed at 2315 hours.

The 6th Green Howards on the right breached the minefield and then became engaged in heavy fighting. The east end of 'The Moor' was taken and they advanced to within three hundred yards of their final objective, where they became pinned down by shelling and mortar fire.

The 5th East Yorkshires reached their assault positions but then two of the three Bren-gun carriers, leading the attack with grappling irons to remove the wire protecting the minefields, were destroyed by mines. When the assaulting companies came up against barbed wire defences of the minefield they came under very heavy cross-fire from small arms and heavy mortars. With men falling casualties to the Shue-mines hidden beneath the surface, and others caught up on the barbed wire and mowed down by the enemy machine gunners, the attack stalled. The acting commanding officer, Major Andrew Edgar, then called on the artillery to

EIGHTH ARMY

PERSONAL MESSAGE

from the

ARMY COMMANDER

(To be read out to all Troops)

1. When I assumed command of the Eighth Army I said that the mandate was to destroy ROMMEL and his Army, and that it would be done as soon as we were ready.

2. We are ready NOW.

   The battle which is now about to begin will be one of the decisive battles of history. It will be the turning point of the war. The eyes of the whole world will be on us, watching anxiously which way the battle will swing.

   We can give them their answer at once: " It will swing our way."

3. We have first-class equipment; good tanks; good anti-tank guns; plenty of artillery and plenty of ammunition; and we are backed up by the finest air striking force in the world.

   All that is necessary is that each one of us, every officer and man, should enter this battle with the determination to see it through — to fight and to kill — and finally, to win.

   If we all do this there can be only one result — together we will hit the enemy for " six," right out of North Africa.

4. The sooner we win this battle, which will be the turning point of the war, the sooner we shall all get back home to our families.

5. Therefore, let every officer and man enter the battle with a stout heart, and the determination to do his duty so long as he has breath in his body.

   AND LET NO MAN SURRENDER SO LONG AS HE IS UNWOUNDED AND CAN FIGHT.

   Let us all pray that " the Lord mighty in battle " will give us the victory.

B. L. Montgomery

Lieutenant-General, G.O.C.-in-C., Eighth Army.

23-10-42
Middle East Forces.

General Montgomery's Order of the Day for October 23rd, 1942.

put down a barrage to assist, but the 25-pdr high explosive shells intended to cover the attack fell short on top of the men close up to the minefield causing further casualties. The Brigade Commander ordered the Battalion to withdraw to a reverse slope four hundred yards from the 'The Cape' and dig in.

The only chance of success was for a heavy artillery bombardment followed by an attack by a new company. Unfortunately there was a breakdown of wireless communications between the Battalion and 69th Brigade H.Q. necessitating an officer having to be sent for instructions, but when these were received there was insufficient time before first light to make the arrangements. Orders were received to withdraw to a defensive position and harass the enemy by fire; the withdrawal being accomplished just before dawn on 26th October. The attack on 'The Cape' cost the East Yorkshires some hundred casualties in dead and wounded, one fifth of its strength.

At 1500 hours on the 26th 'A' Company of the 6th Green Howards renewed the attack and advanced across the bullet-swept plateau. The objective had almost been reached when the enemy put down a concentration of very accurate artillery and mortar fire. During the two days of fighting the casualties of the 6th Green Howards numbered one hundred and sixty. As there was little hope of success the Divisional Commander, Major-General Nichols, called off the battle, and for the next two days the 69th Brigade had to be reconciled with harassing the enemy with mortar and small arms fire.

On the night of the 28th October, the 151st Brigade was taken out of the Munassib line and sent north to reinforce XXX Corps which so far had failed to make a gap sufficiently wide for X Armoured Corps to pass through.

The 69th Brigade was relieved in the Munassib position by the 2nd French Brigade on the 29th October and moved to the rear for two days to reorganise. In the first days of November the 7th Armoured Division moved North to take up its position with X Corps, leaving XIII Corps with only the 50th Division, made up of only the 69th Brigade, the 1st Greek Brigade and the 2nd Free French Brigade, and the 44th Division.

Meanwhile, by early morning on the 2nd November, the infantry of XXX Corps to the north attacked, following a heavy artillery barrage. A bitter battle ensued but a gap was made sufficiently large for the 1st and 10th Armoured Divisions to pass through. Throughout the day a tank battle raged with heavy losses on both sides. The Eighth Army communiqué of the 5th November claimed that two hundred and sixty German and Italian tanks had been destroyed.

On the morning of 4th November an Indian Brigade attacked south of Tel el Aqqaqir. A gap was made in the defences. This was soon widened into a corridor, allowing XXX Corps and X Armoured Corps to sweep forward; Rommel saw that he was beaten and began to fall back. The Italians in the south and centre of the Axis line were cut off. Abandoned by the Germans who had taken all their transport, hardly a man of the six

Italian divisions escaped. XIII Corps collected droves of prisoners who surrendered. Although the Germans were the first to retreat after the battle was lost they left behind 8,000 prisoners apart from killed and wounded. Among the prisoners were General Ritter von Thoma, commanding the *Afrika Korps,* Major Burckhardt, commanding the German Paratroops, and the commanders of the Pavia and Trento divisions.

The Battle of Alamein had been won. On the night of the 6th November General Alexander announced the victory on BBC radio, and telegraphed a message to the Prime Minister: 'Ring out the bells! Prisoners estimated at 20,000, tanks 350, guns 400, motor transport *several thousand.* Our advanced mobile forces are south of Mersa Matruh. 8th Army is advancing.' But the church bells were not rung in England as the next day the Allied Force under General Eisenhower would land, and it was thought that, should any accident then occur, the ringing of bells would not seem appropriate.

On the 12th November, Lieut.-General Montgomery was promoted General for 'distinguished services in the field' and appointed a Knight Commander of the Order of the Bath.

The Battle Honour **El Alamein** (23rd October-4th November 1942) was won by the 5th Batallion, the Regiment electing it to be carried on the Colours.

* * * * *

Meanwhile on the 2nd November, the 69th Brigade, having spent two days reorganising after being relieved by the Fighting French in the Munassib line, moved up to the Ruweisat Ridge to relieve troops of the 4th Indian Division. There it was faced by strong defences on the western edge of the ridge with Deir el Shein immediately to the north.

The 5th East Yorkshires experienced some enemy shelling, but a patrol soon discovered that the enemy opposite had gone. A carrier patrol from the 6th Green Howards went forward as far as Deir el Shein, reporting signs of enemy withdrawal.

Next day from 0630 hours, explosions were heard coming from the direction of the enemy. On the night of the 3rd/4th November, patrols all along the front reported signs of enemy withdrawal. Although it was not known to the Brigade, there had been a breakthrough in the north, the enemy being hotly pursued.

Orders were given to the 69th Brigade to strike west with the utmost speed as far as the Rahman Track and seize a commanding feature some twelve miles east of the Ruweisat Ridge, but the 50th Division having received orders to hand over its second line transport to the 44th Division, only a further limited advance could be made on foot.

On the morning of the 4th November the Brigade moved forward in a column which included artillery, anti-tank guns and a field ambulance. By nightfall the western edge of Ruweisat Ridge had been secured. The next day the Brigade struck out for the Rahman Track and hill feature. Progress was slow, minefields were extensive, some being seventy yards in extent. The hill feature was reached before dark on the 6th November, but further progress was halted at 1700 hours when orders were received to return the next day to the area around Deir El Mireir to take part in salvage operations, with the exception of one company from each of the three battalions in the Brigade.

Major-General Nichols ordered Brigadier Cooke-Collis to form separate mobile columns of these companies together with the carriers of each battalion and supporting arms and strike hard due west with the utmost speed, cross the Rahman Track at 0800 hours on the 7th and intercept an enemy column to the north. The orders given were to 'Advance as fast as possible; accept big risk and attack the enemy with the utmost dash.' Every available vehicle was sent to the 69th Brigade during the night, and by speedy organisation all was ready for a start in the early hours of the next morning.

At the given time the columns set off. After proceeding for some six miles they came up against a small enemy defensive position. With anti-tank guns firing at point blank range, the infantry swept through, firing from their vehicles. The position was taken without any casualties being sustained.

The mobile column from the 5th East Yorkshires, led by Major Andrew W. Edgar, went west across the desert in pursuit of the enemy. A short way out he found a few Italian stragglers and, taking them along, went on until a point was reached some twenty miles south of Sidi Barrani. Running short of petrol the column eventually returned with the stragglers to the Battalion.

The two columns from the 6th and 7th Green Howards, having made contact with the enemy, captured some sixty officers and seven hundred men from the Italian Brescia, Folgore and Pavia Divisions, including the Divisional Commander and staff of the Pavia Division. During the next three days thousands of prisoners were taken and sent on foot to the rear.

On the 8th November these columns reached Minqar Abu Mukhaiyet without incident and early on the evening of the 9th arrived at Minqar Falma on the Mersa Matruh-Siwa track, level with the leading troops of the X Armoured Corps, but, since no prisoners had been collected during the last twenty-four hours and no enemy met with, they were recalled, rejoining the 50th Division at Deir el Mireir on the evening of the 12th November. At the same time the 151st Brigade also returned from its spell of action with XXX Corps, and the Greek and Fighting French Brigades left the Division. For the next three weeks the 50th Division was employed in clearing the battle area of Alamein and salving all the war material of the enemy and our own forces. When this was completed the Division was reorganised, some training carried out, and companies given a period off-duty by the sea at the Divisional Rest Centre at Imayid.

* * * * *

As the 2nd New Zealand Division, the 51st (Highland) Division of XXX Corps, and the Armour of X Corps pursued the *Afrika Corps* across Cyrenaica, an Anglo-American force under the American General Eisenhower landed in Morocco and Algeria on 8th November, and the Axis forces were forced to fight on two fronts.

Changes in command now took place; Montgomery, dissatisfied with the way in which Lieut.-General Lumsden had conducted command of X Corps, relieved him and sent him back to England to take up a role in training armour. He was replaced by Lieut.-General Brian Horrocks from XIII Corps, and Major-General Miles Dempsey came out from England to take over XIII Corps. The 50th Division left XIII Corps to join XXX Corps.

* * * * *

Having completed the salvage work and benefited by the rest, the 50th Division left XIII Corps and moved by stages to join XXX Corps and concentrate on the 1st December at El Adem, south of Tobruk.

Driven back to El Agheila, the Germans made a stand from the 13th to the 17th December, then withdrew to Buerat, the next good defensive position at the western end of the Gulf of Sirte. The 50th Division received orders to take part in the attack there, halting on the way at Agėdabia.

On the 4th December, a storm began to rage in the Mediterranean. Heavy seas caused ships in the harbour at Benghazi to break loose, and tugs and lighters were smashed. Most of the breakwater was destroyed, considerable damage done to the inner harbour and port installations. Benghazi was considerably reduced as a supply base for troops in the forward area. The capacity of the port having been brought up to 3,000 tons a day, only 1,000 tons could now get through. The main supply would have to be transported from Tobruk.

X Corps in the area of Jebel Akhdar was given the task of bringing forward all requirements for the forthcoming advance on Tripoli. The 50th Division, crossing the desert at Msus, having sent its carriers on to Agedabia, was halted and sent on to Benghazi, from where it could obtain supplies from the port with its own transport, and carry out work in the docks.

Arriving in Benghazi around the 12th December, there was much to do. The town had suffered badly from bombardment by air and gunfire, the docks were in a battered state; troops had to be found for guard duties, and all others available were employed unloading supplies from the ships in the docks. This was work to which many of the men of the 5th East Yorkshires were accustomed, having worked in the Hull docks. The unloading of cargoes had to go on through Christmas Day, and in consequence dinner, usually taken around midday, had to be postponed until the evening. Nevertheless a small party was detailed to decorate the dining rooms, and, when in the evening the Christmas Dinner was served, the men enjoyed a plentiful supply of poultry, good rations and a quantity of beer and some spirits. A contrast to the previous one in the cold camp at Kirkuk.

Leaving some men behind to carry on with guard duties and dock work, the Brigade moved out of Benghazi on the 6th January, 1943, to Regima fifteen miles to the east to bivouac in the hills. A varied programme of training began: N.C.O.s cadres, instruction and practice in the laying of mines, and in breaching minefields; parties were sent to attend a three-day course at the Street Fighting School in Benghazi. In order to maintain fitness there was cross-country running, football and sports competitions. Brigade exercises were carried out, but somewhat handicapped by the absence of the carrier platoons which had gone on to Sirte when the Division had been diverted from the intended action at Buerat.

On the 15th January, 1943, the leading units of the Eighth Army began the advance of some 200 miles to Tripoli, the last town left of the Italian overseas possessions. The Axis forces were soon in disarray and, apart from a stand at Homs-Tarhuna, made little attempt to stand and fight until west of Tripoli, which fell on the 23rd January.

The 50th Division in reserve began its move westwards on the 28th February. The 5th East Yorkshires together with the rest of the 69th Brigade left Regima in lorries, arriving at Tripoli on the 7th March, and moved the next day to a spot north of Zarzis in southern Tunisia where they arrived on the 9th March.

CHAPTER VII

THE CAMPAIGN IN TUNISIA

With operations about to begin by Eighth Army in Tunisia there were changes in command. At a conference at Casablanca on the 19th January, 1943, it was unanimously agreed by the Combined Chiefs of Staff that, after the clearing of the enemy from Libya, General Eisenhower should become Commander-in-Chief of the whole of North Africa, General Alexander, his Deputy, Commander-in-Chief and commander of the land forces; Air Chief Marshal Tedder, Commander-in-Chief of all air forces in the Mediterranean theatre of operations with Air Marshal Coningham as commander of the Tactical Air Forces, Air Marshal Harry Broadhurst taking his place as commander of the Desert Air Force.

THE BATTLE OF MEDININE

By the 4th of February Libya had fallen into the hands of the Eighth Army. Before the army could move forward in large numbers the port of Tripoli needed extensive repairs, having been disabled by the retreating Axis forces. By the end of February the port had been restored to a workable order.

The 7th Armoured and 51st (Highland) Divisions together with a further brigade of tanks were sent forward to secure the road centres of communication at Ben Gardene, Foum Tatahouine and Medinine and the lateral roads and airfields there.

Rommel, having planned to make a stand on the Mareth Line, hoped to cause the Eighth Army to withdraw from its positions by an attack from Medinine

Early on the morning of the 6th March the 10th, 15th and 21st Panzer Divisions attacked the sector held by the 7th Armoured Division. By 1000 hours the attack was beaten off. At 1430 hours a further attack was made by those divisions supported by infantry, and later in the afternoon there were two further attacks. All were repulsed. After dark the enemy withdrew and the battle was over. The Germans lost fifty-two tanks; none were lost by 7th Armoured Division, and British losses were minimal. Rommel was to take no part in future operation in north Africa. A sick man, he left for Germany on the 9th March.

The Axis forces in north Africa now had General Jurgens von Arnim in overall command with General Albert Kesselring commanding the Germans in the east and General Giovanni Messe commanding the 1st Italian Army.

THE BATTLE OF THE MARETH LINE AND THE CLEARING OF THE WADI ZEUSS 16th-23rd March, 1943

The Mareth Line had been constructed by the French in Tunisia in 1939 against any incursions by Italian forces from Libya, when Italy, having entered into an agreement to join with Germany in any future war, began to take a hostile attitude towards the French. The line stretched for twenty-two miles from the sea near Zarat on the eastern coast, ending just beyond the Mareth-Medenine road, two miles south-east of the town of Mareth in the Matmata hills in the west. A switch line ran north-west from Matmata following the line of the Wadi Merteba between Djebel Melab and Djebel Tebaga to a gap south-west of El Hamma.

The Matmata hills, 2,300 feet at their highest, dominate the western end of the defences and, with only a few tracks running through narrow passes, formed a natural barrier to wheeled vehicles. The country to the west of the hills, mostly salt marsh and soft sand, stretched westwards for many miles. The French had always maintained that it was impassable to any large force, but in early January, 1943, a reconnaissance by the Long Range Desert Group found a way through.

The Mareth defences comprised a number of concrete and steel pillboxes about 5 feet thick, sunk low into the ground, connected by slit trenches linked with dugouts and covered by wire entanglements and mines. When France surrendered to the Germans in July, 1940, the fortifications were partially dismantled in accordance with the terms of the Armistice Treaty; weapons were taken out and the wire and mines removed. As the Axis forces began to retreat from the Western Desert the fortifications were hastily restored from the partially dismantled state, and considerably strengthened with blockhouses, gun emplacements, new minefields and deeper trenches.

In the coastal sector the line based on the Wadi Zigzaou, a mud-bottomed ravine with steep banks was itself a natural obstacle Where it ran into the sea it was tidal, with a stream fifteen feet wide in its bed. On the Wadi Zigzaou a stand would be made by German and Italian divisions with supporting arms; the armour in reserve at Gabes.

General Montgomery's plan was for XXX Corps to deliver a frontal attack on the eastern flank at 1030 hours on the 20th March, with the 50th, 51st and 4th (Indian) Divisions: General Freyberg's New Zealand Corps (consisting of the 2nd New Zealand Division reinforced with the 8th Armoured Brigade, General Leclerc's Free French and other units, to sweep round the western and southern flanks and 'break-in' behind the Matmata Hills, then to push on to an objective in the Gabes area: X Corps (1st and 7th Armoured Divisions) in reserve to follow up on either flank dependent on the way the battle turned; the whole operation to be supported by concentrated strikes by the Western Desert Air Force

The sector allotted to the 50th Division ran from the sea to the strong point at Zarat Sud Est, and along this line to the west of the wadi were a number of redoubts which faced the 50th Division from right to left; viz. Ksiba Est, Ksiba Ouest, Ouerzi, and Zarat Sud Est., all having been built by the French. These redoubts were covered by an anti-tank ditch twelve feet deep which ran along the western side and extended past Zarat sud Est to Zarat Sud. This ditch had been newly made by Italian labour under German direction when the Axis forces began to retreat from Tripoli, as the sides of the wadi had fallen in and was no longer effective. Behind these were two strong points Ouerzi Est to the north-west of Ksiba Est on the right, and Oerzi Ouest north-west of Ksiba Ouest on the left, about a mile apart. A new mine field of Teller, anti-personnel and shrapnel mines was laid between the anti-tank ditch and the wadi.

On the eastern side of the wadi the Germans had built a redoubt, 'The Bastion'. This was forward of Zarat Sud Est and was covered by another anti-tank ditch running south-east and then south-west to just beyond Garact Djedla, thus encircling 'The Bastion', from which the approaches to the wadi in front of Ouerzi and Ksiba Ouest were dominated by enfilade fire.

Defending the Mareth Line from right to left were the Italian Young Fascist Division – the best of the Italian army (the sector to be attacked by the 69th Brigade), the 90th Light Division, the Italian Spezia and Pistoia Divisions and the 164th German Infantry Division. In reserve behind the Mareth Line defences was the 15th Panzer Division.

Some three miles to the front of the Wadi Zigzaou was the Wadi El Zeuss with a bog at its lower end, and further inland the sides had been steepened, making it almost impossible for patrols to cross. On the western side lay a line of outposts striking back in depth to the main line. These outposts were protected by unmarked minefields.

The G.O.C. 50th Division assigned the 69th Brigade to secure the outposts and reconnoitre the approaches to the Wadi Zeuss in preparation for a frontal attack by the Division.

CLEARING THE OUTPOSTS ALONG THE WADI ZEUSS

Just before midnight on the on the 12th March, the 69th Brigade took over positions from the 51st (Highland Division) facing the Wadi Zeuss in preparation for an attack planned for the 16th March. The Brigade was disposed with the 5th East Yorkshires on the right, the 6th Green Howards in the centre, and the 7th Green Howards on the left. The approaches, dominated by artillery fire, made it impossible to assemble the attacking force, and reconnaissance could only be carried out at night. It was therefore decided that reconnaissance could best be carried out by small 'Thug patrols' each made up of one officer and selected N.C.O.s with Sappers, the infantry to engage the enemy at close quarters while the Sappers cleared and taped narrow paths through the minefields for later attacks by the companies.

During the next three nights reconnaissance patrols went out. The Wadi Zeuss was reached and at various points was found to have banks between five and twenty feet in height, a width of sixty yards, and a stream of water in the bed twenty yards wide. It would be almost impossible to get vehicles across. A number of minefields were found, one eighty yards deep, another two hundred yards in length consisting of anti-personnel mines laid with trip wires to a depth of twenty yards. The wadi was covered by machine-guns and wherever the patrols tried to cross they came under fire.

On the morning of the 13th March a patrol of one officer and six N.C.O.s and men of the 6th Green Howards went out to the forwards trenches of the 5th East Yorkshires to reconnoitre a feature some two hundred yards long with a small re-entrant in the centre, which lay about two hundred yards ahead. After spending the day viewing the area with binoculars they moved out when darkness fell, crossing a salt marsh strewn by bushes and scrub. A single strand of barbed wire was found some fifty yards from the enemy's position leading to the north-east. With this information the patrol returned to the defence line. The next night the party went out again and followed the wire to its end. It was presumed that the wire marked a minefield running parallel to the enemy's position, and as the ground was broken and suitable for the starting point of an attack it was decided that an assault planned for the next night should start from there.

At 2015 hours on the 16th March, two patrols, each of one officer and fourteen men of the 6th Green Howards, set off from east of Point 6 to cross the Wadi Zeuss to the starting point towards the edge of the minefield, arriving there at 2100 hours. An artillery barrage had been planned but Lieut.-Colonel R. B. James, D.S.O., commanding the 5th East Yorkshires, had asked for support from the Machine-Gun Battalion of the 2nd Cheshires with 12 Vickers Medium Machine Guns. At 2130 hours the Cheshires directed fire on the enemy's positions south-east of the wadi. When the barrage lifted at 2150 hours the patrols attacked. The enemy offered little resistance. One officer and twenty-three prisoners were captured. At around 2230 hours the leading company of the 5th East Yorkshires came up and secured their objectives with minimal losses. At 1000 hours on the 17th the enemy was found to be holding a strongly defended post at Point 16 some 1,000 yards in front of the main position. The company put in an attack and the position was captured.

The 6th Green Howards were set to attack Points 26 and 27 to the left of the 5th East Yorkshires at Point 6. As during the three preceding days much of the reconnaissance work had been carried out by patrols from the 7th Battalion and as they had knowledge of the enemy dispositions, it was decided that two strong 'Thug Patrols' should lead the attack by two companies of the 6th Battalion.

At 2015 hours on the 16th March the two patrols, together with Sappers to clear gaps in the minefields, set off and crossed the Wadi Zeuss for the starting point at the edge of the minefield, arriving there at 2100 hours. At 2130 hours 120 guns of five regiments of artillery laid down a tremendous barrage to 'soften up' the attack. When the barrage lifted at 2150 hours the Sappers began lifting the mines to clear a way for the 'Thug Patrols'. The enemy opposition was found to be stronger than had been anticipated. The Sappers suffered many casualties in clearing the mines, and, although the patrols fought with determination and considerable courage, they too sustained heavy casualties. As the objectives could not be captured unaided the companies went forward to join the survivors of the 'Thug Patrols'. Making their way through the gap in the minefield under heavy small arms and mortar fire the two companies of the 6th Green Howards suffered some eighty casualties. By next morning they were established at Point 26.

The East Yorkshires remained in their positions throughout the 17th and 18th until relieved by the 9th Gurkha Regiment soon after midnight on the 19th, marching to new positions near Chet Meskine, some two thousand yards in front of the main Mareth defences.

The 7th Green Howards were given orders to attack another point numbered 26 on the left flank of the 6th Battalion and join up with them. At 2125 hours on the 16th, 'A' Company formed up behind Point 12 and, after the artillery barrage, crossed the Wadi Zeuss and launched its attack. By 2230 it had reached and consolidated on the objective but had not made contact with the 6th Battalion on its right. Aware that the 6th Battalion was fighting a difficult battle and making slow progress, the Brigade Commander ordered 'C' Company of 7th Green Howards to assist by taking Position 27 on the left flank of the 6th Battalion. By the next morning they had arrived and taken up positions there. Later in the day they were relieved by 'C' Company of the 6th Green Howards and rejoined the rest of the battalion behind the Wadi Zeuss. At mid-day on the 18th March they marched to join up with the 6th Battalion at Chet Meskine.

The 69th Brigade had successfully driven in the outposts, and was established within a thousand yards of the ridge which overlooked the Wadi Zigzaou, and enabled reconnaissance of the wadi. On the night of the 18th/19th, patrols of the 151st Brigade reconnoitred the front to find a suitable place for the main assault and crossing of the Wadi Zigzaou. The bed of the wadi was crossed and the anti-tank ditch beyond was examined. It was found that the slopes leading down to the Wadi were mined as was the Wadi itself. The bed of the wadi was found to have water running through it, but there were places with a firm bottom.

THE ASSAULT ON THE MARETH LINE

The attack by XXX Corps on the Mareth Line was timed to begin at 2230 hours on the 20th March. The attack to breach the defences was entrusted

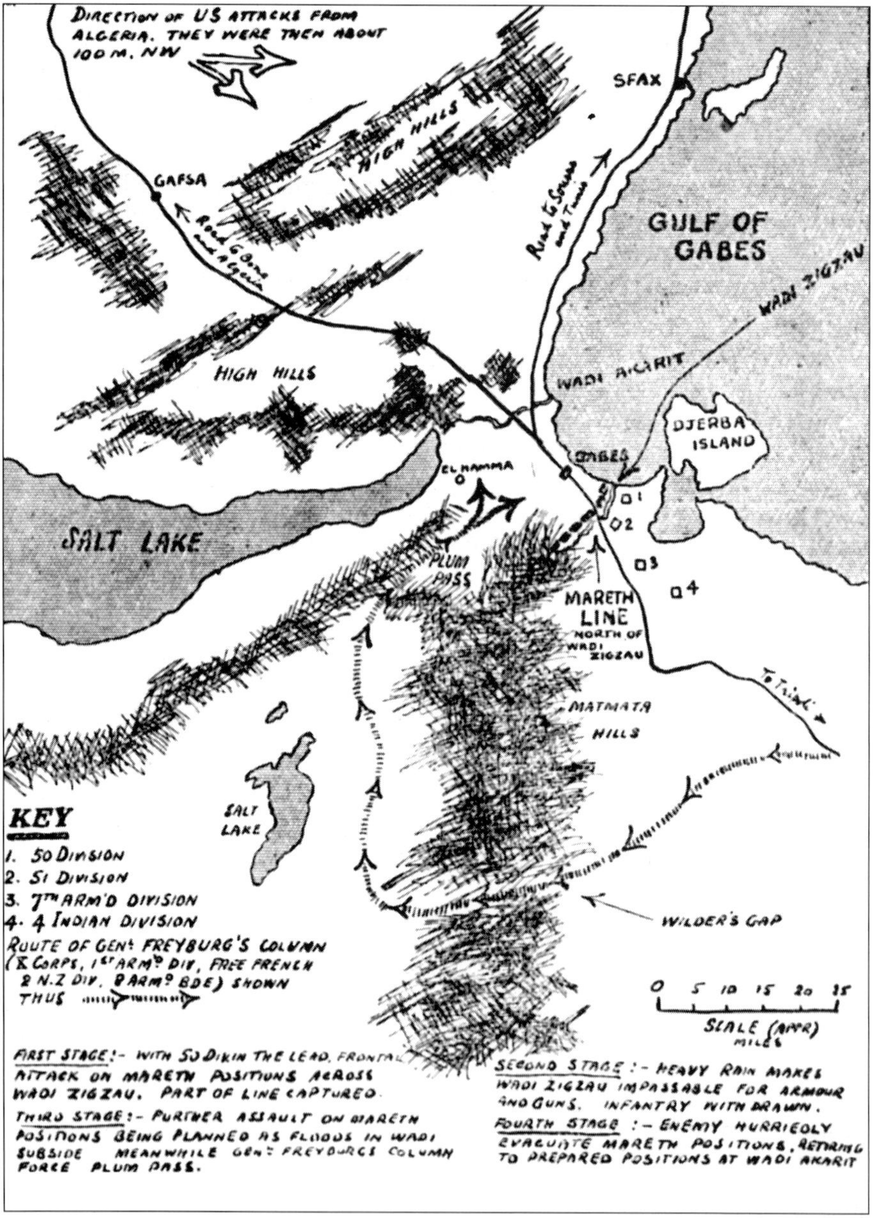

The Tunisian Battlefield.

to the 50th Division and was to be the responsibility of the 151st Brigade. The sector selected lay between Ksiba Ouest and Ouerzi; it had the advantage of not being covered by an advanced main position as at Zarat Sud Est, but was dominated by The Bastion on the left flank. The Bastion was protected by an anti-tank ditch, twelve-feet wide and eight-feet deep, with minefields on both sides; and was one of the redoubts built by the Germans as the Axis Armies fell back from Egypt. This had to be secured before the 151st Brigade could advance and the task was allotted to the 7th Green Howards.

The 5th East Yorkshires had set up Headquarters on the eastern side of the wadi along the line of advance of the 151st Brigade with a post some two hundred yards from the wadi. During the morning the Divisional Commander, the Brigade Commanders and the C.Os of the attacking battalions had all used a stretch of trench in the vicinity to reconnoitre the wadi and the defences on the far side. The movement attracted the attention of the enemy who brought down artillery fire on the position.

In the afternoon a further reconnaissance was made by company commanders of the 8th Durham Light Infantry destined to cross the wadi at this point. The section commander of the 5th East Yorkshires expressed his views. 'I don't mind who comes up here,' he said, 'as long as they keep their heads down, but when "Crasher" (Major-General Nichols) and "Beako" (Brigadier D. M. W. Beake, commanding 151st Brigade) came up here, they bobbed about all over the place and didn't even take the tabs off their ruddy hats!'

At 2215 hours the 7th Green Howards and 5th East Yorkshires moved up to attack The Bastion and, on reaching the start line, some five hundred yards from the anti-tank ditch, came under heavy fire from artillery, machine-guns and mortars, causing some casualties. At 2230 hours the Corps artillery and Vickers machine-guns of the 2nd Cheshires laid down a barrage on the 69th Brigade front. 'Thug parties' of the 7th Green Howards went forward to lay tapes to guide the attacking companies, accompanied by a party of sappers to clear the minefields and lay scaling ladders across the ditch, then make a bridgehead. As the assaulting companies advanced they came under intense enfilade fire from artillery, machine-guns and mortars on the flanks. Throughout the night they fought with amazing zeal, and in hand-to-hand fighting worked their way through the complex system of trenches and defence works of The Bastion. Casualties were heavy but by first light The Bastion had fallen. The Commanding Officer, Lieut.-Colonel Derek Seagrim, showing exemplary courage, inspired the men, resulting in his being awarded the Victoria Cross. When daylight came on 21st March, The Bastion had fallen: despite fierce counter-attacks it was held throughout the day.

Meanwhile, at around 1930 hours, the 151st Brigade left the assembly area reaching the Forming-Up-Position on the Chet Meskine at 2130 hours and began to prepare to launch the main attack. The 9th D.L.I had been given the task of capturing Ksiba Ouest on the right flank, whilst the 8th D.L.I. captured Ouerzi and a strong point to the right of the fort known as Little Ouerzi. When these objectives had been accomplished, Valentine Tanks of the 50th Royal Tank Regiment would cross the wadi by means of causeways; the 6th D.L.I. would then attack through the 8th and 9th to deepen the bridgehead.

The forming-up position was packed with troops, and movement was made more difficult by disused enemy slit trenches and old gun positions. The Durham Light Infantry assembled together with 2nd Cheshires and other arms. The Sappers moved forward to improve the roads, and parties aided by 'Scorpions' – old Matilda tanks fitted with flails – made gaps in the minefield, and built causeways over the salt flats. Mines previously undiscovered lay on the tracks leading to the forming-up place, causing casualties. Enemy shelling on the forming-up place resulted in more casualties. Fire from artillery, mortars and machine-guns rained down but fortunately casualties were few.

At 2000 hours artillery and fifty Vickers machine-guns of the 2nd Cheshires laid down a barrage on the front of the sector of the 151st Brigade. This continued for some ninety minutes.

It was a full moonlit night when, at 2300 hours on the 20th March, the 8th and 9th Battalions of the Durham Light Infantry moved off for the main attack: the 9th Battalion to capture Ksiba Ouest on the right, the 8th Battalion Ouerzi to the left. As they moved to the forming-up place enemy shelling caused casualties as did mines on the tracks leading up to it.

As the Durham Light Infantry approached the Wadi they met a hail of fire from artillery, mortars and machine-guns; but fortunately a great deal of it was inaccurate. Scorpion tanks fitted with flails and gapping parties of Sappers went forward to clear the way through the minefields, which was successfully cleared.

The wadi was reached and found to be wider and deeper than anticipated. On the far side was a high embankment made from soil thrown up when the enemy had made the anti-tank ditch. Wading across the water (which in some places was up to the chest) and holding rifles and machine-guns above their heads, they clambered up the steep side while rifle and machine-gun fire came down in enfilade along the wadi. The anti-tank ditch was reached and crossed by means of ladders. The Battalions fanned out and attacked the concrete fortifications and strong points. The Italians suffered heavy casualties and a considerable number of prisoners were taken. By daylight the fortresses were in the hands of the Battalions. Beyond the wadi all was quiet and there was no sign of an enemy counter-attack.

While the D.L,I. were crossing the wadi and carrying out their attack, enemy artillery and machine-gun fire enfiladed the crossing place where British and Indian Sappers were laying brushwood fascines as a base for a causeway for the follow-up by tanks, artillery and machine-guns. They suffered many casualties, not only from this fire but also from anti-tank and anti-personnel mines strewn around the area. Their work was to little avail, as when the causeway was completed only three Valentine tanks of the 50th Royal Tank Regiment got across, a fourth broke the fascines, sunk in the wadi and held up further crossing not only by the remainder of the Valentine tanks but also by other vehicles, anti-tank guns and carriers of the 8th and 9th D.L.I. The 2nd Cheshires, needed by the D.L.I. for support in case of counter-attack, unable to get guns and ammunition across by trucks, gallantly manhandled them over and established themselves along the sector to the front of the anti-tank ditch

Although a counter-attack was expected it was not launched and the day of the 21st was quiet, except around Ouerzi where some Italians attacked the 8th Battalion's positions, but they were soon overcome. There was no activity on the front of the 9th Battalion until 1900 hours when two hundred and fifty Bersaglieri came in and surrendered.

In order to enlarge the bridgehead the 151st Brigade was ordered to attack and capture the second line of defences at Ouerzi Est and Ouerzi Ouest, and Zarat Sud Est on the left flank. Ouerzi Est was to be the responsibility of the 9th D.L.I. and they were relieved at Ksiba Ouest by the 5th East Yorkshires. The 6th D.L.I. was to pass through the 8th D.L.I. positions and then, following a heavy artillery barrage, deepen and widen the bridgehead on the left flank. One of the companies of the 9th D.L.I. and a company of the 5th East Yorkshires were to broaden the base of the bridgehead.

As darkness fell the 8th and 9th D.L.I. were called forward to the anti-tank ditch which was to be their starting line. The attack by the 9th Battalion went in behind a heavy barrage at 0130 hours on the 22nd. By this time the Young Fascist Division had been reinforced by German troops and it was not until after three hours of hand-to-hand fighting that the task was successfully accomplished. Although more than a hundred and twenty Italians were captured, losses were heavy, the troops exhausted and with a shortage of ammunition they could do little more.

The 6th D.L.I. suffered heavy casualties from artillery fire on the anti-tank ditch but secured their objectives with little difficulty. The 5th East Yorkshires had crossed over the wadi on the evening of the 21st and hastened forward to relieve the 9th D.L.I. in Ksiba Ouest. The advance was held up as artillery support was insufficient to put out of action strong points to their front.

During the 21st the enemy continued to lay down enfilade fire on the crossing place and, under this fire, parties of Sappers worked in the wadi to improve the crossing. By nightfall the causeway was repaired and forty-two more Valentine tanks of the 50th Royal Tank Regiment crossed into the bridgehead, but so damaged the causeway that it was not possible to get much needed anti-tank guns across, or wheeled vehicles to bring adequate supplies of ammunition for the infantry.

In the early hours of the 22nd March the 15th Panzer Division together with a regiment (equivalent to a British brigade) of the 90th Light

Division and parachutists of the Rameke force, now used as infantry, moved from Gabes to Zarat. Their presence was reported by the Royal Air Force. Around 1100 hours they were seen to be forming up, but attempts to move forward were held off by artillery.

Light bombers of the Desert Air Force had been briefed to break up the counter-attack as it formed up, but a heavy rainstorm broke which transformed the half-dry wadi into a raging torrent. The 'planes were temporarily grounded and the enemy was able to move tanks into the open and at 1330 hours a counter-attack was launched. The counter-attack would have to be faced with only the Valentine tanks, the supporting weapons still on the other side of the wadi, and no air support. This began with shelling of the crossing place in the wadi by heavy artillery, and a concentrated bombardment and bombing from aircraft on the infantry positions, followed by a move forward by three columns, each of Mark IV tanks, anti-tank guns and infantry on Ouerzi Est and Ouerzi Ouest and along a shallow valley between Ouerzi Ouest and Ouerzi.

The first objective was the British armour, the battle going on throughout the afternoon, but the German 88-millimetre guns were too good for the old Valentine Infantry tanks of the 50th Royal Tank Regiment. Soon a number were ablaze, thirty of the forty-five were put out of action and most of the crews killed, including the commanding officer, Lieut.-Colonel T. Cairns, M.C. The remainder withdrew to the wadi. The D.L.I. were engaged in tough battles and, having fired off all their ammunition, were driven out of all positions to the west of the wadi and then, on the orders of Brigade H.Q., fell back on the anti-tank ditch. Much of the ground gained by the 151st Brigade had been lost. All that was left was Ksiba Ouest, held by the 5th East Yorkshires.

Meanwhile, the 5th East Yorkshires, still well forward, found food and ammunition running low. Carrying parties were sent back over the wadi to obtain supplies. Captain A. A. Blackwell together with his party managed to get through with food, but an ammunition party under Major F. R. Yorke, the 2 i/c of the Battalion, ran into an unmarked minefield, and in an explosion R.S.M. C. J. Rennison, (who had been a P.S.M. in 'B' Company and later C.S.M. of Headquarters Company) was killed and Major F. R Yorke severely wounded. There was now only a small bridgehead and the 69th Brigade was ordered up to support the 151st Brigade on the line of the anti-tank ditch.

Around midnight on the 22nd/23rd March the 151st Brigade was withdrawn to reorganise and refit, leaving the 5th East Yorkshires alone on the west side of the Wadi Zigzaou to hold Ksiba Ouest as a position from which a further attack could be made, the 6th and 7th Battalions of the Green Howards taking up a position on the east bank of the wadi which they held throughout the 23rd March.

During the 23rd March the enemy put down a tremendous bombardment on Ksiba Ouest, and an infantry attack which followed succeeded in getting a foothold in the position. The 5th East Yorkshires held on with grim determination. Captain Alexander S. A. B. Macdonald (whose family had long owned the estate at Rudston, East Yorkshire, and who later succeeded to the baronetcy as Sir Alexander Bosville, The Macdonald of the Isles), with 'B' and 'C' Companies counter-attacked and threw back the enemy. Soon after dark orders were received to withdraw to the other side of the Wadi. As they moved out the companies walked into a minefield, Captain Macdonald and one soldier being wounded. Major H. N. Wallace then led the companies in single file through the danger area. Both of these officers were later awarded the Military Cross for Gallantry.

* * * * *

At 0200 hours on the 23rd March, General Montgomery gave orders to cease all attacks in the coastal sector, the frontal attack by the 50th Division having forced the enemy to reinforce the coastal attack with German troops. He ordered the 50th Division to withdraw east of the Wadi Zigzaou, replacing it with the 51st (Highland) Division with orders to take deceptive measures to pin down the Germans on the coast, leading them into thinking that the Eighth Army was reorganising for another attack across the wadi. By this deception he hoped to continue the involvement of the 15th Panzer Division in the coastal sector and reinforce the outflanking movement in the El Hamma-Gabes axis with a decisive blow before the Germans could move reserves to oppose it.

At the same time, seeing that there was no chance of reviving the coastal attack, he decided to concentrate all his resources on the inland flank where a renewed attack might break through at El Hamma. Lieut.-General Brian Horrocks was ordered to switch that night H.Q. X Corps together with 160 tanks of 1st Armoured Division (Major-General Raymond Briggs) and 8th Armoured Brigade to reinforce the newly formed New Zealand Corps (including the Free French Brigade) which was blocked at the 'Plum' defile between Djebel Tebaga and Djebel Melab, north-west of the Matmata Hills. Simultaneously, the 4th Indian Division (Major-General Francis Tuker) to move westwards from Medenine and clear the Hallouf Pass through the Matmata Hills advancing northwards past the flank of the Mareth Lie.

At 1500 hours on the 26th, Air Marshal Sir Harry Broadhurst sent in the Western Desert Air Force using twenty-two squadrons of Spitfires, Kitty bombers and Hurricane tank-busters, operating beyond the artillery barrage. The ground attack followed; the New Zealand Corps (with the 8th Armoured Brigade) leading, breaking into the enemy defences. Three hours later the 1st Armoured Division passed through them and penetrated some 6,000 yards. During the night they drove through the enemy and by first light on the 27th March had reached the outskirts of El Hamma where they were held up.

The next day, the New Zealand Corps, in fighting more intense than in the Battle of Egypt, held off attacks by the 15th Panzer Division, while the

1st Armoured Division repulsed attacks by the 21st Panzer Division and broke through at El Hamma. Some 2,500 prisoners, mostly German, were taken. British casualties were 600, and only eight pilots of the Desert Air Force were lost. The 15th and 21st Panzer Divisions had been seriously mauled and the 164th Division lost most of its heavy weapons and vehicles.

Three Italian divisions lost so many prisoners that they were of no future consequence, and by the 28th March the total enemy casualties in killed and prisoners totalled 7,000. But the bulk of General Giovanni Messe's 1st Italian Army escaped to positions behind the Wadi Akarit north of Gabes on the orders of Colonel-General Jurgen von Arnim.

Meanwhile to avoid being cut off by the attack north of the Mareth Line the German and Italians on the XXX Corps front evacuated their position on the night of the 27th/28th March. So hurriedly did they go that they made no attempt to hold the Gabes Gap, although this was a strong natural defensive position. Patrols sent out at dawn on the 28th discovered that they had gone. By 0900 hours on the 28th March the Mareth Line had fallen, and by the next day the Eighth Army had captured El Hamma and Gabes. The enemy forces, depleted and disorganised, withdrew to take up a defensive position on the Wadi Akarit, fifty miles west of the Mareth Line. They were closely followed by XXX Corps taking up a position between Mareth and Gabes.

* * * * *

During the night of 23rd/24th March, the 69th Brigade was relieved by troops of 51st Highland Division, and 50th Division placed into reserve. For the 50th Division the Battle of Mareth was over. Major-General Francis de Guingand (General Montgomery's chief of staff) paid tribute to the Division: 'It was sad that that gallant formation had not reaped more tangible signs of the hard fighting but in the big scheme of things they had nobly played their part.' On 25th March the Brigade went into a quiet sector of the line south of the town of Mareth, and carried out reconnaissance raids and patrols. These revealed that the enemy was thinning out, and on the 27th March it was discovered that the enemy had abandoned its positions. The next day the town of Mareth was entered unopposed, and the next four days were spent in cleaning up the battlefield around Zarat, reorganising, re-equipping and allotting reinforcements to companies and platoons.

The 50th Division in its determined stand north of the Wadi Zigzaou against overwhelming odds had greatly contributed to the successful conclusion of operations. It had drawn off the German 15th Panzer Division and 90th Light Division, reserves which might otherwise have been used to meet the New Zealanders in their flank attack.

The 5th East Yorkshires gained for the Regiment the Battle Honours **Mareth** (16th-23rd March 1942) and **Wadi Zigzau** (20th-23rd March 1942). **Mareth** was elected to be carried on the Colours.

THE BATTLE OF AKARIT
6th – 7th April, 1943

When the Axis forces evacuated the Mareth Line they gathered for the defence of the Gabes Gap, along the Wadi Akarit, a strong natural defence line fifteen miles wide running from the sea along the coastal plain north of Gabes and El Hamma to Shott el Fejadji. This was held by Italian divisions, the main reserve being the 15th Panzer and 90th Light Divisions.

From the sea, the wadi ran at right angles into the foothills of the Djebel er Roumana, a steep feature some two thousand feet high. On the left was the Djebel Fatnassa, hills almost as steep and perhaps as high and with a sheer face. There was a gap of two miles between them and where they butted on the valley the ground level was some two hundred feet. Between these two points lay the Hachana Ridge and the Mesreb El Alig, a thousand yards apart, to which the ground sloped up steeply reaching a height of some eight hundred feet. The left was secured by the Shott el Fejadj, an impassable region of salt lakes and marshes some fifteen miles wide. From just to the front of the Djebel er Roumana, running across to a point just south of the Hachana Ridge, ran an anti-tank ditch which extended from the Wadi Akarit. This was protected by minefield and wire. One thousand yards forward of the eastern part of the anti-tank ditch was an outpost, Point 85.

On the 2nd April Sir Oliver Leese, commander of XXX Corps, gave out his plan to breach the defences of the Wadi Akarit: the 51st Division to attack on the Djebel er Roumana and a line to the sea; the 4th Indian Division on the left to attack the Fatnassa Hills. The respective divisional commanders sent out reconnaissance parties and as a result it was decided that there were too few troops to cover such a wide distance. The next day a revised plan was issued; the 51st Division to attack the Djebel er Roumana feature and any enemy positions found between there and the sea, the 4th Indian Division the Fatnassa Hills; the 69th Brigade of the 50th Division to be brought in to make a frontal attack on the comparatively low line of the anti-tank ditch in the gap in the centre. The boundary line between the 69th Brigade and the 51st Division would be that section of the Gabes road running north from Oudref. The attack of the two Divisions would be launched in darkness; that of the 4th (Indian) Division would be silent and without artillery preparation; the 69th Brigade to launch its attack just before first light.

The order for the attack on the anti-tank ditch given by Brigadier E. C. Cooke-Collis, commanding the 69th Brigade, was for the 7th Green Howards on the right to make a preliminary attack with 'C' Company on Point 85. It was essential that this should be eliminated before the main attack, as it lay on the flank of the rest of that Battalion and the 5th East Yorkshires, who were to attack the anti-tank ditch. After its capture the 6th Green Howards would pass through the 7th Green Howards to

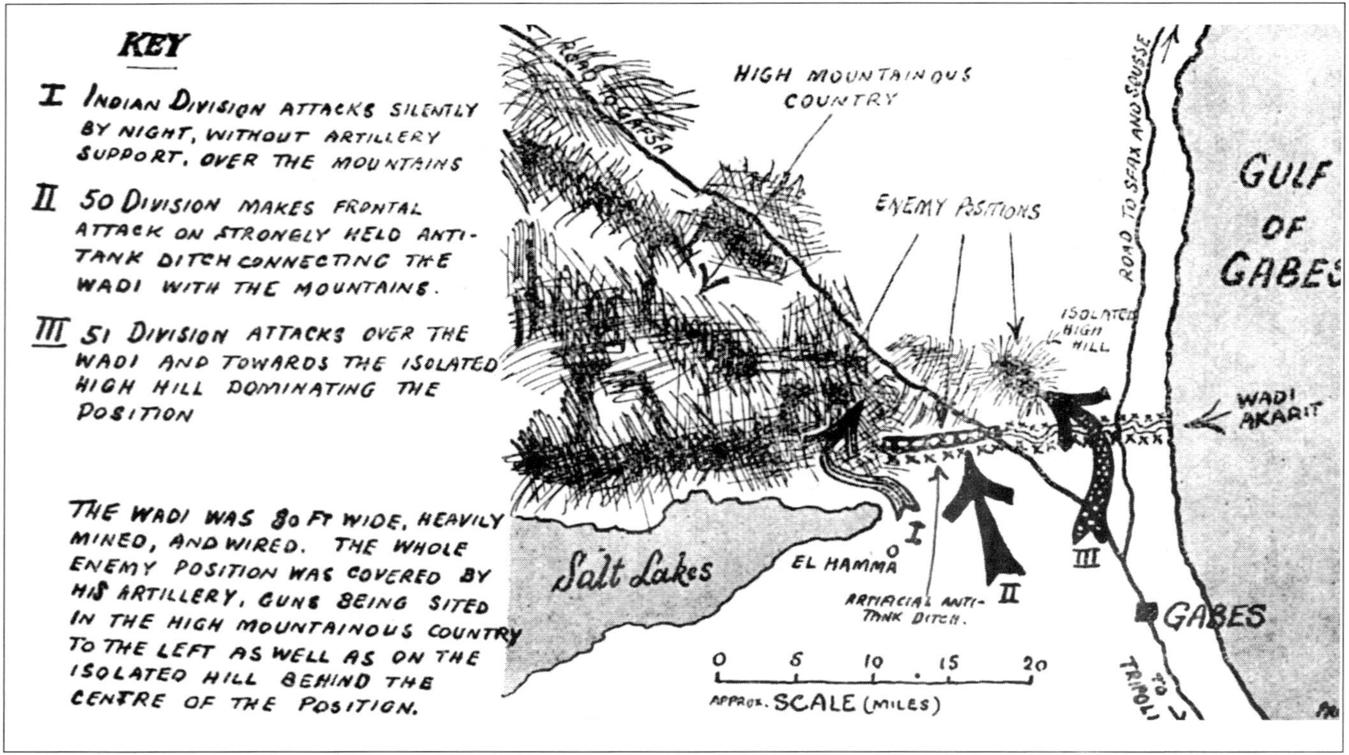

The site of the Wadi Akarit.

capture the furthest edge of the ridge of the neck of low ground two thousand yards farther on, the Start Line to be laid and lighted by the Intelligence Officer of the 5th East Yorkshires in conjunction with the 7th Green Howards. This to be ready by 0330 hours on the 6th April.

On the morning of the 3rd April the 69th Brigade began its move forward along the Gabes-Sfax road. At Metoula they turned off to take the road for Gafsa, reaching Oudref at around 1600 hours. After a reconnaissance, as darkness fell, a further move forward of three miles found the battalions taking up their positions. The next morning it was found that these positions were out in the open and overlooked by the enemy. Later in the morning the area was mortared and there was a short period of shelling. At nightfall a troop of artillery which had come up opened fire resulting in enemy counter-fire. The next two days were spent in preparing for the battle. A reconnaissance showed that the first line of the enemy defences behind the anti-tank ditch consisted of machine-guns, infantry, and anti-tank guns sited to fire down the ditch.

At nightfall on the 5th April, 4th Indian Division started its advance and before dawn on the 6th April had penetrated the Fatnassa hills, capturing some 4,000 prisoners, mainly Italians.

The attack by the 69th Brigade and the 51st Division was scheduled to begin at 0430 hours on 6th April. The 69th Brigade left the Concentration Area at 2100 hours on the 5th April, and arrived at the Assembly Area just before midnight.

At 0200 hours the Intelligence Officer of the 5th East Yorkshires together with an officer of the 7th Green Howards, a few men and a covering party, went forward to lay the Start Line. At 0300 hours, 'C' Company of the 7th Green Howards moved to the Start line, and thirty minutes later advanced on Point 85 to eliminate it, before the attack on the anti-tank ditch by the 5th East Yorkshires and the remaining companies of the 7th Green Howards which was scheduled to take place an hour later. This early start was made in order to give artillery support to the company as all the artillery was required to support the main attack an hour later. When the assault was made it was met by heavy rifle and machine-gun fire and grenades. In fierce fighting large numbers of the enemy were killed, and eighty prisoners taken, but in the successful capture of the strongpoint the company suffered severe losses, only two officers and twenty-two other ranks remaining.

In the meantime, the 5th East Yorkshires who were to attack on a two company front – 'A' Company on the right, 'B' Company on the left – had split 400 yards apart at the Assembly Area in readiness for the move to the Start Line.

The Start Line having been completed by 0330 hours, the attacking companies advanced from the Assembly Area in column of threes, each company preceded by Sappers with mine-detecting equipment, covered by a well-armed protection party. During the advance the enemy dropped flares from aircraft, first over the sector of the 4th Indian Division, then the 51st (Highland) Division, then the 69th Brigade. It seemed that the large concentration of vehicles must be discovered, but the distance from the enemy lines was so great that the flares were ineffective. The illumination of the area also 'grounded' the companies for some time but did not prevent the crossing of the Start Line at the scheduled time of 0415 hours.

At 0430 hours the 5th East Yorkshires and 'A' and 'B' companies of the 7th Green Howards began their advance on the anti-tank ditch and the objective which lay some two hundred yards beyond it. Artillery fire had already opened up on Point 85 at 0330 hours in support of 'C' Company of the 7th Green Howards so silence was no longer necessary.

At 0445 hours, artillery commenced a creeping barrage, lifting at the rate of 100 yards every three minutes. Enemy defensive fire was almost negligible and the advance was made close to the barrage. By 0500 hours, 'A' and 'B' Companies of the 7th Green Howards on the right and the 5th East Yorkshires on the left, with their supporting arms, had covered the distance indicated on the map which should have brought them to where the anti-tank ditch should have been found, but there was no sign of it. A message was sent back to the artillery who confirmed that this was where they should be, but artillery had the mapped position as their target, and shells were falling so close that loose shots were coming down amongst the forward troops. The advance continued at the pace permitted by the barrage. There was no small arms fire from the enemy, only defensive fire from mortars and artillery which was completely ineffective. It seemed that the enemy had withdrawn, but this was soon found to be wrong as, after crossing a small ridge, they came upon the anti-tank ditch and met heavy fire from machine-guns to the north-east of the ditch. The forward troops on the ridge were quickly disposed on the reverse slope and waited for the artillery barrage to move forward onto the enemy machine-guns, thus enabling the advance to continue to the final objective – the high ground two hundred yards beyond the ditch. But the artillery barrage should by this time have been falling on the enemy line well behind the ditch in its final phase, whereas in fact it was still concentrated on the ditch. Furthermore it had not been sufficiently strong to subdue the enemy forward troops and any forward movement brought intense small arms fire and direct fire from 47 mm guns and other close support artillery. Enemy mortar and long range artillery fire from the high ground to the north-east then hailed down and heavy casualties occurred.

In their advance 'A' and 'B' Companies of the 7th Green Howards ran into an anti-personnel minefield and were pinned down in an exposed position to the front of the ditch. Lieut.-Colonel Seagrim, commanding the 7th Green Howards, paid a visit to the 5th East Yorkshires to inform them of the situation. The situation was made even more difficult as the 4th and 51st Divisions had not cleared the tops of their respective hills.

At daylight the whole front was subjected to heavy enemy fire from small arms, machine-guns mortars and artillery. Lieut.-Colonel Seagrim went forward with his Intelligence Officer and started to lead his men down into the anti-tank ditch. He was wounded, and died the following day, the 7th Green Howards losing their new holder of the Victoria Cross. Command of the Battalion was temporarily taken over by the 2 i/c, Major Andrew William Edgar, M.C., an officer of the East Yorkshire Regiment.

Meanwhile on the 69th Brigade front, 'D' Company of the 7th Green Howards had gone up to Point 85 to reinforce 'C' Company of the 6th Green Howards. The remainder of the 6th Green Howards followed up the 7th Battalion and at daybreak took up a position about a thousand yards short of Point 85. They should have moved forward at 0630 hours but, being held up by the 7th Battalion, came under enemy observation and were shelled, suffering heavy casualties. It was now 0700 hours and the anti-tank ditch was still not crossed.

On the front of the 7th Green Howards, when 'A' and 'B' companies moved forward they were met by heavy machine-gun fire and on getting into the ditch were enfiladed by a machine-gun firing along the ditch from a position about two hundred yards away. Casualties were heavy and at 1730 hours Major Edgar received orders to withdraw these companies to the positions on which they originally formed up. Although they had failed to reach their final objective they fought with determination and bravery and suffered heavily. 'D' Company, which had gone up to Point 85 to reinforce 'C' Company, remained there during the night of the 6th/7th April and withdrew on the afternoon of the 7th, rejoining the rest of the Battalion.

Meanwhile on the left the East Yorkshires ran into difficulties as they crossed the first subsidiary ridge. Lieut.-Colonel James withdrew 'A' and 'B' Companies, leaving behind a number of wounded men on the crest.

The stretcher bearers showed much courage, tending those wounded and evacuating casualties. In any attack stretcher bearers are particularly vulnerable. Moving to and fro with long stretchers or running forward to give aid they stand out and can easily be casualties of enemy fire. Although wearing Red Cross armbands indicating they were non-combatants, this did not always give them protection, and they might well be shot at deliberately by enemy riflemen not respectful of the laws of war.

Private Eric Anderson, a stretcher bearer with 'A' Company, went forward alone through intense enemy fire and single-handed carried a succession of wounded men from the slope. He was killed at the fourth attempt. His courage saved the lives of three of his comrades.

In a letter to his wife, Captain R.F. Clark, R.A.M.C., the Battalion's Medical Officer, wrote:

> 'It was on one of these occasions that Private Anderson was mortally wounded and was buried on the ridge, which saw so much of his fine work, beneath the sands of the desert we know so well. I have nothing but admiration for the way in which he conducted himself both in and out of battle. I came to know him well and I found him to be a man of outstanding character, with lofty ideals which he gave his life to uphold.

Our small squad (the medical section) has lost a friend we could ill afford to lose, whose dauntless courage and untiring devotion to duty was out of the realms of men to fathom. His memory will always be hallowed in our ranks.'

He won for the East Yorkshire Regiment its only Victoria Cross of the Second World War. (See Honours and awards on page 198).

To return to the action. Having withdrawn 'A' and 'B' Companies, Colonel James brought forward 'C' and 'D' Companies, which up to that time had been held fairly well back. Under cover of smoke from the battalion's mortars and artillery, 'C' Company began the advance round the right, over the ridge and down the re-entrant to the ditch. The enemy concentrated its fire on 'C' Company. Only Major H. N. Wallace with a few men succeeded in reaching the ditch. Captain G. D. Wood and Lieutenant Beaty were killed on the way there and Lieutenant Smurthwaite was killed on arrival in the ditch. The position was covered by enemy weapons and, as no advance was possible, 'C' Company was withdrawn to its former position. Lieutenant-Colonel James was wounded in the thigh whilst endeavouring to observe the situation, but remained on duty.

There was now an improvement in the position of the troops as the 4th (Indian) Division on the Fatnassa Hills to the left, and the 51st (Highland) Division on the Dejebel er Roumana on the right appeared on their respective hill tops. The 4th (Indian) Division had reached its objectives, causing such trouble to the enemy that they began to evacuate the position. At 0845 hours General Horrocks commanding X Corps came to headquarters of the 4th (Indian) Division to be told by Major-General Francis Tuker that the enemy had been broken and, if X Corps was immediately brought forward, to take up the offensive, the campaign in north Africa could be brought to a quick end. Lieut.-General Horrocks requested permission for X Corps to put in, but when approval was given there was a delay in starting, and, when the move began, the enemy counter-attacked; the gap made by 4th (Indian) Division was not exploited.

Soon after 0900 hours when Point 85 had been cleared, the Divisional Commander, Major-General J. S. Nichols, the Brigade Commander, Brigadier E. C. Cooke Collis, Lieut.-Colonel S. V. Keeling commanding the 2nd Cheshires, and Lieut.-Colonel G. C. P. Lance of the 6th Green Howards assembled at the top of the strongpoint to view the enemy's positions on the far side of the anti-tank ditch and give orders to Lieut.-Colonel Lance for its crossing. Suddenly Sherman tanks from the 3rd County of London Yeomanry came up and, ignoring the enemy minefield, passed straight through, two were either blown up on mines or hit by an 88-mm which fired straight across the front. The two leading tanks then went on, crossed the anti-tank ditch, and turned on the enemy position lining the anti-tank ditch. They were followed by others and, although two were knocked out and on fire on the further slope behind the enemy's forward positions, the threat resulted in some of the enemy surrendering.

The tanks had created a gap through the enemy minefield. The Brigade

Commander ordered Lieut.-Colonel Lance to take 'A' and 'C' Companies through the gap in single file, cross the anti-tank ditch to the east of Point 85 and then advance for almost a mile to a plateau: support to be given from the other two companies. Not wishing to draw attention to the move it was decided that no artillery barrage should be put down on the gap and the only support should be from two tanks of the 3rd County of London Yeomanry firing from a hull down position.

This was a very daring move, as, to the left, the 5th East Yorkshires and 7th Green Howards were still fighting a fierce battle in front of the anti-tank ditch, with Bren gunners assisted by machine-gunners of the 2nd Cheshire Regiment engaging the enemy at every opportunity, on both the front of the anti-tank ditch and at Point 85.

The leading companies of the 6th Green Howards went quickly through the gap with little opposition, but as soon as the enemy became aware of the situation a heavy concentration of fire from tanks and high velocity guns was brought down on the gap causing considerable casualties to the rear companies as they passed through.

The forward companies made good progress, overrunning the enemy reserve positions with little difficulties. Many Italians surrendered but a few showed fight. Soon after 1100 hours it was clear that enemy resistance had been broken, but in the afternoon when the lower slopes of the Djebel er Roumana were reached heavy fire was met with from machine guns on both flanks and mortars in front. The machine-guns of the 2nd Cheshires were turned on them, allowing the 6th Green Howards to establish themselves on the forward edge of the basin which formed their final objective and from which they commanded the plateau for some 800 yards. As the position was exposed to artillery and mortar fire from the surrounding high ground, they were forced to withdraw slightly to the ridge to the rear which gave better protection.

Just before nightfall enemy infantry were seen advancing across a ridge and with increased shelling it seemed that a counter-attack was likely. Casualties during the day had been very heavy, particularly in the forward company which the Battalion commander wished to relieve, and the men were tired. Soon after darkness the noise of tanks was heard and infantry supported by tanks advanced under high velocity fire to within four hundred of the front of the company's position, where they were halted by fire from anti-tank guns, tanks and artillery. The rest of the night passed without incident.

Returning to the front of the 5th East Yorkshires and 7th Green Howards. After the 6th Green Howards and tanks of the 3rd County of London Yeomanry had crossed the anti-tank ditch on the right flank, enemy resistance lessened, due in no small measure to the machine-guns of the 2nd Cheshires. The enemy was subdued, allowing some progress to be made,

At midday the 5th East Yorkshires moved forward to bridge the ditch. This was done without difficulty, except for heavy mortar and artillery fire which came down on the ditch. Machine-gunners of the 2nd Cheshires ably assisted by Bren gunners of 'A' and 'B' companies continuously engaged the enemy and by 1430 hours the two Rifle companies had crossed the ditch and taken up positions on the objective, followed by tanks of the Northumberland Hussars and the Battalion's anti-tank guns. The enemy was found to have fallen back, abandoning guns, ammunition and equipment.

Later that evening, as food arrived and was being sent out to companies, a German aircraft dropped three bombs on the headquarters of the Battalion, resulting in the deaths of Major H. N. Wallace, Captain A. A. Blackwell, Lieutenant and Quartermaster A.S. James, Lieutenant J. A. Atkinson and Privates A. Blackmore, E. Bolton and J. W. Bousfield.

On the night of the 6th April, two of the three Panzer Divisions, the 10th and 21st, were drawn off to hold the American attack on the rear. General Giovanni Messe, who had succeeded Rommel as commander-in-chief of the First Italian Army, (the renamed Axis force on the eastern Tunisian front), finding it impossible to hold out with only one division, obtained the agreement of his superior, Colonel-General Jurgen von Arnim, to withdraw 150 miles from positions on the Wadi Akarit to Enfidaville, the next natural defence line along the coastal plain.

At first light on the 7th April, finding that the exhausted and demoralised Axis troops had abandoned the Wadi Akarit, tanks of the 8th Armoured Brigade passed through the gap created by the 4th (Indian) Division, followed by the 2nd New Zealand Division and the 7th Armoured Division.

This had been one of the most successful battles of the campaign. Casualties had been high. In twenty-four hours two infantry divisions and the 69th Brigade had broken through and driven back three enemy armoured and sixteen infantry divisions from what was considered an extremely strong defensive position. The 69th Brigade had played a conspicuous part in the battle, the 5th East Yorkshires and 6th and 7th Green Howards destroying the Italian Spezia Division, and capturing all of its weapons. Over 7,000 prisoners (mostly Italian) were taken. The Brigade was now pulled back for a much earned rest.

The East Yorkshire Regiment gained the Battle Honour **Akarit** (6th/7th April, 1943).

Within hours of breaking through the Wadi Akarit, forward elements of X Corps came into touch with the U.S. II Corps on the Gabes – Gafsa road and XXX Corps had reached Cekhira. On the 9th, XXX Corps fought an engagement near Agareb just short of Sfax, held by the 15th Panzer Division. The port of Sfax, taken by XXX Corps on the morning of the 10th April, was a key to future operations as supplies could be brought there instead of Tripoli, some three hundred miles distant. Sousse, further north, fell to X Corps on the 12th April and the next day X Corps was up against the enemy anti-tank defences at Enfidaville.

After Akarit, the 5th East Yorkshires, together with the rest of the 69th

Brigade moved to Sfax. Command of the 50th (Northumbrian) Division passed from Major-General J. S. (Crasher) Nichols to Major-General Sydney G. Kirkman, who had been General Montgomery's C.R.A. in South-Eastern Command and in August, 1942, been brought out from England by him to take up the appointment of C.R.A., Eighth Army.

The enemy now prepared to make a stand on a line in the Zaghouan Hills in the north-eastern corner of Tunis, from Sedjenane in the north-west, to Enfidaville in the south-east. The plan was for the British First Army with General Eisenhower, which had been fighting its way through difficult mountainous country to the north, to attack from the west, as the plain there was most suitable ground for armour. To give help, the 1st Armoured Division and the 1st King's Dragoon Guards, an armoured car regiment, were transferred to IX British Corps. XXX Corps was to exert pressure on the Enfidaville position to make the enemy think that the main attack would be delivered there.

On the 14th April, the 50th Division moved forward, reaching a concentration area north of Sousse on the 17th. Three divisions of Eighth Army – 4th Indian, 2nd New Zealand and the 50th – attacked the Enfidaville position on the night of the 19th/20th April, joined during the day by the 201st Guards Brigade. The enemy – Italians as well as Germans – resisted strongly, causing heavy casualties. Enfidaville fell and an advance of three miles was made through the mountainous country around Takrouna.

The 69th Brigade moved forward on the 20th April to take over reserve positions left by the 201st Guards Brigade just south of Enfidaville. On the 21st April a defensive position was adopted in the expectation of a counter-attack. Several enemy counter-attacks followed but were repulsed. With mounting losses, and being aware that further fighting would result in high casualties, on the 23rd April the attack was suspended.

The 50th Division was relieved on the 23rd April by the 56h (London) Division, brought forward from Tripoli; the 69th Brigade being transported back to the 50th Divisional concentration area about twelve miles north of Sfax.

When the attack north of Enfidaville was renewed on the 29th April it was quickly checked. General Alexander arrived the next day to discuss the situation with Montgomery and, having decided that the operations at Enfidaville had not been successful in breaking through the enemy defences, gave orders that the two best available divisions be switched to IX Corps for a thrust against the Medjez el Bab sector to strengthen the operations of the First Army. Subsequently Montgomery selected the 4th (Indian) Division and 7th Armoured Division, adding the 201st Guards Brigade. Lieut.-General Horrocks also went over to command IX Corps in its attack on Tunis, as Lieut.-General J. T. Crocker had been disabled by an accidental injury incurred in demonstrating a new mortar.

The days of the Axis forces in North Africa were now numbered. The

First and Eighth Armies having regrouped were to deal the final blow. The attack on Tunis began on the 6th May breaking through the defences west of Tunis, and on the 7th May, Bizerta and Tunis were captured, the first troops to enter Tunis being the 11th (Prince Albert's Own) Hussars, of 7th Armoured Division, which looked upon themselves as part of the Eighth Army. The enemy fell back on Cap Bon Peninsula. Mopping up operations took place, some 248,000 being taken prisoner, and all stocks of stores heavy weapons and equipment were captured. Enemy resistance came to an end on the 12th May, with Field-Marshal Messe, the Italian C-in-C. who had succeeded Rommel in overall command, surrendering on the 13th May. Only a few hundred of the enemy had escaped by air or sea to Sicily, thus depriving the enemy of troops hardened and experienced in battle, who would have been used to resist an invasion of Italian territory in the Mediterranean. The Eighth Army had advanced some 1,850 miles from El Alamein. General Alexander cabled to England: 'We are masters of the North African shores'. A further Battle Honour for the campaign, **North Africa 1940-43,** was awarded to the Regiment.

The days of fighting for the 50th (Northumbrian) Division in North Africa were over. The next assignment was not known. There were rumours that the Division was to move to Kabrit in Egypt for combined operations training. There was some disappointment that this, the longest serving Division in the Eighth Army, should not be allowed to take part in the final defeat of the Germans and Italians in North Africa.

On the 25th April it set out on a journey of nearly 2,000 miles to the Egyptian Delta to prepare for the assault on Sicily.

CHAPTER VIII

ALLIED PLANS AND STRATEGY FOR THE FUTURE OF THE WAR

With the decisive defeat of the Axis armies in Egypt in October, 1942, and the landing in the early hours of Sunday the 8th November of an Anglo-American force under General Eisenhower at Algiers, Oran and Casablanca, it would be only a matter of time before the enemy was cleared from the shores of North Africa.

Attention was now directed to further operations to relieve the pressure on the Russian front. A landing in north-west Europe was out of the question, but there were other possibilities.

In a telegram which reached the British Prime Minister on the 12th November, President Roosevelt set out the 'possibilities' of 'a forward movement' against Sardinia, Sicily, Italy, Greece and other 'Balkan areas'. The views of the British Prime Minister were similar – to attack either Sardinia or Sicily, from where air attacks could be made to support subsequent amphibious landings on the Italian mainland. The Joint Chiefs of Staff were directed to draw up the necessary plans.

Mid-December found Eisenhower's armies being held by German counter-attacks. The attempt to take Tunis was postponed.

On the 21st December, the Prime Minister readily agreed to President Roosevelt's suggestion for a meeting to discuss future strategy. The conference would take place near Casablanca on the 13th January, 1943 – the first plenary meeting on the 15th.

Churchill and the British Chiefs of Staff, Admiral Sir Dudley Pound, General Sir Alan Brooke and Air Chief Marshal Sir Charles Portal, arrived on the morning of the 13th, and in the afternoon went into conference with Field Marshal Sir John Dill, head of Britain's Joint Staff Mission in Washington. Churchill joined them later and their thoughts were for an attack on Sicily. The next day, President Roosevelt arrived with the American Chiefs of Staff.

On the morning of the 15th January, Mr. Harold Macmillan, Minister of State for the Middle East, General Eisenhower, Air Marshal Sir Arthur Tedder and General Sir Harold Alexander arrived at Casablanca.

The first plenary meeting headed by President Franklin D. Roosevelt began that afternoon. The discussions considered whether, when North Africa was cleared, the Allied Forces should attack Sardinia or Sicily. The Joint Planning Staffs favoured Sardinia where it was thought there would be less opposition on the beaches, and the aerodromes better placed for air action against Italy, and the operation there could start three months earlier than an attack on Sicily. Eisenhower was also favourably inclined to Sardinia. The next day after studying these plans the combined Chiefs of Staff recommended to the President and Prime

Minister a preference for Sicily, the distances being shorter, landings easier to support, and it was on the direct route to Italy. Agreement to this was given at the second plenary meeting on the afternoon of the 18th January. It was also agreed that General Sir Harold Alexander should become Eisenhower's deputy Commander-in-Chief of the whole of North Africa and for the eventual landings in Sicily with direct control of ground operations of the 15th Army Group (comprising the 7th U.S. Army under command of Lieut.-General George S. Patton, and the British Eighth Army under General Bernard Montgomery); Admiral Sir Andrew B. Cunningham, to be Naval Commander; Air Marshal Sir Arthur Tedder, Air Commander.

The two previous sea-borne landings in the war, at Madagascar on the 5th May, 1942, and Morocco and Algeria on the North African coast on the 8th November, 1942, had not been strongly defended. The landing in Sicily, with the Italians fighting on their own territory. supported by strong German forces would prove to be harder. The invasion was to call for the largest force so far assembled for a sea-borne operation, with 150,000 men and more than 3,000 ships, the largest amphibious operation ever taken in the history of war.

An outline plan code-named 'Operation Husky' for the assault on Sicily had been drawn up by the Joint Planning Staff in London. This was sent to General Alexander at his headquarters in Tunisia and received the approval of the President and Prime Minister. A detailed plan was made by Alexander's staff and submitted by General Eisenhower to the Allied Combined Chiefs of Staff in Washington in April. This was modified as were others, and eventually finalised at the eighth attempt.

The plan provided for the United States 7th Army to assault the north-west corner of the island near the port of Palermo, the 8th Army in the south-east between the Gulf of Catania and the Gulf of Gela. The plan was sent to General Montgomery who was with his Corps and Divisional commanders at Cairo. After much discussion the sites for the landings were found wholly unacceptable and Montgomery was convinced it would not succeed. He wished to draw up his own plan for the Eighth Army which would concentrate his forces in an initial assault between Syracuse and Pachino: the American 7th Army to move from the north-west and land alongside the British forces in the Gulf of Gela, west of the Pachino peninsular. Thus the U.S. 7th Army and the Eighth Army would land side by side in a concentrated attack. He made his views known to Alexander on the 24th April and two days later left for Tunisia. Alexander called a conference on the 29th April, but Montgomery, suffering from influenza, was unable to attend and, as Alexander was unable to get the agreement of the service chiefs, the conference broke up.

Time was getting short and Montgomery pressed Alexander to call another conference. This was held on the 2nd May. Montgomery put forward his views. They had the full support of Admiral Sir Bertram Ramsey who would have the sole responsibility for getting the force ashore. Approval was given by Eisenhower on the 3rd May – only two months away from 'D' Day. There was still much to do.

The final plan provided for the invasion of Sicily by the Eastern Task Force (Eighth Army) in the south-east of the island from a point just south of Syracuse, southwards round the Pachino peninsula, the Seventh U.S. Army (Western Task Force) to land to the west from just east of Gela to Licata. This was based on the assumption that resistance would be slight as only small numbers of the Axis forces had escaped from Tunisia and the island could be captured easily. But the time taken by the Allies in mounting an attack enabled the Axis powers to strengthen the defences of the island and send reinforcements of three German Panzer Divisions and Italian troops from Italy.

The two armies would form 15th Army Group under the operation control of General Alexander and would comprise Eastern Task Force (British) under command of Lieut.-General Montgomery and Western Task Force (American), under Lieut.-General George S. Patton.

Eastern Task Force was comprised of:

XIII Corps (Lieut.-General Miles Dempsey) made up of the 5th Division (Major-General Berney-Ficklin): and 50th Division (Major-General Sidney C. Kirkman) Dempsey also had control of the 1st Airborne Division and a Commando Brigade.

XXX Corps (Lieut.-General Sir Oliver Leese, Bart., comprising 51st (Highland) Division (Major-General Douglas Wimberley): 1st Canadian Division (Major General Guy Simmonds): 78th Division (Major-General Vyvyan Evelegh) and 231st Infantry Brigade (Brigadier R.E. Urquhart). This brigade had been in Malta from June, 1939, and styled 1st Malta Brigade. It had been responsible for the south-eastern defences of the island and had no previous experience of fighting, but with the clearance of Axis forces from North Africa was released and sent to the Egyptian Delta for training.

X Corps in reserve in Tripoli was made up of the 1st and 7th Division and the 56th Division.

The Western Task Force (Seventh U.S. Army) under command of Lieut.-General George S. Patton comprised four infantry divisions, one armoured division, and the 82nd U.S. Airborne Division.

At Eighth Army Headquarters the planning staff drew up detailed plans for the assault. The 1st Air Landing Brigade Group would drop west of Syracuse between 2210 and 2330 hours on the 9th July to capture an important bridge, the Ponte Grande over the Anapo river; the coastal batteries to the north, and a seaplane base. A Commando Brigade would then land from the sea four hours later to capture the coastal battery at Capo Murro di Porco just south of Syracuse. XIII Corps would then assault the Gulf of Noto on a frontage of twelve thousand yards with the 15th and 17th Brigades of the 5th Division landing in the Cassibile and Casanuova area, then turning due north to capture Syracuse, while the 151st Brigade (6th, 8th and 9th Battalions, Durham Light Infantry) of the 50th Division landed near Avola and Noto to capture the towns and protect the bridgehead from the west and south-west. XXX Corps plan would provide for a landing by the 231st Brigade Group to the east of the

Pachino peninsula south of Marzememi to establish a beachhead and join up with the 50th Division at Avola, with the 51st (Highland) Division landing at the south-east point of the peninsula to capture the town of Pachino. The 1st Canadian Division to the west to establish a beachhead to protect the flank of the 51st Division and capture the Pachino airfield, the Seventh U.S. Army still further west on the Gulf of Gela, at Licata and Gela.

THE 50TH DIVISION PREPARE FOR SICILY

Having been relieved from operations in Tunisia on the 25th April the 50th Divisions wended its way over 2,000 miles to the Egyptian Delta. The 5th East Yorkshires moved in motor transport, by easy stages, as far as Tobruk, which had now become a railhead, and here the Battalion entrained for Alexandria, the transport continuing by road. After a short rest at Alexandria it reassembled on the 13th May with the 69th Brigade eight miles east at Sidi Bishr, to re-equip, reorganise and train for the next phase of the war. The camp was pleasantly situated, surrounded by palms and only half a mile from bathing beaches. There was also time to relax. Whilst training was confined to mornings, the afternoons were free for bathing and visits to nearby Alexandria, and four days leave was granted to those who wished to visit Cairo.

Once again the 50th (Northumbrian) Division was placed under command of XIII Corps (Sir Miles Dempsey). The other division in the Corps, the 5th, had been out of the line since El Alamein, clearing the battlefield.

Meanwhile, the 50th Division having been re-equipped, was reorganised with three brigades. The 69th remained under command of Brigadier E.C. Cooke-Collis, D.S.O. Command of the 6th and 7th Battalions, The Green Howards, had passed to Lieut.-Colonels D.J.M. Smith, D.S.O., of The Essex Regiment and D.G. Jebb, D.S.O., of The Cameronians. The 5th East Yorkshires remained under command of Lieut.-Colonel R.B. James, D.S.O. The 151st was under command of Brigadier Ronald H. Senior, D.S.O., T.D., who had taken over from Brigadier Beake shortly after the Battle of Mareth. The 150th Brigade, lost at Gazala, was replaced by the 168th Brigade, under command of Brigadier Kenneth C. Davidson, M.C., a former officer of the Gordon Highlanders. The battalions forming this brigade were:

The 10th Battalion, The Royal Berkshire Regiment.
The 1st Battalion, The London Scottish, The Gordon Highlanders.
The 1st Battalion, The London Irish, The Royal Ulster Rifles

Major-General S. G. Kirkman, O.B.E., M.C., who had been appointed G.O.C. during the latter part of the North African campaign, remained in command.

But the period of rest and relaxation was not to last for long; work had to be put in hand for future operations. Orders were received to replace worn and damaged vehicles, overhaul those fit for service, carry out waterproofing and remake camouflage nets. On the 30th May a 'dock party' left the 5th East Yorkshires with some of its transport for an 'unstated destination.'

The 69th Brigade left Sidi Bishr on the 5th June to journey to Kabrit by road and railway. Here, at the Combined Operations Training Centre on the Suez Canal, a week's training in combined operations was carried out. There were exercises in beach fighting, mountain climbing, 'dryshod' and seaborne landings, loading and offloading of vehicles. A good deal of time was spent in experimenting with the amount and weight of equipment each man could take on to L.C.A.'s (Landing Craft Assault), also what could be carried on landing, as in assault landings it would be some time before vehicles were ashore.

The course completed there was a thirty-mile march in intense heat along the banks of the Suez Canal to a tented camp just south of the oil refineries at Ataqa, near Suez, where there was a further ten days of training.

While at Ataqa there were visits from Sir James Grigg, the Secretary of State for War, and General Montgomery, who gave a short speech to the men. The 5th East Yorkshires also had the very great pleasure of a visit by Captain The Lord Middleton, the former C.O. of the Battalion, who, in order to go overseas had relinquished the rank of Colonel, as well as command of the 6th Battalion, and had to seek and obtain the approval of H.M. The King, to temporarily relinquish the office of Lord Lieutenant of the East Riding of Yorkshire.

While the 50th Division was busy carrying out its training, H.M. The King left London on the 11th June for Algiers to visit General Eisenhower and the Allied Armies. The first days were spent inspecting the American forces. On the 19th June the King moved on to Tripoli to visit General Montgomery and the Eighth Army. Shortly after his arrival at the aerodrome at Castel Benito, in the lunch marquee, His Majesty conferred on General Montgomery the accolade of Knight Grand Cross of the Order of the Bath in recognition of his services in the victory at El Alamein.

The 69th Brigade remained in camp on the shores of the Red Sea until the 29th June, when it marched to the nearby docks at Ataqa, and went on board a troopship, sailing the next day through the Suez Canal to Port Said. Here the 5th East Yorkshires remained in dock aboard its L.S.I. (Landing Ship Infantry), while further training took part in the adjoining waterways, embarking onto L.C.A.'s (Landing Craft Assault), and disembarking ashore. The Divisional Commander came on board the Battalion's transport, and explained the operations in which they would be engaged, but gave no hint of the destination.

On the morning of the 5th July the convoy moved off, and it was only after reaching the open sea that the destination – known hitherto to only a few – was given to everyone – Sicily. During the four days journey the battalions of the 69th Brigade had a restful time, apart from daily physical training and exercise. There were games and competitions, talks and lectures. In fact everything was done in free time to keep minds occupied and away from the task to be undertaken. Officers and men were each given a copy of a small booklet, 'A Soldiers Guide to Sicily'. It told of the climate of the country, the history, geography and topography and the people; the protective attitude of the Sicilians to their womenfolk and when their jealousy was aroused they were known to resort to the use of knives and daggers. While at sea General Montgomery's message to the Eighth Army was received.

The ship had a well fitted Intelligence Room in which scale models, aeroplane photographs, maps of the coastline at Avola and Noto (the landing area of the 50th Division), and the interior could be studied, as were aerial photographs of the beaches. There were lectures on the form of attack and briefing of companies and platoons.

Soon after midday on the 9th the convoy was joined by others from North Africa and Malta, a vast armada of some 2,400 ships. For the first four days the weather had been perfect, the sea calm; then there was a change, a brisk wind blew and a heavy sea was running. In the evening of the 9th July just as Mount Etna was sited a strong north-easterly wind turned into a gale with a heavy swell of the sea. At midnight the convoys anchored seven miles off shore. As the invasion force converged on either side of Malta the wind reached gale force, and it seemed that the landings might have to be called off, but Admiral Sir John Cunningham, the Naval Commander-in-Chief, decided that the armada should go on and was supported by Eisenhower. Zero hours was set for 0245 hours on the 10th July. A rum ration and cocoa was issued before embarkation on assault craft.

Before the landing could be made it was necessary to capture the small fortified island of Pantelleria which lay on the sea route to Sicily and was an air and submarine base of the Italians. The island had to be neutralised and its defences destroyed. From 1st June it was subjected to intense and prolonged bombardment by Fortresses of the U.S. Air force until ten days later it surrendered.

CHAPTER IX

THE ASSAULT ON SICILY

SATURDAY 10th JULY, 1943

The airborne assault by the 1st Airborne Landing Brigade Group from Tunisia began two hours before midnight on the 9th July: the object was to create a diversion and capture the Ponte Grande, the bridge across the Anapo River, near Cassibile. Weather conditions and insufficiently trained pilots of towing aircraft resulted in gliders being cast off at sea with forty-seven failing to reach land, while seventy-five scattered their passengers over such a wide area of the mountainous interior that they were unable to take part effectively in the day's operations. Only twelve gliders landed in the neighbourhood of the objective, but the eight officers and sixty-five men who reached the Ponte Grande fought a hard battle for eighteen hours and by removing the demolition charges prevented the destruction of the bridge by the Italians.

The 82nd U.S. Airborne Division also suffered from the gale and their parachute troops were dispersed over an area of fifty miles. They did, however, manage to form small groups which attacked enemy posts and key points, surprising and causing confusion amongst those inland.

The seaborne landings were also made in hazardous conditions, but the landings of the 5th Division went well and by 1000 hours the 17th Brigade had captured Cassibile: Casanuova followed. In the afternoon the 17th Brigade arrived at the Ponte Grande to rescue the survivors, crossed the bridge without delay, and by nightfall Syracuse had been entered, the Italians failing to put up a fight. The port was seized undamaged, the peninsula overrun and a thousand prisoners taken.

The 51st (Highland) Division of XXX Corps landed on the southern tip of the island just west of Cape Passero, the 1st Canadian Division a little further west. The Italians were not expecting a landing in such adverse weather conditions, although during the previous day the convoys from Malta were clearly visible, and in consequence they were surprised and disorganised, putting up little opposition. The coastal guns and inland artillery were soon accounted for from supporting fire of the Royal Navy. By 0730 hours the 51st (Highland) Division had taken possession of Pachino airfield and work had started to put it into a usable state. The 1st Canadian Division had captured the town of Pachino. At 1145 hours the airstrip was ready for use and the town had been cleared of the enemy by 0130 hours. Some one thousand prisoners had been taken by XXX Corps at the end of the first day.

The Americans were less fortunate in the landings in the Gulf of Gela. The 1st U.S. Infantry Division had landed at Caltagirone, overlooking the Gela Plain, but the heavy sea had held up the unloading of anti-tank guns and artillery and only a few tanks had got ashore. The Herman Goering Division, equipped with the new 56-ton Tiger Tanks, one of three Panzer Divisions rushed over to the island by Hitler, counter-attacked, penetrating almost to the beaches, but was broken up by guns of the Royal Navy and when darkness fell the Americans were firmly established.

Although 'H' hour for the landings was 0245 hours, the 151st Brigade, the assault brigade, was delayed due to the high seas and the long distance from the shore where the transports had anchored. At 0030 hours, after cocoa and stiff tots of rum, the L.C.A.'s were boarded and moved off. But the distance from the shore meant a run-in of several miles causing the craft to be scattered, and uncertainty by naval officers in charge as to landing places resulted in groups being put down some distances from the right places. By 0415 the leading battalions, the 6th and 9th D.L.I., were ashore, moved forward and reached the outskirts of Noto and by 1000 hours were established in the town of Avola. The 8th Battalion landed at dawn, but not on the intended beach, in fact in the area of the 5th Division, but quickly moved south to Avola. By midday the battalions of the Brigade had reached and taken their objectives, and, having moved forward to the concentration area, the 69th Brigade was called forward.

The 69th Brigade was not in the first part of the assault, having been given the task of following up the landings of the 151st Brigade. In the late hours of the 9th July the ship carrying the Brigade anchored seven miles off shore of Sicily. Soon after midnight the leading assault troops boarded the landing craft and made for the shore. At 0800 hours the assault craft of the 5th East Yorkshires lay off the beach in the Gulf of Noto, just north of Avola which was the southern boundary of XIII Corps landing area. The shore was clearly visible and quiet, no sound of guns, or small arms; no aircraft overhead. At 0830 hours they went ashore. The beaches were quickly overrun and a beach-head established. Some of the transport of the 5th East Yorkshires was put ashore, together with its baggage, but, as the rest of the transport was being unloaded from the ships, an enemy aircraft came over and dropped bombs. One of these fell on a ship which caught fire and six 15-cwt trucks and a jeep were lost. There were no casualties to personnel. By 1000 hours the 69th Brigade had reached a point west of Avola, astride the road leading to the interior.

It had been intended that the Brigade should move on to take up a position to defend Syracuse against enemy counter-attacks, but when this failed to develop there was a change of plan. At 1330 hours General Dempsey arrived at Divisional Headquarters and on being told that other than the forward area was clear of the enemy, except in the Noto region, gave orders that the 69th Brigade would move north, relieve the 17th Brigade (5th Division) and take over a defensive position south of Floridia, where an attack by tanks was expected, and that the 15th Brigade (5th Division), holding a defensive position north-west of Cassibile, should come under command of the 50th (Northumbrian) Division.

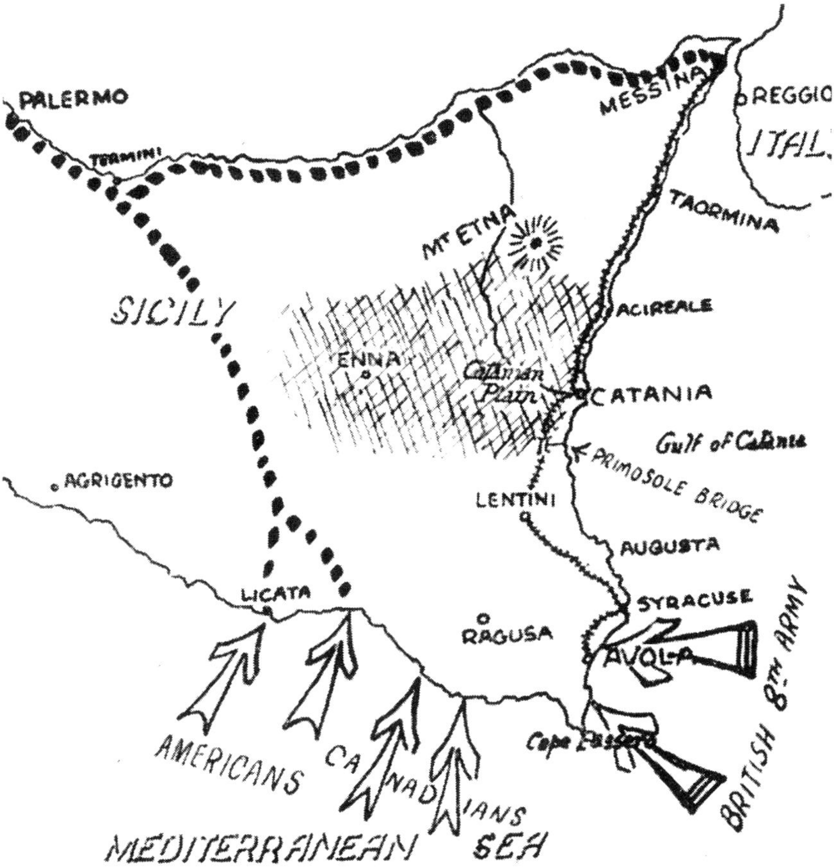

Route taken by 5th East Yorkshires

Area of heaviest fighting

Route of advance by U.S. Forces

The 69th Brigade moved off, to begin a march of twenty miles. There was a shortage of transport and this was supplemented by requisitioning and collecting Sicilian country carts, horses, mules and donkeys, the Brigade headquarter's wireless sets being carried in a donkey cart requisitioned at Avola. It was very hot and the road was dusty, narrow and winding. There was a shortage of water due to there being no water carts and, although orders had been given that water from wells should not be drunk until tested, the orders were unenforceable. On arrival at 2300 hours the 69th and 151st Brigades of the 50th Division, together with the 15th Brigade (5th Division) under command, took up a defensive position facing west on a very wide front between Floridia and Noto, but the anticipated counter-attack did not materialise.

All being quiet on the front, the men, tired out from the day's activities. the long march in considerable heat, and having gone without sleep for twenty-four hours, were able to get a good night's rest. Patrols were sent out and advanced some four thousand yards but made no contact with the enemy. At dawn carrier patrols went out and reported all was clear as far as Canicattini Bagni, twelve miles west of Syracuse.

SUNDAY 11th JULY

General Montgomery arrived on the island during the morning of the 11th July and spent the morning visiting the front. In his book, *El Alamein to the River Sangro*, he wrote:

> 'I was confirmed in my view that the "Battle of Sicily" would be primarily a matter of securing the main centres of road communication. Movement off the roads and tracks in the hilly country was very difficult and often impossible, so that if nodal points were gained it was clear that the enemy would be unable to operate.
>
> 'My orders on the 12th July were for the advance to continue on the two axes, 13 Corps along the coast to Catania and the north, 30 Corps to Caltagirone, Enna and Leonforte . . . On the 13th Corps flank, I decided that we should make a great effort to break-through into the Plain of Catania from the Lentini area and ordered a major attack for the night of the 13th/14th July. A parachute brigade and a commando were made available for the operation, in which the main problems were to force the bottleneck through the difficult country between Carlentini and Lentini and to secure two bridges: one north of the Lentini ridge and the other, the Primosole, over the River Simeto.
>
> 'The plan was to land the parachute brigade during the night near Primosole bridge with orders to capture it and establish a small bridgehead on the north bank. Contact was then to be made with the commando whose task, having landed west of Agnone, was to secure the other bridge. The main thrust, directed on Catania, was to be delivered by the 50th Division with an armoured brigade leading. Naval support for the air and sea landings was arranged.'

At 0700 hours the Corps Commander arrived at Headquarters 50th (Northumbrian) Division to outline plans for the day. The 50th Division was to be relieved by two brigades of the 51st (Highland) Division of XXX Corps. On completion of the relief the 151st Brigade would take over from the 13th Brigade of the 5th Division in the Floridia-Solarino area: the

69th Brigade would take over from the 151st Brigade and that brigade would relieve the 15th Brigade (5th Division) north-west of Cassible, allowing that Brigade to return to the 5th Division. The 69th to concentrate south-east of Floridia.

The moves in relief of Brigades began in the afternoon, and at the same time the 69th Brigade was ordered to advance three miles westwards and take up a more advantageous position into more open country in the foothills.

At 1930 hours General Dempsey again visited the Divisional Headquarters to give orders for the 12th July. The Division would advance along the inland road, through Syracuse, along the road to the west running through the hills from Floridia through Solarino, Sortino, Carlentini to Lentini, then along the road which crosses the Simeto River by the Primosole Bridge into the Catania plain.

MONDAY, 12th JULY
THE CAPTURE OF SORTINO

At 1145 hours, the G.O.C. 50th Division received further orders from Corps by wireless not to wait to be relieved in the positions around Floridia-Solarino but to start the moves at once. The 69th Brigade to move to an assembly area near Floridia from where it would lead the advance of the 50th Division to Lentini and Sortino, it being essential to occupy the Catania Plain before the enemy could become established in a strong defensive position.

In the afternoon the 69th Brigade moved to the assembly area and the 151st Brigade, having relieved the 13th Brigade, moved forward and occupied positions in and around Floridia and Solarino. The 6th Durham Light Infantry, having relieved the 2nd Wiltshire Regiment (5th Division), found themselves facing the Italian Napoli Division in front of Solarino. An enemy attack was stopped by artillery. The presence of this division constituted a threat to the line of communications and would have to be eliminated.

At 0445 hours on the 13th the 6th D.L.I. supported by the 98th Field Regiment, R.A. and the 44th Battalion, The Royal Tank Regiment, attacked the Italians and by 0530 hours had overrun their positions. At 0800 hours two sections of carriers and a troop of tanks went along the road to Palazzola, and, finding the enemy completely disorganised, attacked and destroyed the Italian Napoli Division. Three hundred and twenty prisoners were taken, including the Divisional Commander, General Porgini. Sixteen R35 tanks were taken together with field and anti-tank guns and fifteen lorries – a welcome addition to the limited resources of the Division

Meanwhile the 69th Brigade had concentrated south-east of Floridia in readiness for the advance on Lentini, and orders were given to the 5th

East Yorkshires and a field artillery battery to lead the Brigade advance and capture Sortino before dark.

During the advance a mobile column consisting of one squadron of Sherman tanks, a battery of self-propelled guns and the carrier platoon of the 7th Green Howards, was to move through the Canicattani Bagni, cut the Solarino-Palazzolo Road, then attack Solarino from the rear and if possible capture Sortino.

The column advanced to a point west of Solarino where there was a short but sharp fight. The carrier platoon of the 7th Green Howards circumvented the Italian position and entered their transport lines. A large number of prisoners were captured and taken aboard the carriers. An 88mm gun then fired on the carriers and three were put out of action. The prisoners were killed but the crews, unharmed, drove away a number of Italian lorries and several score of mules, a valuable addition to the battalion transport. The column then began to withdraw the way it had come.

The Italian troops west of Solarino then made two unsuccessful attacks: first an infantry attack, then with tanks. Five French R35 tanks, manned by Italians, came down the road from Palazzolo to Solarino in line and at full speed. Four were put out of action but one got through Solarino and made its way to Floridia firing its machine-gun at anything in sight. Lieut.-Colonel James, commanding the 5th East Yorkshires, riding a motor-cycle, accompanied by his Intelligence Officer in a wireless carrier, met with the French R35 tank which had run amok the mobile column. It hurtled down the road, firing as it came. Its first target was a 15-cwt truck loaded with ammunition. It exploded and the advancing troops of the 5th East Yorkshires ran for cover behind the stone walls and fell into ditches on the roadside. Lieut.-Colonel James and the carrier turned and returned the way they had come with the tank in pursuit. A shell knocked a track off the carrier, the unharmed crew scrambling out as it careered onto the verge. It then followed Colonel James half a mile down the road, firing machine-gun bursts at him until reaching Floridia where a Sherman tank blocking the road caused the tank to collide with a lamp-post. The Italians left the tank and surrendered. The Italians, coming under heavy artillery fire, pulled back.

Orders were then received by the 69th Brigade to capture Sortino before dark, then advance on Lentini; the 151st Brigade to occupy Sortino after it had fallen. The advance of the 69th Brigade was led by the 5th East Yorkshires followed by the 6th Green Howards with the 7th Green Howards in reserve. The 5th East Yorkshires moved off; ‘C’ Company commanded by Captain J.R.H. Owen in the lead; ‘D’ Company commanded by Captain D.J. Penwill, D.S.O., following; the remainder of the Battalion coming on behind.

Since landing, little opposition had been met, and was not expected, and since speed was important they advanced along the mountain road giving no attention to the possibility of enemy troops concealed in the olive groves, vineyards and scrub bordering the roads.

At 1820 hours, one mile south-east of Sortino, the Battalion fought its first battle on Sicilian soil. Advancing through a narrow gorge, they were ambushed by German troops to the north and Italian troops to the south on both sides of the road. The enemy opened fire on 'C' Company which was the only part of the Battalion within enemy range. An anti-tank transport had come too far up the column and reached the head of 'D' Company which was turning a bend in the road. A German Spandau gave a long burst of fire and the Italians, in stone houses on the left of the road, opened fire on 'C' Company. They were quickly cleared from the houses and taken prisoner. 'D' Company had halted when the firing broke out but Colonel James sent his Intelligence Officer to order 'D' Company to come forward. It entered the stretch of road dominated by the enemy and was allowed to moved forward unmolested. 'C' and 'D' Companies were then ordered to deploy to the right of the road, move up the steep slopes and concentrate an attack on the enemy, fleeing to the hills. The enemy then opened fire from both sides of the gorge – small arms, mortar bombs and Spandau. A platoon of 'D' Company gave covering fire whilst 'C' Company together with the remainder of 'D' Company went forward. The effect of the enemy fire prevented the rest of the Battalion from closing up, resulting in the Battalion being virtually cut into two parts, one past the gorge, the other approaching it. Both halves of the Battalion then attacked: 'C' and 'D' companies on the enemy front, the rest of the battalion on the rear. The enemy then fled to the hills and at midnight began to withdraw, enabling the high ground on each side of the village to be occupied. Some of the Italians were seen to be changing into civilian clothes in order to get away; large numbers came into the Battalion's area and surrendered. They were identified as being from a German battle group which had been hurried forward with French R35 tanks from Catania to support the Italian Napoli Division. Sentries were posted and the rest of the Battalion were able to get a few hours' sleep after a long and tiring day.

An account of this action has been given by Major K.C. Harrison, an officer of The West Yorkshire Regiment, at that time serving as a Platoon Commander with the 5th East Yorkshires:

> 'Sudden and exciting, I heard from my position in 'B' Company the unmistakeable purr of Spandaus. Bren guns replied from our leading companies, the heavy thumps of German mortar bombs echoed down the valley. We halted for a while, hoping that 'D' and 'C' Companies might soon overrun the enemy. But the noises of battle continued spasmodically, and without knowing much about the situation 'B' Company was told to advance further down the narrow valley. Further ahead at a road junction we were ordered to establish ourselves on a hill to our right.
>
> 'The enemy could not see to fire its spaundaus at us, as we were still climbing the slopes and hidden by stone walls and trees, but a regular procession of mortar bombs hit the valley below, near the road junction we had just left. Dusk was rapidly approaching and, in my platoon area, I found the CO with my Company Commander. The CO's plan was that 'B' Company should occupy one of the enemy hills during the darkness, while 'D' and 'C' Companies were given similar assignments.
>
> 'Although the men were tired, hungry and thirsty after the long march in the

> almost tropical sun, they welcomed the move and set off with a great heart. The CO led us in the darkness, the Company Commander with him. I was immediately behind with my platoon, but the exceedingly rough ground and the many stone walls made it hard going for my men with their rifles, Brens and other platoon weapons.'

Meanwhile, the 6th Green Howards had been held up by mortar fire when entering Solarino at 1800 hours the previous day. The C.O., Lieut.-Colonel D. J. M. Smith, went forward with his Intelligence Officer to make a reconnaissance. Finding the 5th East Yorkshires held up outside Sortino, he received orders to pass through, continue the advance, and capture the village. By 1000 hours on the 13th July, Sortino had fallen to the 6th Green Howards who were given an enthusiastic welcome from the population.

TUESDAY, 13th JULY

The bridgehead in Sicily could now be regarded as firmly established. The Eighth Army held two supply ports, Syracuse and Augusta, and a stretch of coast some thirty miles long with numerous beaches for landing.

General Montgomery issued a message to be read out to all of his divisions:

> 'The beginning has been very good, thanks to your splendid fighting qualities and to the hard work and devotion to duty of all those who work in the ports, on the roads and in rear areas. We must not forget to give thanks to "The Lord Mighty in battle" for giving us such a good beginning towards the attainment of our objective, and now let us get on with the job. Together with our American Allies we have knocked Mussolini off his perch. We will now drive the Germans out of Sicily. Into battles with stout hearts, good luck to you all.'

The 50th Division was now on the high ground north of Sortino and out of touch with the fleeing Axis forces. The 168th Brigade, having that morning landed at Syracuse and moved to a concentration area East of Floridia, the Division was complete.

It had been the intention that the 151st Brigade should occupy Sortino once it had been captured by the 69th Brigade, but being delayed through mopping up at Solarino, Major-General Kirkman, the Divisional Commander who was present with 69th Brigade, ordered Brigadier Cooke-Collis to continue the advance on Lentini, leaving one battalion at Sortino, to be relieved by the 151st Brigade. The Brigade Commander detailed the 5th East Yorkshires to hold Sortino until the 151st Brigade came up, the 6th Green Howards to lead the advance on Lentini, followed by the 7th Green Howards.

Around 1415 hours the Divisional Commander, who had been to a meeting with General Montgomery and the Corps Commander, arrived back to tell Brigadier Cooke-Collis that the 69th Brigade must capture Carlentini and Lentini during the night, and on the next day take over the Primosole Bridge some seventeen miles ahead. During the night of the 13th/14th the 1st British Parachute Brigade would be dropped by plane and gliders around Primosole to capture the bridge over the Simeto River: No. 3 Commando to land from the sea to seize the bridge over the Leonardo River some three thousand miles north of Lentini. Both bridges must be taken intact as no Bailey bridging was available.

The 6th Green Howards moved off at 1330 hours, screened by the mortar and carrier platoons. They were soon held up when the carriers and the mortar platoons were attacked by an armoured car and a 75-mm self-propelled gun. The mortar platoon went into action and blew up the self-propelled gun which blocked the road. At 1700 hours, the carriers having cleared the obstruction, the Battalion moved off. Almost at once, when just three miles south of Carlentini they were held up by machine gun fire from a low hill astride the road and from a hill on the left of the road called Mount Pancali. It was now obvious that the capture of Lentini that night could not be achieved and any postponement might result in the bridges being destroyed by the enemy. The Divisional Commander gave orders for 69th Brigade to delay the attack until after darkness, then eject the enemy from the positions on Mount Pancali.

It was not known that one battalion of the German 115th Panzer Grenadier Regiment was on the road in front, another battalion of the same regiment in Carlentini and Lentini, while Mount Pancali was held by a hundred Germans with machine-guns under cover and well concealed, and a troop of self-propelled guns and tanks.

At 2115 hours the attack was launched, with support by the 124th Field Regiment, R.A., and 'C' Company the 2nd Cheshire Machine-Gun Battalion. By midnight the hill astride the road was taken and the enemy fled across the road towards Mount Pancali. The Battalion moved back to the road and attempted to continue the advance by going round the hill. But coming under heavy enfilade machine-gun fire from this feature, they could make no progress and returned to the ridge which had recently been captured to hold a firm base.

At 0530 hours on the 14th the 7th Green Howards were brought up and ordered to attack Mount Pancali. At the foot of the hill was a flat plain some two thousand yards in length which would have to be crossed before the hill could be ascended. The attack, supported by the 98th and 124th Field Regiments, R.A., and the machine-guns of 'C' Company of the 2nd Cheshire Machine-Gun Battalion was timed for 0800 hours, but at the request of the artillery put off until 0830 hours. The support fire could not be very effective owing to the concealment under cover and the positions of the enemy unknown.

The frontal assault began under cover of artillery and mortar fire, and when the foot of the hill was reached the British barrage ceased and the advancing troops, covered by steep sides and boulders, began to climb. When they reached the summit enemy machine-guns swept the area. As they advanced they came under fire from Spandaus, but went forward and soon the enemy gave up, some surrendering and other making away. There were many dead and wounded. By 1000 hours Mount Pancali had fallen.

Before continuing the advance it was necessary to collect and reorganise the Battalion, and it was not until 1300 hours that the advance was resumed. By 1500 hours Lentini and Carlentini were in the hands of the 69th Brigade, and the 7th Green Howards passed through on to the Catania road. When three miles north of Lentini the carrier platoon ran into an ambush of three German tanks, but withdrew after knocking out the leading carrier. The Battalion then took up a defensive position four miles north of Lentini. The 6th Green Howards who had remained in their positions at Mount Pancali advanced to Lentini and took up a defensive position to the west of the village.

Three miles north of Lentini the Malati Bridge crosses the Leonardo River. Possession of the bridge was vital as it formed part of Highway 114, the only direct road to Catania. If in British hands, troops, guns, tanks and supply vehicles could be got across and the plain cleared in a very short time. Should the enemy succeed in destroying the bridge, the British might be held up on the Simeto sufficiently long for reinforcements to be brought up and the position around Mount Etna consolidated.

The capture of the bridge intact was to be the objective of No. 3 Commando. The first commandos landed at 2200 hours on the 13th July in the Agnoni Bay to force march five miles to the bridge. Instead of the expected Italians, they found themselves up against the newly arrived 3rd Parachute Regiment and the 3rd Battalion the Herman Goering Regiment. They battled their way forward until at 0300 hours the bridge was reached and, having driven the Italian defenders away, removed the demolition charges, and the bridge was captured intact.

The Commando was to be relieved by the 50th Division at dawn, but the units were still fighting their way forward and could not meet the agreed time. The Germans pounded the bridge with an 88-mm gun and laid down mortar fire and swept the area with rifle and machine-gun fire. After holding out for the best part of the day and with heavy casualties the commandos were compelled to withdraw.

In the early afternoon of the 13th the 5th East Yorkshires set off from Sortino to relieve No, 3 Commando. With the Germans in retreat the line of advance was covered with booby traps. There were small ambushes, mines, road blocks and craters which slowed down the advance, resulting in a number of casualties. Lentini was reached by 1700 hours and it was found that the Germans had withdrawn.. All three battalions of the 69th Brigade were now together and were placed in defensive positions. The 7th Green Howards holding the area of the Leonardo bridge some two miles north of Lentini; the 6th Green Howards to the western flank of the town and the 5th East Yorkshires in brigade reserve just north of Lentini with one company covering the town from the east.

At dusk the 5th East Yorkshires concentrated in some orange groves on the right of the main road just north of Lentini. The area was thickly wooded, and here – as on the 28th May, 1940 near Poperinghe – unknown to the Battalion the other end of the orange groves were occupied by three hundred German paratroops with three self-propelled 75-mm guns of the Herman Goering Division. On some hilly ground about three miles east of Lentini was a battalion of Germans. There was also in the area an Italian mobile column which had earlier been rounded up by the 124th Field Regiment, R.A. and as a result the Regiment asked for infantry protection.

'C' Company of the 5th East Yorkshires under command of Captain J. R. H. Owen was sent out at about 0200 hours to a position roughly two miles east of Lentini, and about two miles south-west of the German battalion referred to above. At midday a platoon patrol established contact with the Germans in the hills. Captain Owen who accompanied the patrol was killed as was 2/Lieut. D.G. Stanley, and some of the men were wounded. Eight men were captured by the enemy. They were locked up in a farmer's barn, the farmer being told to release them next morning, after which the men returned to the Battalion.

Concerned at what had happened, the C.O., Lieut.-Colonel James, moved his reserve company to the scene of the action. The departure was seen by the three hundred German paratroops in the north of the orange groves and a raid was made on Battalion Headquarters. At about 1500 hours the headquarters was fired on from the east at a range of about one hundred and fifty yards. Those remaining at the headquarters charged the enemy, who withdrew. For the loss of one man wounded, twenty Germans, some wounded, were captured.

Soon afterwards, a soldier from the Commandos, wandering through the orange groves quite by chance, came upon the German headquarters in the northern part. A platoon from 'D' Company was sent to mop it up. The platoon commander, Lieutenant G. M. Dunkeld, was killed and the platoon met with fierce opposition and was beaten back. As the platoon retired Private J. Bailey distinguished himself by holding off the superior numbers of enemy with a Bren gun, until five minutes fire from four 3-inch mortars drove the Germans off. In recognition of this act of bravery he was awarded the Military Medal. When the position was occupied the next day the barns were found to have been destroyed and a number of Germans killed.

The actions of one platoon are told below:

> 'We spent a night amongst the orange trees, and the next morning we were static. We began weapon cleaning and washing of clothes, but before long my platoon was given its first job of what later proved to be one of our busiest days. The order was to go out as a fighting patrol over ground where there were supposed to be pockets of enemy resistance, but although we combed the suspect area for 2 or 3 hours we saw no sign of the enemy, and returned to our leaguer about midday.
>
> 'The orange groves we were in were rather thick with trees and undergrowth and, generally speaking, it wasn't possible to see more than 20 yards. After lunch, however, the C.Q.M.S. drew my attention to movements about 200 yards away: a lane of trees in the grove afforded us this long view. Some troops were moving alongside a small wall, and we felt certain that they weren't Eighth Army, as they were wearing khaki drill slacks and not shorts. Whilst we were debating who they might be, the question was solved by the rapid burr of a Spandau not very far away. The bullets did not come in

our direction, but we immediately stood-to and the company's 2 i/c led my own platoon and 10 platoon to overrun the enemy.

'Amongst the thickening groves we came to a house surrounded by a high wall, and from the wall a British paratrooper hissed to me to look out. He pointed in the direction of the enemy. We advanced a little further, and I suddenly saw that one of my section commanders had grabbed a German officer and was propelling him in front. The German officer was yelling something, but my men were right on top of their form now, and the air was ringing with shouts of "Come out, you bastards" and similar remarks. I felt sure that the officer was calling upon his men to surrender, so I shouted to my men to stop the noise. Soon the Boches appeared, several from a deep ditch and others from various hiding places in the undergrowth. We combed the area and our final bag was the officer and 18 men, with one Spandau.

'We had no sooner reorganised than up came the company commander in a hurry and told us to get ready for another job. This time we had to go out as a company mobile column to put in an attack on a farmhouse where a respectable number of Germans were holding out. We went off on portees (truck-mounted anti-tank guns) but when we reached the area the C.O. had decided that the battalion was already strung out too far, and in any case the attack was more than a company could tackle, so it was called off.

'Once again we returned to our orange grove, and once again we found a job already 'lined-up' for us. This time we had to attack a farmhouse where a small number of enemy paratroops had been holding out. Fortunately for us, the C.O. decided to try his mortars first and our mortar platoon laid down such an effective 'stonk' that the Boches came out and surrendered, obviating the necessity for our attack. Some British paratroopers who had been captured came out with them and testified to the deadly accuracy of our mortars.

'Our last assignment on this busy day was to go a little further north and provide protection for the artillery supporting the D.L.I. This was necessary owing to the numbers of enemy paratroops that had been dropped. Another task here was to ambush any enemy who might be driven into our area by the advancing troops of 5 Div. on the coastal sector. We spent a chilly and sleepless night, disturbed by the guns, which were firing all the time. We were not involved with the enemy, but 'A' Company and the anti-tank platoon fought a confused action in the darkness, capturing some enemy paratroops and releasing some British paratroops.'

The 69th Brigade, having borne the brunt of the fighting during the advance, was given a rest. The advance to the Primosole Bridge was taken over by the 151st Brigade. A mobile column was formed of the 9th D.L.I., the machine-guns of No. 6 Platoon of 'A' Company The 2nd Cheshire Regiment and a troop of 6-pdr anti-tank guns which set out from the Sortino area along the twenty-five miles winding pass to the River Simeto: the 8th D.L.I. to follow in a forced march, then the 6th after completing the clearing up at Sortino. From Sortino to Primosole is a distance of twenty-five miles. The 5th East Yorkshires were attached to the Brigade in reserve.

Late in the afternoon the 9th D.L.I. passed through the 6th and 7th Green Howards at Lentini and by 2130 hours had joined up with the 4th Armoured Brigade, a mile south of Primosole bridge. The 9th D.L.I. established contact with troops of the 1st Parachute Brigade who had a sorry tale to tell. For thirty-six hours they had battled for the bridge against the German 3rd Parachute Regiment, seasoned veterans of the Crete and Russian campaigns, who had been flown from the Italian mainland with orders to halt the Allied advance. Four times they had repulsed the attacks of the enemy, with mounting casualties; but only two hours earlier, shortly before dusk, under pressure of a fifth assault, and with ammunition running short, in order to keep the force in being at all, the commander had withdrawn across the bridge to the southern bank. But the bridge had not been destroyed, the demolition charges had been removed and the paratroopers were close enough to prevent the enemy planting any more.

The commander 151st Brigade, Brigadier R. H. Senior, D.S.O., T.D., decided that an attack that night was not possible; darkness had fallen, the 9th D.L.I. were very tired; the 8th even more so after a forced march, and the 6th would not arrive until midnight. He would attack the next day at 0730 hours with the 9th D.L.I.: this would give time for a reconnaissance of the Simeto River, to find possible crossing places in order to make a bridgehead.

THE BATTLE OF PRIMOSOLE BRIDGE 13th-18th JULY

The airborne assault to open the way for XIII Corps to break through into the Plain of Catania from the Lentini area began at 2200 hours on Tuesday, 13th July, when the 1st British Parachute Brigade under command of Brigadier G. W. Lathbury, flying from its base in North Africa, dropped troops by plane and glider around the Primosole Bridge. The bridge, with a superstructure of iron girders some 240 yards long, spanned the sluggish reed-bordered River Lentini to the east of the confluence of the Rivers Gornalunga and Simeto, over which Highway 114 passes to the city of Catania some seven miles away. The task was to seize the bridge, prevent its destruction, establish a small bridgehead on the north bank, hold off any enemy advance from Catania, and hold the south bank until the leading ground force of No. 3 Commando, 4th Armoured Brigade and 151st Brigade, advancing from the River Lentini after capturing the Malati Bridge, made contact some time in the afternoon of Wednesday, 14th.

The night was calm, but as the aircraft approached the coast line they were mistakenly fired on by Allied ships lying off Sicily and Malta, together with a considerable amount of enemy anti-aircraft fire. Of the 107 planes taking part, three were lost at sea, eleven were brought down by anti-aircraft fire, twenty-six found the flak too strong and returned to base with their loads still aboard, and only fifty-six successfully put their troops down in the Gerbini plain. Only twelve of the seventeen '*Horsa*' gliders carrying anti-tank guns and artillery got through. Only 295 out of the 1,856 men who set off from base landed close to or around the Primosole Bridge.

A glider collided with the bridge and the Italian troops fled. Small groups who had fallen farther afield came into the area. The bridge was seized and a small party of fourteen engineers removed the demolition charges from the steel girders. When dawn came the bridge was held undamaged and the paratroops extended on either side.

Almost simultaneously with the dropping of the British airborne troops, German airborne troops dropped behind the Axis line to reinforce it. The small force holding the bridge was attacked but the enemy was repulsed. There was still no sign of the relieving force. There were three more enemy thrusts; all were repulsed. When a fifth attack was launched around 1930 hours the commander decided that in order to keep his small force in being the bridge must be abandoned, and a withdrawal began to the south bank, leaving no bridgehead on the north side. At 2130 hours the vanguard of the 50th Division, the 44th Royal Tank Regiment and the 9th Durham Light Infantry made contact with the parachutists south of the bridge. It was found that the enemy had retaken the bridge, but the parachutists were holding on.

* * * * *

As decided by Brigadier Senior the previous night, the attack by the 9th D.L.I., supported by the fire from Priests (self-propelled 25-pdr guns mounted on tank chassis) of the 24th and 98th Field Regiments, R.A., started as planned at 0730 hours on Thursday the 15th July. As the companies advanced in open formation over the open ground they were heavily machine-gunned before they reached the river. A number of men were lost. Some platoons were able to get across but many were drowned. Those that crossed came up against fierce resistance from German paratroops concealed in vineyards and lining a sunken road some four or five hundred yards north of the bridge, the existence of which was unknown. After fierce hand-to-hand fighting those who had managed to get across were driven back leaving their wounded and dead behind them.

At 0930 hours the remnants of the 9th Durham Light Infantry holding the ground on the southern bank of the river were subjected to heavy German mortar fire, and although able to mount an attack were able to break enemy attempts to place charges to blow up the bridge.

At 1000 hours Major-General Kirkman arrived at 151st Brigade Headquarters and gave orders for an attack by the 8th Battalion at 1600 hours, but soon afterwards the Corps Commander arrived and decided that another daylight attack would be suicidal. As there was no urgency for the capture of a bridgehead the attack was postponed until 0200 hours on the 16th when the attacking force would have the advantage of a full moon. It would be satisfactory if a footing could be established on the other side. A plan was drawn up for a frontal attack as by the 9th Battalion Durham Light Infantry on the day before. It did not find favour with Lieut.-Colonel R.P. Lidwill, commanding the 8th Battalion Durham Light Infantry.

Fortunately, Brigadier G. W. Lathbury, the commander of the 1st

British Parachute Brigade, was still in the area with Lieut.-Colonels Alastair Pearson, D.S.O., M.C., and J. Frost, the commanders of the 1st and 2nd Battalions, Parachute Regiment, who had taken part in the capture of the bridge the previous day. Colonel Lidwill put the plan to them. Colonel Alastair Pearson had a clear understanding of the nature of the ground and particularly a point some four hundred yards west of the bridge where the river could be forded, and where the enemy were fewer in numbers. Furthermore he offered to guide the attacking companies over the river. Two companies were to cross, move back to the bridge and, when it was captured, the rest of the Battalion would cross over it.

The final plan for the assault was for two companies to ford the river at 0210 hours, turn eastwards through an area of vineyards towards the bridge, and, if captured intact, the rest of the Battalion with supporting arms would cross over and establish a bridgehead; an artillery concentration would commence eighty minutes earlier in the area of the bridge and the vineyards immediately north of the river, extending to five hundred yards west of the bridge. For the last ten minutes fire would be directed on the northern end of the bridge. The artillery barrage would be strengthened by machine-guns of Number 2 Platoon of the 2nd Cheshire Regiment on the high ground to the south of the river overlooking the bridge and a squadron of Sherman tanks on the low ground.

At 2200 hours 'A' and 'D' Companies guided by Lieut.-Colonel Pearson moved off. Arriving at the crossing point they lowered themselves into the Simeto River. In single file, at two points fifty yards apart, they waded the thirty yards across. The water was four feet deep with a muddy bottom, and, other than at deep holes where shells had fallen, no difficulty was encountered. Most of those falling into the holes were quickly rescued, but some were submerged.

On reaching the far bank they formed up, wheeled eastwards and advanced with difficulty through the thickly planted vineyards. On reaching the bridge, the few Germans encountered, greatly surprised, were quickly disposed of with bayonets, grenades and small arms fire. Those defending the bridge had suffered heavily from the artillery fire and the main body had withdrawn. The first phase having been successfully completed, the companies dug in, established themselves across the Catania road about one hundred yards north of the river bank.

Colonel Lidwill then attempted to bring up the rest of the Battalion but all prearranged methods failed. He set off to walk across the bridge and at this critical moment met a Major Wigram (a War Office 'observer') riding a bicycle, who at Lidwill's request went back to the Battalion to tell it to come forward.

The plans were now considerably delayed and it was not until daybreak that 'B' and 'C' Companies were across. As they advanced up ditches on either side of the road they came upon withering small arms fire from a concealed sunken track. Hand-to-hand fighting broke out with bayonets, hand-grenades and automatics, and casualties were heavy. Concealed

Spandaus opened fire at point-blank range on the leading sections of 'B' and 'C' Companies, wiping out the whole of the leading platoon of 'B' Company, and, but for the ditch, hardly a man in either company would have survived. A small party from 'C' Company charged the leading posts; most were killed but the enemy was compelled to withdraw

Both companies rallied quickly. 'C' Company took to the fields on the right to outflank the enemy. Heavy casualties had been suffered from Spandau fire and the remnants were reduced to such an extent that, scattered in small groups and with no officers left, they no longer fought as a company. From the ditch on the left of the road 'B' Company returned the fire of the Spandaus; then went into the vineyards and almost immediately met with the paratroops. Both sides set to with bayonets in close hand-to-hand fighting but within twenty minutes had fought to a standstill.

The enemy still held the sunken road, the existence of which was not known. On being discovered 'B' Company withdrew to the embankment opposite the sunken road and the remnants of 'C' Company took up a position on their left, while 'D' Company took up positions on the right side of the road, in line with 'B' and 'C' Companies. 'A' Company moved to the right of the road but back towards the river. The Battalion then established itself in a position three hundred yards to the north of the bridge and waited for the inevitable counter-attack.

Soon after first light the enemy launched a counter-attack. It fell on 'A' Company which was outnumbered. Two platoons were overrun and after more hand-to-hand fighting were forced back to the river, some swimming across, while others withdrew towards a farmhouse. By 0600 hours the Battalion held a small bridgehead three hundred yards in depth and an equal width, and held on waiting for reinforcements to arrive. Throughout the day the Germans launched a number of attacks with tanks and infantry, but all were repulsed. At the end of the day the Battalion was still where it had been in the morning.

Meanwhile at 0600 hours, General Kirkman, the Divisional Commander, arrived at 151st Brigade Headquarters, and having acquainted himself of the situation went back to Divisional Headquarters to inform the Corps Commander that the Division would not be able to operate efficiently in the plan for the capture of Catania. When informed, General Montgomery postponed the time for the capture of Catania by twenty-four hours, and gave the 151st Brigade the task of enlarging the bridgehead during the night. This was to be accomplished by the 6th and 9th Battalions and 'H' hours was set for 0130 hours on the 17th. As the bridge was still under fixed machine-gun line, the crossing would be by the ford where the 8th Durham Light Infantry had crossed the night before.

At around 2330 hours, as the 6th and 9th Battalions Durham Light Infantry began the approach march to the ford, a barrage was put down on the enemy's bank of the river to left of the bridgehead. As they formed up it was lifted two hundred yards north of the river and continued during the crossing.

At 0130 hours on the 17th July the river was forded without difficulty and they formed up on the other side and made their way to join the 8th Durham Light Infantry holding the small bridgehead. But as they moved forward through the vineyards they met with German paratroopers determined not to give ground. The fighting was fierce and, as the companies went through the thick vineyards, the Germans to the fore were cleared, but pockets of resistance were left on the flanks and they got split up. Intense automatic fire came from a sunken road causing heavy casualties, but they fought on and cleared the enemy from the sunken road. Using bayonets and grenades they moved forward and took up a position beyond the sunken ditch on the left of the Catania road. The Germans then attacked towards the sunken road. They were kept at bay for three and a half hours and eventually driven off. At around 0600 hours the Germans counter-attacked with tanks down the road from Catania but the attack was broken up by the artillery. Soon afterwards the 6th and 9th Battalions were well beyond the bridge. At 0700 hours Bren carriers were sent across the bridge to draw enemy fire while the Sherman tanks of the 44th Royal Tank Regiment came over. They were joined by tanks of the 3rd County of London Yeomanry, crossed into the bridgehead and cleared the Germans from the vineyards. Very soon resistance by the enemy lessened. One hundred and fifty-five German parachutists were captured and the enemy dead numbered about three hundred. The German forces began to withdraw into the north-east of the island, pivoting on Catania. Mopping up continued until 1000 hours and, when completed, resistance in the area ceased. The battle for the bridgehead was over.

By 1100 hours the 151st Brigade had established a strong bridgehead some three thousand yards deep, with the 9th Battalion Durham Light Infantry entrenched on the right of the road to Catania, the 6th Battalion Durham Light Infantry on the left, the 8th Battalion to their rear just north of the bridge in close defence. There was sufficient depth to mount a full-scale attack towards Catania.

The enemy consisting mainly of elite German parachute troops were still landing on Catania airfield to reinforce those holding the line astride the main road, half-way between Primosole and Catania. At 1000 hours on the morning of the 17th July, the 5th East Yorkshires as reserve battalion to the 151st Brigade was ordered to move forward. It passed over the bridge and into the bridgehead with few casualties and that night joined up with the Durham Light Infantry. That night an attack was made and the enemy driven back. The next two days were spent in repulsing strong enemy counterattacks. Threatened by an outflanking movement, the enemy withdrew.

While in this position parties of men were withdrawn to bathe in the river a mile away, returning with bunches of grapes and tomatoes which they found growing in abundance along the riverside. Mosquitoes were troublesome and an issue of mosquito nets was made.

Although the Primosole Bridge had fallen on the 17th, another day was included in the official dates of the battle to include those units which crossed and formed the immediate bridgehead. It had been a hard fought 'soldiers' battle' and, with the possible exception of Centuripe, a fortnight later, the hardest fought in the Sicilian campaign. The three Battalions of the Durham Light Infantry had lost between them five hundred killed, wounded and missing.

The official history of the East Yorkshire Regiment hardly mentions the activities of the 5th Battalion in the battle for the Primosole Bridge although it brought to The East Yorkshire Regiment the Battle Honour **Primosole Bridge** (13th-18th July, 1943), granted to only three other infantry regiments, The Durham Light Infantry, The 1st Battalion The London Scottish (The Gordon Highlanders) and The Cheshire Regiment, the latter having played a major part with its machine-guns.

* * * * *

Meanwhile at 1000 hours on the 17th July the Commander XIII Corps, General Miles Dempsey, visited the Headquarters of the 50th Division and gave orders to the G.O.C., Major-General Kirkman, to enlarge the bridgehead a further two thousand yards up to the Fosso Bottaceto, a ditch forming the defence line on the southern edge of the Catanian airfield. The third brigade of the 50th Division, the 168th, (Brigadier K. C. Davidson, M.C.), which had been in reserve after landing, was now called forward. It was to pass through the 151st Brigade on the night of the 17th/18th, with its centre line on the main road: its objective the Fosso Bottaceto. The 69th Brigade would then pass through, swing to the west, capture the line of the railway and screen the left flank of the 168th Brigade. The attack was to be supported by eight field regiments and one medium regiment. The German 4th Parachute Regiment had been landing on the airfield at Catania all day to reinforce those who had withdrawn from the bridge, placing the enemy in a stronger position than anticipated.

At 2200 hours on Saturday, 17th July, the 168th Brigade moved off with the 1st Battalion, The London Scottish (The Gordon Highlanders), T.A., on the right and the 1st Battalion The London Irish (The Royal Ulster Rifles), T.A. on the left. The initial advance proceeded with little difficulty, but when just short of the Fosse they met heavy small arms and machine-gun fire and were mown down. It was the Brigade's first battle and it was soon in disarray. At 0300 hours on the 18th the Divisional Commander ordered the brigade to fall back a thousand yards and take up a defensive position.

Thirty minutes after the 168th Brigade had left to cross the bridge, the 69th Brigade began crossing. The 7th Green Howards moved up the Catania road, to a point about one hundred yards short of the Fosso

Bottaceto. It was now 0130 hours on the 18th and the Battalion turned towards the western end of the Fosso Bottaceto, the railway line and the railway bridge which crossed the ditch.

Having reached its objectives the Battalion met with very heavy machine-gun fire and was pinned down; losses were very heavy. That night there was a withdrawal to more suitable positions. The 6th Green Howards, having crossed the bridge, turned, to the north-west reaching its objective, the railway bridge to the south of the western end of the Fosso Bottaceto, at dawn. The approach had been observed by the enemy who launched an attack on one company The main body then withdrew up the railway line and took up the intended position on the flank of the 7th Green Howards. During the next three days both Battalions were actively engaged in defending the bridgehead. They remained in the positions they held until midnight on the 21st July when the 8th Battalion Durham Light Infantry arrived to relieve the 7th Green Howards, the 6th Battalion Durham Light Infantry relieving the 6th Green Howards. On relief both battalions moved to rest areas until the 25th July when they returned to the line to relieve the 8th and 9th Battalions Durham Light Infantry

That day, Benito Mussolini, the *Duce* (Leader and Prime Minister), returned from a meeting with Herr Hitler in northern Italy and was presented with a demand for his resignation by the Italian Fascist Grand Council, supported by King Victor Emmanuel and Marshal Badoglio. Marshal Badoglio was appointed his successor. The King ordered Mussolini's arrest and he was confined to a house in the Appenine mountains. He was to die on the 27th April, 1944, when shot by Italian partisans on the shore of Lake Como.

Badoglio opened secret negotiations for an armistice which were signed at Cassible by General Castellano on the 3rd September. The formal unconditional surrender took place on the 8th September.

Four days later, on the 29th July, the 5th East Yorkshires received news that Private Eric Anderson, the stretcher bearer who had distinguished himself at the Battle of the Wadi Akarit, had posthumously been awarded the Victoria Cross.

THE ADVANCE TO MESSINA

The next objective of 50th Division was Catania, but the coastal road was heavily defended by the bulk of the Herman Goering Division, particularly so in the area of the aerodrome, where some time before the invasion Italian engineers had constructed concrete fortifications surrounded by barbed wire entanglements and strategically placed minefields.

At 0900 hours on the 18th July, General Dempsey arrived at Headquarters 50th Division to inform the Divisional Commander that, as the infantry of XIII Corps had been engaged in continuous fighting for many days, General Montgomery had changed the plan for the Corps. The attack would be switched to the left flank and taken up by the 5th Division of XXX Corps, on the left flank of 50th Division, to broaden the front, breaking through to the west of the foothills of Mount Etna and turn the aerodrome defences to enable XXX Corps, reinforced by the 78th Division, to attack the rear of the enemy's positions. The 50th Division would assume a defensive role and for the time being would experience a period of static warfare.

The town of Adrano was the key to the Mount Etna position, and XXX Corps moved forward to launch attacks; on the 28th July Agira was captured. On the 29th July attacks were launched on Adrano, Catenanuova and Regalbutto. Catenanuova fell on the 30th July, Regalbutto on the 3rd August, thus opening the way to Adrano, and on the 3rd August the town of Centuripe, five miles south-west of Adrano was captured after four days' fighting, by the 78th Division. The enemy, fearing being split in two, began to withdraw on the 4th August, and on the 6th Adrano was entered. The Mount Etna defences collapsed on 7th August and with lessening resistance the final advance of the campaign began, with thrusts on both sides of Mount Etna to converge at Catania.

With the enemy strongly engaged by XXX Corps, those to the front of the 50th Division began to withdraw and on the 3rd August, XIII Corps received orders to go over to the offensive and advance along the coastal road towards Messina, with Catania as the objective. The 50th Division began its move at 0730 hours on the 4th August, advancing across the Bottaceto Ditch with the 151st Brigade on the right, the 69th Brigade on the left and the 168th Brigade in reserve. The 69th Brigade, led by the 7th Green Howards, was followed by 6th Green Howards and the 5th East Yorkshires.

The road and fields on either side were mined and there were numerous booby traps. Enemy troops, well concealed, held up progress with mortars, machine-guns and ambushes. The Adjutant of the 5th East Yorkshires, Captain L. E. L. Steele, an attached officer of the Royal Berkshire Regiment, was fatally wounded when a road mine exploded. Having advanced some six thousand yards, both brigades were held up in front of Catania by determined resistance

In the late afternoon, Brigadier Cooke-Collis, commanding the 69th Brigade, ordered the 6th Green Howards to pass through the 7th Battalion and attack next morning, but there was no fighting. The enemy had abandoned the pill boxes on the outskirts of the city and fled.

At 0830 hours on the 5th August, the 6th Durham Light Infantry were moving down the road towards the Piazza del Duomo in the centre of the city, when Lieut.-Colonel W. I. Watson was handed a note which said:

> 'The authorities and functionaries of the city of Catania are in the barracks of the Carabiniere in the Piazza Giovanni Verga awaiting orders.' It was signed by the Mayor of Catania, the Marquis di San Giuliano, and was the unconditional surrender of the city.'

The 50th Division found the roads blocked by craters or fallen houses, the streets empty, the shops closed and the trams stationary where they had stopped when the current from the generating plants had ceased on their destruction. Within a short time everyone came out of their homes and buildings, and cheered the conquering troops. Only a quarter of the population, some fifty thousand, had remained in the city; the rest had fled to the hills and neighbouring villages when bombing and shelling began.

The 168th Brigade now passed through the 69th Brigade and advanced along the inland road, the 151st Brigade along the coastal road. The day's advance of six thousand yards took the brigades to a position one thousand yards north of the outskirts of Catania.

During the next seven days progress was slow. north of Catania the plains come to an end and the ground from the lower slopes of Mount Etna falls steeply to the sea. It is intensively cultivated with vineyards, olive groves and citrus fruits except where it is covered with lava. Much of the ground is terraced with lava walls often ten feet high. The roads are intersected by deep river beds, nearly all dry in summer but difficult for tracked and wheeled vehicles to negotiate when crossing owing to the steep sides. Most of the roads are bordered by lava walls four to twelve feet in height.

Past Riposto a narrow, intensely cultivated coastal plain runs on to Taormina, and, beyond, a road thirty-five miles in length leading on to Messina is dominated by hills rising to some three thousand feet above sea level. Almost all of the principal bridges over the main roads had been blown up and half the small ones. The roads were strewn with mines as was the adjacent cultivated land and areas of demolitions. As the enemy withdrew it had the advantage of concealment causing surprise to the advancing forward troops who suffered fairly heavy casualties. Throughout the withdrawal they fought in small numbers, then hastily retired so that at no time was it possible to mount a brigade attack.

From the outskirts of Catania, the 151st and 168th Brigades moved forward and on the 7th August the 151st Brigade advanced without much opposition to a mile short of Acireale; the 168th Brigade operating in more difficult country was three thousand yards to their rear.

On the night off the 7th/8th August the enemy withdrew a short distance allowing the 151st Brigade to move into Acireale, while the 168th Brigade, echeloned behind the 151st Brigade, was in touch with the enemy at Acis Antonio. A longer advance was made on the 9th August and at the end of the day both brigades were in touch with the enemy on the Mangano River. There was a further withdrawal by the enemy on the 10th August and as they withdrew they blew the bridges over the Mangano and Leonardello just to the north.

On the night of the 11th August the enemy withdrew to a position around Riposto and the next day these brigades came into contact with the enemy on the line of the River Macchia north of the towns of Giarre and Riposto: the 151st brigade held up in the northern outskirts of these two towns, the 168th Brigade in Macchia and on the Mascarello ridge.

Meanwhile the 69th Brigade had followed up and, apart from one action at the foothills off Mount Etna when the 7th Green Howards were pinned down by mortar, machine-gun and artillery fire, the advance continued slowly and uneventfully. San Anonio was reached on the 8th August and on the 12th August the Brigade moved across to the coastal road to take over from the 151st Brigade

The date for the landing on the toe of Italy having been brought forward to the 1st September, on the 12th August General Montgomery, regrouped the Army. The 231st Brigade was placed under command of the 50th Division and the Division was to come under command of XXX Corps, commanded by Lieut.-General Sir Oliver Leese, Bart., at 0600 hours the next day. The 168th Brigade was at the end of its present operations to return to the 56th (London) Division, the 231st Infantry Brigade Group (Brigadier R. E. Urquhart) to replace it.

During the night of the 12th/13th August the enemy broke contact at all points along the whole of the Eighth Army front. At first light on the 13th August, the 69th Brigade continued the advance, making good progress until 1700 hours on the 14th August, when approaching Taormina it was found that the enemy had vanished. A patrol of the 7th Green Howards went into the town and found the civic authorities were prepared to surrender the town. However, the enemy in retiring had carried out extensive demolitions including two bridges, and it was impossible to move forward with road transport until bridges had been rebuilt. In the early hours of the 15th August, forward troops of the 7th Green Howards occupied Taormina and the town surrendered.

At 0630 hours the rest of the 7th Green Howards moved off, but, just short of Taormina, found the road blocked by demolitions. The rifle companies made a detour over the hills, rejoining the road a mile to the other side of the block. Having proceeded some six miles north of the city, approaching Cape San Alessio at 1500 hours, they came upon the enemy holding a strongly built medieval castle turned into a strong point. The leading troops came under close-range fire from Spandaus and mortars. The Battalion was then pinned down by heavy artillery, mortar and machine-gun fire. It held on until at 1930 hours but when the enemy launched a counter-attack it was forced to withdrew a a short distance to take up a new position for the night. At 2100 hours the enemy's fire ceased and demolitions were blown on the road. In the meantime the 6th Green Howards and 5th East Yorkshires had advanced from Catania and by the 13th August had reached Piedmonte. The next day Giardini was entered, unopposed.

At dawn on the 16th, the 6th Green Howards were ordered to pass through the 7th Battalion near Forza d'Agro. On arriving at around 0900 hours they found the enemy had withdrawn during the night. Setting off in pursuit, by evening they reached a point some five miles short of Capo d'Ali where they were held up by mines and demolitions.

On the 15th August, General Montgomery gave orders for No. 2

Commando with supporting troops to land in the rear of the enemy in the Marina d'Ali area on the night of the 15th/16th, to prevent the enemy carrying out demolitions at Capo d'Ali by blowing up the cliff face and blocking the advance. The 69th Brigade would then join up with this force and advance on Messina.

The force, under command of the 4th Armoured Brigade (Brigadier Curry), sailed from Augusta on the east coast late at night on the 15th and landed at 0300 hours on 16th August, not at Marina D'Ali but at Capo D'Ali, to the north of the position. The landing was too far distant to be reached by the 69th Brigade so the force went on alone towards Messina, but the road came under shell-fire and the force was held up.

It was decided to reinforce the first expedition during the night of the 16/17th with a second force from the 50th Division consisting of the 5th East Yorkshires with supporting troops. On landing, this force would come under command of the 4th Armoured Brigade which would come under command of the 50th Division. The 5th East Yorkshires were to be organised so that they could, if necessary, take to the hills and continue the advance by an indifferent mountain road which joins the Messina-Palermo road some three miles west of Messina, but entire discretion as to how Messina should be captured was left to the commanding officer, Lieut.-Colonel James, and Brigadier Curry, when Colonel James should have got in touch with him.

At 2100 hours on the 16th, the 4th Armoured Brigade advanced but was subjected to mortar and shell fire, some from German batteries on the Italian mainland, and was held up until 0430 hours on the 17th. The enemy rearguard could not be cut off and demolitions had been carried out to the north and the south.

The 5th East Yorkshires landed before dawn on the 17th at Scalata to find the enemy had gone. The two forces made their way inland on foot to Messina. Here the 5th East Yorkshires made contact with men from General George Patten's American Seventh Army who had advanced rapidly from Palermo along the northern coast, and, having arrived at 2200 hours the previous day, claimed to have beaten the British. However, the 5th East Yorkshires were able to claim to have been the first *British* troops to enter Messina.

Unfortunately most of the German troops had got away across the Straits of Messina to Italy, leaving the broken and shattered Italian forces remaining in the island. On the 17th August 1943, after thirty-eight days fighting since the landings in Sicily, all resistance ceased and Sicily was in the hands of the Allies. This marked the end of the Sicilian campaign; the Germans had lost 24,000 killed. With the ending of enemy resistance the 5th East Yorkshires were given the role of coastal defence against raids from the Italian mainland, detachments being sent to points between Messina and Scalata.

The Battalion gained for the Regiment the Battle Honour **Sicily 1943** (9th July-17th August 1943).

The Sicilian campaign had also come to an end for the other two battalions of the 69th Brigade. We left the 6th Green Howards on the morning of the 16th August some five miles short of Capo d'Ali. The next morning they went forward to join No. 2 Commando reaching Marina d'Ali next day at 1000 hours and Capo d'Ali at mid-day. Here, they met Brigadier E.C. Cooke-Collis, the Brigade commander, who told them Messina had fallen and the campaign had ended. The 6th Green Howards at Capo D'Ali marched back to Forza D'Agro on the 17th August, and then proceeded by motor transport to Letojanni Gallodoro.

At the beginning of September the Battalion was then split up, one company to Catania and two companies to Syracuse to construct convalescent camps. The 7th Battalion, having retired from action around Forza d'Agro on the 16th August, went back in the afternoon to a rest area south-west of Taormina.

With the Allied troops having landed on the Italian mainland on the 3rd September, Sicily became a peaceful place, the 5th East Yorkshires enjoying sports and leisure, whilst also carrying out some training. Lieutenant-Colonel R.B. James, D.S.O., who had recently received a second Bar to his Distinguished Service Order, relinquished command of the Battalion on taking up a Staff appointment. Command now devolved on Lieutenant-Colonel G.W. White, M.B.E., an officer of the King's Royal Rifle Corps.

On the 19th September the 50th Division received a signal indicating that it was to return to England on the 25th September. The 5th East Yorkshires moved down the coast to the Port of Augusta on the 17th October, and the next day, together with the 6th and 7th Battalions the Green Howards, embarked on the *H.M.T. Otranto* and joined a convoy which sailed at midday on the 23rd October. The convoy anchored off Algiers on the 25th, sailing again on the 27th to Gibraltar. north of Ireland the convoy split up, ships going to Bristol, Glasgow and Liverpool

The Troopship *Otranto* sailed into the Mersey Estuary in the early hours of the 5th November 1943 and was guided by tugs to a berth in Liverpool. It was a wet and misty day and Liverpool had been shattered by bombs since the 69th Brigade left there in the spring of 1941, a contrast from the sunshine and warmth of north Africa and Sicily.

On leaving for the Middle East the battle experience of the Brigade had been limited to actions in France and Flanders; now they were war-hardened veterans. The composition of the Battalions had also changed. Although reinforced on a number of occasions by men from all over the country, there was still a core of men from Yorkshire, veterans of the hard days in the desert battles.

The 5th East Yorkshires still retained the old Territorial Army characteristics with veterans from North-West Europe and North Africa; Majors A. M. N Rice, H. C. Cocking. Captain E. J. Crews, Captain A. Consitt, Captain W. Sugarman, Lieut. T. A. J. Hill, M.T.O.,

R.S.M. F. Gibson, M.C., M.M., C.S.M. W. E. McDougal, C.Q.M.S. Barraclough, Sergeants Dooley and Gaunt and Pte. Taylor, a Company Clerk.

The next day they disembarked and entrained on 8th November for Thetford in Norfolk, from where they went on two, three or four weeks' leave according to the length of service abroad.

By the 6th December the Brigade had reassembled, and it was known that the 50th Division was to form part of the force to land in north-west Europe, with the *role* of following up the initial landings on Day 3.

At Thetford there began a programme of strenuous training aimed at bringing every one to a hundred per cent physical fitness. There was the usual early morning physical training, and long route marches in full eqipment.

CHAPTER X

OPERATION 'OVERLORD'

THE LIBERATION OF NORTH-WEST EUROPE FROM THE GERMANS

PLANNING AND PREPARATION

Germany having launched an invasion of Russia on the 22nd June, 1941, most of the best forces in France and North-West Europe had been withdrawn to the eastern front, leaving only second-rate troops to hold down the population. There was now little likelihood of any invasion of Great Britain. Attention was then turned towards a cross-Channel attack.

In July, 1940, Sir Roger Keyes had been appointed Director of Combined Operations, with the object of planning raids on the French coast to gain experience for a large landing in 1941. He was replaced in October, 1941, by Commodore Lord Louis Mountbatten R.N., who under the general direction of the Chiefs of Staff was to 'Act as Technical adviser on all aspects of, and at all stages in, the planning and training for combined operations' and 'Direct and press forward research development in all forms of combined operations varying from small raids to a full-scale invasion of the Continent.' Further strategic planning was carried out by General Sir Bernard C.T. Paget, Commander-in-Chief Home Forces, Admiral Sir Bertram C. Ramsey and Air Chief Marshal Sir Sholto Douglas. But it was not until April, 1942, that the British and American Governments agreed that in order to defeat Germany there must be a cross Channel invasion of North-West Europe.

On the 12th August, 1942, the Prime Minister. Winston Churchill, accompanied by Mr. Averell Harriman, President Roosevelt's Special Representative to the U.K., arrived in Moscow to discuss with Marshal Stalin the overall war situation. The Germans were advancing on Moscow, while in the south the German offensive was not being held. Stalin pressed Churchill to open a second front in North-West Europe. Churchill explained that at that time there were insufficient British and American forces in Britain to launch a cross-Channel offensive, those available having been committed to Operation 'Torch,' the landings in north-west Africa. But later sufficient U.S. forces would have been built up and a second front would be opened as soon as practically possible.

Then, at a conference at Casablanca on the 15th January, 1943, code-name 'ANFA', attended by the United States President, Franklin D. Roosevelt, and Prime Minister Winston Churchill and the Combined American and British Chiefs of Staff, it was decided that the time had come to prepare a definite plan for a cross-Channel landing. An Allied Inter-Service Staff would be set up to work in London.

Following these discussions Lieut.-General Frederick E. Morgan, at that time G.O.C.-in-C of I Corps in Scotland, was appointed to head a staff composed of British and United States personnel to plan the assault and later given the appointment of Chief of Staff, Supreme Allied Commander (designate). From the initials of this title the organisation was called COSSAC).

General Morgan took up the appointment on the 1st April, 1943. With the target date of the 1st May, 1944, for the cross-Channel invasion, he was faced with a Herculean task. The landings were to be made by units of the British Home Forces under General Sir Bernard Paget and those of the Americans forming the European Theatre of Operations under General Jacob L. Devers.

The British units would form the Twenty-first Army Group, the Americans the First United States Army Group (subsequently 12th Army Group). Meanwhile General Paget would command Twenty-first Army Group; General Devers, First United States Army Group. General Morgan's task could prove difficult, as all military and political decisions would have to be made by him and he would have to anticipate that these would meet with the approval of the Supreme Allied Commander who had not yet been appointed

It had been thought that General Sir Alan Brooke, Chief of the Imperial General Staff, might be given the Supreme Command in Europe to balance the commands in other theatres; Eisenhower in the Mediterranean, Douglas MacArthur in the South-West Pacific, Lord Louis Mountbatten in South-East Asia. But the Chairman of the American Joint Chiefs of Staff, General George C. Marshall, was also a likely choice. In the end the British Prime Minister was unwilling to part with Sir Alan Brooke, and President Roosevelt felt it better to retain General Marshall. No decision was made as to the Supreme Commander for Europe.

On the 2nd December, 1943, Winston Churchill arrived in Cairo from Teheran where he had been conferring with Stalin and President Roosevelt, to continue the series of meetings codenamed 'Sextant' which had begun in Cairo on the 23rd November.

During a drive to the Pyramids, Roosevelt told Churchill that he had decided upon the Supreme Allied Commander of the Allied Expeditionary Force in Western Europe. It was to be General Dwight D. Eisenhower, currently in supreme command of the Allied forces in the Mediterranean. On the 15th January, 1944, Churchill's nominee, Air Chief Marshal Sir Arthur Tedder, was appointed Eisenhower's Deputy Supreme Commander, 'on account of the great part the air will play in this operation'.

As a result of a meeting in Algiers on the 14th December Churchill set out his views in a telegram to the War Cabinet as to the future organisation of the campaign in the Mediterranean: should Alexander succeed Eisenhower or General Sir Henry Maitland Wilson? who should command the Expeditionary force in Europe under Eisenhower – Montgomery or Alexander? Eisenhower would have preferred Alexander. The next day the War Cabinet decided on Montgomery, because, as Churchill told Roosevelt, 'the War Cabinet consider that the public confidence will be better sustained by the inclusion of the well-known and famous name of Montgomery, and I agree with them as the operations will be to many people heart-shaking.' Alexander should succeed Eisenhower. Admiral Bertram C. Ramsey was appointed Commander of the Allied Naval Expeditionary Force; Air Chief Marshal Sir Trafford Leigh-Mallory, Commander of the Allied Expeditionary Force.

On the 24th December Montgomery was ordered to return to England to succeed General Sir Bernard Paget as G.O.C.-in-C 21st Army Group. Handing over command of the Eighth Army to Sir Oliver Leese on 31st December, he left Italy for Marrakesh to confer with the Prime Minister who was convalescing there after a recent illness, and on the night of 1st/ 2nd January, 1944, departed for England, to prepare for the initial landings in Normandy. The American armies in England were also placed under his command for the landing and subsequent operations until an American Army Group could be deployed. Eisenhower did not leave for England to take over his new command until the 15th January,1944.

The forces taking part in the assault, designated 21st Army Group under General Sir Bernard Montgomery were initially:

The United Sates First Army under General Omar Bradley, comprising the 1st, 7th, 8th, and 19th Corps, and attached airborne troops of the 82nd and 101st Divisions

The 2nd Corps of the First Canadian Army under Lieut.-General Harry D.G. Crerar.

The British Second Army under Lieut.-General Miles C. Dempsey comprising I, VIII, XII, and XXX Corps, with the 1st and 6th Airborne Divisions under Lieut.-General Sir Frederick A. M. Browning, Bart.

The projected assaults would be on five beaches west of the mouth of the Orne River, ten miles north of the city of Caen. These beaches were code-named from east to west, 'Sword' (*Ouistreham*); 'Juno' (*Courselles*); 'Gold' (*Asnelles*); 'Omaha' (*St. Laurent*) and 'Utah' (*Varreville*). 'Sword' would be the landing site of the 3rd British (Iron) Division; 'Juno' the 3rd Canadian Division; both supported by the 79th Armoured Division (Major-General Percy Hobart); all part of I Corps commanded by Lieut.-General John Tredinnick Crocker, D.S.O., M.C.; 'Gold,' the 50th (Northumbrian) Division, part of XXX Corps (Lieut.-General Derek Corfield Bucknall). In support the 8th Armoured Brigade from 79th Armoured Division.

The U.S. 1st Infantry Division and U.S 29th National Guard Division would assault 'Omaha' beach; the U.S. 4th Division, 'Utah' beach. The U.S. 82nd and 101st Airborne Divisions were to drop in the area south-east and west of Ste-Mère-Eglise, capture the crossings of the Merderer River with the U.S 101st Airborne Division securing the exits from 'Utah' beach; the U.S. 82nd Airborne Division to secure the line of the Douvre River and prevent German forces moving on to the flanks of the troops coming from 'Omaha' and 'Utah,' then link up with the troops from 'Omaha.'

The British seaborne landings would be preceded at 0055 hours on the 6th June by the dropping of 4,800 parachutists and 3,200 men in gliders of the 6th Airborne Division behind the sea defences on the high ground east of the River Orne; capture the bridge over the Caen canal (Code named 'Cricket' - later to be called 'Pegasus Bridge' from the symbol of the British airborne forces - winged Pegasus), and the bridge over the river Orne (code named 'Rugger') between Caen and the sea, together with the destruction of the Merville Battery (four casemates inside concrete and barbed wire, believed likely to harass the beaches); then form a perimeter east of the Orne, to hold off any counter-attacks.

In his book, *Normandy to the Baltic*, General Montgomery gives the outline of his plan for the Normandy Campaign:

> (1) The Assault Landing. The invading Armies swiftly to 'stake claims' deeply inland after a foothold had been secured on the beaches. If necessary, pockets of enemy resistance to be by-passed and left to follow-up troops to deal with.
>
> (2) To consolidate and link up the beachheads ; to extend them; to continue with the utmost speed, the build-up of troops, ammunition, stores.
>
> (3) To keep the Germans continually on the defensive, by constant attacks on the eastern part of the beachhead ; The U.S. Armies meanwhile to cut off the Cotentin Peninsula - with the deep-water port of Cherbourg at its head.
>
> (4) By means of attacks constantly renewed, to attract to the eastern part of the captured territory (i.e., the British held part) the main German Forces - particularly his Armour - and there to hold it. Meanwhile, the U.S. Forces to reorganise and build up for a break-through.
>
> (5) The U.S. Armies to break out of the beachhead to the south and at speed, to overrun N.W. France as far as the Loire. Then their main force was to turn left, and left again, so coming up northwards from the south, with the idea of pinning the German Armies in the area bounded to the north by the sea ; to the east by the Seine and to the west by the British. In that area it was hoped to exterminate the German Armies.

CHAPTER XI

THE 50th DIVISION PREPARES FOR THE NEXT PHASE OF OPERATIONS

At the beginning of January there were changes in command of corps and divisions. Major-General S. G. Kirkman, O.B.E., M.C., G.O.C. the 50th Division, left to command the XIII Corps, Eighth Army, in Italy and was succeeded by Major-General D. A. H. Graham, C.B.E., D.S.O., M.C., a former officer of the Cameronians; Brigadier E. C. Cooke-Collis, D.S.O., left to command a brigade of the 49th Division, being succeeded in command of the 69th Brigade by Brigadier F. Y. C. Knox, D.S.O., of the Royal Ulster Rifles.

On the 1st February the 5th East Yorkshires moved to nearby Lowestoft, the 6th and 7th Green Howards to Southwold. The Division, having left all transport, stores and weapons, other than rifles, in Sicily, the battalions had to be re-equipped. and found themselves using entirely new kinds of transport and fighting vehicles from those in North Africa and Sicily.

At the same time the Division was told that there had been a change of plan: XXX Corps which had returned home from Italy was to incorporate the 50th Division which would be the spearhead of the landings. Although in June, 1943, the 50th Division had been given training in Egypt in embarkation on to assault landing craft and disembarkation, seaborne landings and beach fighting, and had in fact had already made a seaborne assault at Sicily, the landings in North-West Europe would be far more advanced. As more than half of the Division were reinforcements with no battle experience the next five months would be concentrated on training, not only in the use of weapons, tactics and fitness but specialist training in marshalling and methods of boarding and loading assault craft – the 'craft' being marked out by tapes on dry land – and amphibious operations.

On the 23rd February H.M. The King, Colonel-in-Chief of the East Yorkshire Regiment, inspected the Battalion and spoke to several of the men. His visit was followed by the Commander-in-Chief 21st Army Group, General Montgomery, to witness and direct exercises of the 50th Division.

Addressing the Division he paid tribute to its fighting qualities, and said that, whereas it had been intended to use the Division as part of the follow up force, because of its fighting qualities it was now to be one of three divisions to spearhead the attack on North-West Europe – 'Operation Overlord.'

The announcement was not well received by all. There were a number of divisions in the U.K. which had never seen action and many of those present must have felt that they should have faced the hard and dangerous task of landing, the 50th Division having been in the forefront of battles for more than two years.

The operations allotted to the 50th Division entailed it being strengthened by the addition of the 56th Brigade, under command of Brigadier E.C. Pepper, an officer of the Bedfordshire and Hertfordshire Regiment, as a reserve brigade. This necessitated the formation of an entire new brigade headquarters. The brigade was to be made up of:

2nd Battalion The Essex Regiment
2nd Battalion The Gloucestershire Regiment
2nd Battalion The South Wales Borderers

None of these had been overseas or trained in combined operations and amphibious warfare. They now had only a short period of time to train in this role.

With four brigades the 50th Division became the largest division to take part in the Normandy landings. Other major units and formations were incorporated. These were:

8th Armoured Brigade from the 79th Armoured Division
74th, 86th, 90th 124th and 147th (Essex Yeomanry) Field Regiment, R.A.
102nd Anti-Tank Regiment, R.A, 25th Light Anti-Aircraft Regiment, R.A.
and supporting units from Royal Engineers, Royal Army Service Corps,
Royal Army Medical Corps, Royal Army Ordnance Corps, Royal Signals and
Royal Electrical and Mechanical Engineers.
The 47th (Royal Marine) Commando would come under command for the initial landings.

When the Division sailed from Southampton, on the 5th June, the strength was approximately 38,000.

On the 28th February, the 5th East Yorkshires with other battalions of the 69th Brigade went to the Combined Operations School at Inverary, to take part in amphibious training with live-ammunition and sea-borne exercises, returning to the south of England on 13th March to billets at Bournemouth.

In 1943 the demand for junior officers in the Mediterranean and Far East had caused a shortage of officers in units preparing for the invasion of North-West Europe. With the disbanding of two Canadian Home Defence divisions, and the Canadians only fighting in Italy, they had a surplus of officers with little to do. The Canadian government offered to loan some of these to the British Army on a voluntary basis under the code-name CANLOAN. Early in 1944 they were interviewed by a selection board and on the 7th April the first draft arrived in England.

A move was made to a camp near Winchester on 6th April, where seven Canadian officers, Captain Montague L. Tyrwhitt-Drake, and Lieuts. W. Ballance, Norman A. Brown, Melville A. Guidotti, Gerald D. Hibb, Robert E. Inman, and Laurent Lapierre, joined. In early March, 'Force G' was formed. This was the naval force which was to carry the 50th Division across the Channel, land them on the beaches and give naval gun support as they advanced.

In April large scale exercises were carried out in Studland Bay, part wet-shod and part dry-shod. In the wet-shod exercise, 'Smash I', the troops having embarked and sailed out, returned in their landing craft to assault the beaches and carry out a tactical scheme inland. During this exercise, as the East Yorkshires carriers grounded, the driver of the first carrier thinking this was the beach, drove off and the carrier disappeared into deep water. It was not the beach but a sandbank. The occupants came to the surface together with parts of the wireless apparatus, and were rescued. Orders were then given that in future the Carrier Officer, Captain F. E. Donkersley, an attached officer from the Duke of Wellington's Regiment, would walk off first. On the next exercise, again in Studland Bay, when the landing craft grounded Captain Donkersley walked off first. Once again the landing craft had struck a sandbank and he too disappeared in the deep water. In a later landing exercise, rocket-bearing ships fired salvoes of live ammunition, the Battalion witnessing for the first time the devastating effect of such bombardments. During these exercises the sea was often rough and the troops suffered a good deal of sea-sickness, but everyone took it in good part.

A fortnight later, on the 17th April, the Division took part in a dry-shod operation, 'Smash II', designed to test the naval plan for the landing and handling of the Beach Groups. The infantry were guided by men of the Beach Groups through dummy minefields on the Dorset coast to an assembly area near to Swanage followed by a long strenuous march.

In another exercise one of the company commanders of the 5th East Yorkshires, Major C. W. S. Belas, records that 'wireless operators of the unit were sent out to contact one another with messages *en claire* which could be picked up by German listeners and mislead them to think that the invasion of the Continent was about to begin'.

The Battalions were now divided into shiploads according to the order of going ashore in France, and on the 1st May boarded Landing Ships Infantry, G67 and 68, at Southampton to take part in a final rehearsal in the Solent of the sea-borne part of the Division's role.

On the night of the 3rd/4th May the assaulting divisions, 3rd British, 3rd Canadian and 50th Divisions, began a final full-scale combined services operation codenamed 'Fabius,' designed to test the machinery of movement and embarkation of the troops, vehicles, tanks and stores. The force went to the Hards at Southampton, where the infantry companies boarded the L.C.I.'s while the vehicles were driven onto L.C.T.'s and sailed out into the Solent with a strong naval escort to make landings in a mock invasion; the 3rd British and 3rd Canadian Divisions between Littlehampton and Bognor Regis, the 50th Division on Hayling Island, a few miles east of Southampton.

As the hulls of the craft touched the bottom the ramps went down and the men dropped into water waist high and waded ashore, the vehicles being driven through shallow water to the beach. Units of the force then moved forward to destined assembly areas from where they returned to camps. As the ships were crewed by men of the Royal Navy and Royal Marines who would be with them during the landings there was an opportunity to get to know one another. During the exercise, Captain the Reverend Henry Lovegrove, R.A.Ch.D., Chaplain of the 6th Green Howards, conducted a service on board one of the Battalions L.C.I.'s, taking as his text 'The hour is now come'. The men thought it was his way of telling them that they were on their way to France, but were to be disappointed. The exercise completed, the 69th Brigade went back to their respective camps at Winchester.

There was now a period of waiting until the 16th May when there was a move to the assembly area at Romsey, north of Southampton, tented camps surrounded by high barbed wire fences; on the 25th May these were sealed off. A ban was placed on visitors entering the coastal areas which extended inland to a depth of ten miles. Once inside there was no further communication with the outside world, no one allowed to leave except under stringent security checks. Personnel were given an Army Post Office number, and told that no place names of locations could be given in the address. Here all were issued with anti-sea-sickness pills and lifejackets; new gas-protective battledress; ODs, (a special American assault jerkin); 200 BAFVs (British Army Franc Vouchers) mostly in 5-Franc notes, blue-green in colour, square, with a representation of the French tricolour on the reverse side; briefing orders in the form of a card giving the sections of the ship which each were to occupy and a code word with the time of the landing and beach sector; phrase books (containing phonetically arranged sentences to enable the recipient to cope with any situation with which he might be confronted), and leaflets about how to get on with French civilians. Final arrangement were made. Vehicles and their loads were waterproofed, equipment was brought up to scale, and each soldier and his equipment was finally inspected. The assault companies, 'A' and 'B', were equipped and armed exactly as they would be for the landing, the commander 69th Brigade, Brigadier F.Y.C. Knox carrying out an inspection.

On 30th May the 5th East Yorkshires were trucked down to the Marshalling Transit Area at Southampton. Officers, W.Os and senior N.C.O.s were briefed and the remainder of the unit given their instructions. Here there was an issue of two French Letters (condoms) to protect rifle barrels, watches, cigarettes and matches from sand and seawater; ammunition and grenades also had to be waterproofed. Each man was provided with a tin of 'Taverner and Rutlege' boiled sweets, two 24-hour ration packs, self-heating soup, a light gas respirator, a vomit bag, spare underwear and boots. In all, each man carried a load of about 65lb in weight.

Conscious of the possibility of vehicles stalling with flooded engines, those responsible for motor-cycles, Jeeps, carriers and tanks, aided by R.E.M.E. Light Aid Detachments worked doggedly to ensure safety.

EMBARKATION AND WEATHER DIFFICULTIES.

Thursday the 1st June opened with a fine moon. As the day came the sun shone and the heat was unbearable, but the fine weather was welcome, indicating a good crossing. Those not engaged in work were able to have some time relaxing in the sunshine, until later that day they boarded the L.C.I.'s (Landing Ships Infantry) G.67 and G.68. H.Q. and the two follow-up companies 'B' and 'C' were in one ship, the two assault companies 'A' and 'D' with the 3" mortars in support, in another. This arrangement had been made so that if one ship was sunk the other could do the assault – the follow-up troops having been trained in the assault role as well as their own – the vehicles being at the same time embarked in L.C.T.'s (Landing Craft Tanks). The L.C.I.'s were prefabricated, newly-built, American ships of 7,000 tons, very comfortably fitted out with first-class messes serving peace-time food, and drinking-water fountains; hammocks were provided for sleeping. Each L.S.I. carried eighteen L.C.A.'s (Landing Craft Assault) manned by Royal Navy and Royal Marine personnel, designed to operate in shallow water so that they could get almost on to land, and then, with the front down, the assaulting troops could wade ashore. They were slung in two tiers from davits which could be loaded with men while still on the davits, then lowered into the sea.

The assault was scheduled for 5th June, 1944, a day when the tide and moon concurred. From the 1st June the commanders met with meteorologists to receive weather forecasts from which to base the final decision as to the date of launching the assault. In consequence the ships anchored at Spithead.

The L.S.I.'s sailed out on the morning of the 3rd June for a last practice on that day and the next in the lowering of the assault craft. Later in the day after two months of unbroken sunshine the weather turned squally; the English Channel saw the highest winds and roughest seas experienced in June for twenty years.

In the morning the Prime Minister, Mr. Winston Churchill, arrived at Southampton and in the afternoon, accompanied by the South African Prime Minister, Field-Marshall Smuts, and the Minister of Labour, Mr. Ernest Bevin, saw the embarkation of the 50th Division, and then embarked on a motor launch to view an assembly of landing craft. At a conference at 2130 hours on the 3rd June it was decided to make no change in the plans, and those ships at Spithead sailed on to join the armada in the assembly area in the Solent to the south-east of the Isle of Wight in readiness to sail to Normandy. The days of waiting were spent in physical training, cleaning weapons, eating, sleeping and generally relaxing in readiness for the great ordeal.

At the next meeting held at 0400 hours on the 4th June, Group Captain J. M. Stagg, the R.A.F. meteorologist, gave the Supreme Commander the bad news that the weather on the 5th June would be overcast and stormy and that the situation was deteriorating. Eisenhower decided to postponed the assault for one day. When they met again that day at 2130 hours to consider the situation rain was pouring down and there were strong winds, but the latest weather report indicated a break; the rain would stop in two or three hours, followed by thirty-six hours of more or less clear weather, with the winds moderating. There were only three days in the month when there was a conjunction of tide and moon: the latest possible date on the present tides was the 7th June. A further postponement would mean that the naval task force to bombard the French coast would have to put back into port to refuel, causing a further delay, and on the 8th June the tidal conditions would not be right for landings. The next suitable date was the 19th June, but, with the preparations made, that date was not a suitable alternative.

Eisenhower left the conference, returned to his trailer, and after a short sleep went back at 0330 hours the next day to meet his commanders. The wind was still blowing a hurricane, but the meteorological reports indicated that late on the 5th June the wind would drop and a period of reasonable weather could be expected on the morning of the 6th, but towards the evening of that day there would be a return to high winds and rough sea.

With so many ships at sea, which if delayed would have had to return to refuel, and necessary air cover in place ready to cover the landings, the Supreme Commander with full knowledge of success or failure, for which he alone had the responsibility, decided to let the operation go ahead. His words were, 'I'm quite positive we must give the order, I don't like it, but there it is . . . I don't see how we can possibly do anything else. O.K., let's go.'

At 1700 hours on Monday the 5th June orders were given for the ships to weigh anchor and at 2030 hours the transports, led by mine-sweepers to ensure mine-free passages, cast off and slipped silently out of Southampton Water. Soon after sailing personnel assembled on the decks to hear read the Special Orders of the Day from General Dwight D. Eisenhower, General Sir Bernard Montgomery and Major-General D. A. H. Graham, the Commander of the 50th Division. Maps were issued showing the invasion beaches and the places immediately inland which it was expected would be taken in the first days after landing.

The Order of the Day from Major-General Graham read:

JUNE, 1944

SPECIAL D-DAY MESSAGE FROM THE DIVISIONAL COMMANDER TO ALL RANKS OF THE 50TH (NORTHUMBRIAN) DIVISION

The time is at hand to strike – to break trough the Western Wall and into the Continent of Europe.

To You, officers and men of the 50th (Northumbrian) Division, has been given the great honour of being in the vanguard of this mighty blow for freedom.

It is my unshakeable belief that we, together with Force 'G' of the Royal Navy, the special regiments of the Royal Armoured Corps, the Royal Artillery and the Royal Engineers attached to us and with the help of the Royal Air Force and American Air

Force, will deliver such an overpowering punch that the enemy will be unable to recover. Thus shall we be well set to carry through to a glorious and successful end to all that is now entrusted to us.

Much has been asked of you in the past and great have been your achievements, but this will be the greatest adventure of all. It will add yet another chapter to your already long and distinguished record – the grandest chapter of all.

Very best of luck to every one of you.

D. A. H. GRAHAM, Major-General
Commander, 50th (Northumbrian) Division

Sixty-nine battalions of the British Army were to assault the shores of Normandy on the greatest sea-borne operation the world had known. Only two regiments, the East Yorkshire Regiment and the Green Howards, were to provide two battalions in the first assault wave: the 2nd East Yorkshire Regiment with the 3rd (Iron) Division, the 5th East Yorkshire and the 6th and 7th Green Howards with the 50th (Northumbrian) Division. They constituted one third of the British troops in the initial landing.

CHAPTER XII

THE ASSAULT ON NORTH-WEST EUROPE

'D' DAY – 6TH JUNE
THE NORMANDY LANDINGS

Soon after midnight on the 5th/6th June, 'Operation Overlord' began; R.A.F. bombers headed for the Normandy coast to saturate enemy defences with high explosive bombs; these were to be followed by glider-borne troops of the British 6th Airborne Division to drop six miles inland at Benouville, capture bridges over the Caen Canal and the River Orne at Ranville, and soon afterwards parachutists of the 9th Battalion Parachute Regiment (3rd Parachute Brigade) would drop to destroy the Merville coastal battery (which covered the beaches and would be a major hazard to the main landings), and then secure the high ground east of the Orne. The 50th Division would land on 'Gold' beach between Le Hamel and La Rivière to the east of Arromanches.

'Gold' beach was divided into three sectors; 'King' for the assaulting 69th Brigade (Brigadier F. Y. C. Knox, D.S.O.) and its follow-up brigade, the 151st; 'Jig' for the 231st and 56th Brigades, and 'Item' (Red) for 47th Royal Marine Commando. 'King' and 'Jig' sectors were divided into Red and Green sub-sectors: 'King Red' for the 5th East Yorkshires (Lieut.-Colonel G. W. White, M.B.E.); 'King Green' the 6th Green Howards (Lieut.-Colonel R. H. W. S. Hastings); and the supporting unit, the 7th Green Howards, (Lieut.-Colonel P.H. Richardson). 'Jig' sector also divided into 'Jig Red' and 'Jig Green' sub-sectors, the former for the 1st Dorsets, the latter the 1st Hants.

At 0315 hours reveille was sounded. Throughout the evening of the 5th June the troops suffered miserably as the ships rolled on the journey across the Channel; few slept as most were suffering seasickness despite the anti-seasick pills. Only a few had breakfast but most had recovered before landing. A rum issue was available for those who wished to take it.

Commander H. Wheeler, Captain of L.S.I. (Landing Ship Infantry) G.67, and Chief of the Flotilla – 'Force G', later sent a letter to Major C.W.S. Belas of the 5th East Yorkshires in which he wrote:

> 'We have taken several "loads" over . . . but none of them could compare either for fitness or discipline with your assault troops . . . I must congratulate you and your men on the wonderful show you put up, calling for the utmost bravery and tremendous endurance. Well done!'

The L.S.I.'s of the 69th Brigade reached a point some six miles from the coast at around 0500 hours. The L.C.A.'s were hoisted from their davits and dropped into the rough sea. There were Force-5 winds from the west

(16 to 20 knots) and 4-foot waves causing the craft to roll and bounce up and down some ten feet. The troops off-loaded, scrambling down the netting hanging on the side of the ships. When all were aboard, the craft together with those of the other assaulting battalions formed up to make the journey to the shore. A Naval Motor Launch was ahead to navigate a course to within six hundred yards of the shore where landmarks could be recognised, and when within one hundred yards the troops leapt out, wading through the last hundred yards, behind amphibious tanks. Many were weak from sea-sickness, cold and wet through, the spray from the landing craft drenching them and their weapons.

The beach defences consisted of under-water mines, 'Hedgehogs' made of three strong steel or iron girders joined together at the centre and splayed out to form a sort of single knife rest with 'Teller' mines and explosives fixed to the top. These obstacles were half-covered at high tide and could only be observed at low tide. Ramps were made from baulks of timber 15-16 ft long at a height of 8ft with the lower end of the ramp sloping towards the sea. They were covered by a defence feature covering a wide area along the beach frontage with machine-gun posts in pillboxes, batteries of guns were sited in depth up to three miles inland and anti-tanks guns covered the beaches where many anti-tank traps had been dug. A battery at Longues to the west of 'Gold' Beach consisting of four specially reinforced casemates, each containing a 6-inch naval gun, covered the beach. Deep shelters in the strong points protected the defenders from bombardment. Off the beaches the lateral roads were mined and protected with barbed wire entanglements and beyond the first road there was a minefield

The R.A.F. had for some hours been saturating the coastal batteries and beach area with high explosive bombs and destroying the defences inland, but the morning mist prevented accurate bombing and the beach defences were not demolished to the extent anticipated. Guns from cruisers and destroyers bombarded the shore to clear obstacles and secure exits; rocket-firing ships came to within one-hundred yards of the beach then delivered four salvos a minute of ninety rockets; landing craft carrying 25-pounders also joined in the bombardment.

'H-Hour' was set for 0725 hours. As the L.C.T.'s carrying the DD (Duplex Drive) Sherman tanks of 8th Armoured Brigade (designed to swim ashore after leaving the craft) approached the beaches, the sea was so rough that the tanks could not be launched and had to be taken right inshore to land on the beaches. Their task was to give covering fire to the assaulting troops and clear machine-gun nests and a battery west of the village of Ver-sur-Mer, a mile and a half inland. They were followed at H-Hour (0730) by 280th Field Company, Royal Engineers with Major-General Percy Hobart's 'Funnies': 'Flail' tanks to destroy mines and other obstacles, A.V.R.E,'s – flame throwing 'Crocodiles' and 'Petards' throwing drum bombs.

The 69th Brigade landed at 0735 hours at the eastern end of Gold

Beach on sub-beach King' below the German strong point at La Rivière; the 5th East Yorkshires to the left on 'King Red' beach, the 6th Green Howards about 1,000 yards to their right on 'King Green'. The 7th Green Howards in reserve would land forty-five minutes later and advance through the 6th Battalion to capture the battery at Ver-sur-Mer, the objective being to secure the beach and push on to the Bayeux-Caen road and capture the town of Bayeux by 1100 hours.

The objectives of the 5th East Yorkshires were for 'A' Company on the right and 'D' Company on the left to clear the beaches, 'B' Company in support of 'A' to go on to the further objective of the village of Ver-sur-Mer; 'C' Company, in support of 'D,' to cross-roads east of the village of La Rivière.

The 231st Brigade was allotted the Le Hammel Sector, its objective to secure the beach, then, accompanied by the 47th Commando, push west towards the small port of Port en Bessin. Two hours after the landing of the assault brigades, the follow-up brigades – the 151st and 56th Brigade – were to land, and, as the assault brigades separated and moved away from the beaches, fill the gap.

The approach to 'King Red' beach by the 5th East Yorkshires was met with some shelling from a coastal battery at Longues, four specially reinforced casemates each containing a 6-inch naval gun, but none of the unit's craft were hit. Three of the four guns were put out of action by *H.M.S. Ajax* after firing 114, 6-inch shells in twenty minutes. The remaining gun was finally silenced at 1800 hours after a prolonged duel with the French destroyer *George Leygues,* the gun crews surrendering on D+1.

When the landing craft hit the beach, the men jumped out into water some 4ft deep, waded the last yards to the shore, and ran up the beach some 200 yards to the sea wall at the top. 'A' Company met little opposition as they crossed the beach. A minefield was crossed and the company advanced towards the enemy battery at Mont Fleury some half a mile inland. The battery had been hit by R.A.F. bombing earlier in the morning and soon fell. The enemy came out of their defences and surrendered. Thirty prisoners were taken and the battery commander committed suicide at the sight of the advancing infantrymen. The company suffered only slight casualties. Meanwhile tanks of the 6th Assault Regiment, R.E., cleared machine-gun positions to the west of Ver-sur-Mer, enabling 'B' Company pass through 'A' Company and clear 'C' Company's objective, the crossroads east of the sea-side village of La Rivière from the rear.

Mont Fleury battery was also the objective of the 'D' Company, 6th Battalion, The Green Howards. The company under command of Major R. Lofthouse advanced across the protected minefield of the beach coming under heavy fire from a fortified house. Picking up a Bren gun from the beach, C.S.M Hollis fired on the house, silencing the gun. The company went on to the Mont Fleury battery, which was surrounded by strong pillboxes. Major R. Lofthouse, the O.C. 'D' Company, noticed that two pill-boxes had been by-passed and went with C.S.M. Stanley Hollis to see that they were clear. What followed was to bring to C.S.M. Stanley Hollis the award of the only Victoria Cross on 'D' Day. The citation which appeared in the *London Gazette* on the 17th August, 1944 reads:

> 'In Normandy on 6th June, 1944, during the assault on the beaches and the Mont Fleury battery, C.S.M. Hollis's Company Commander noticed that two of the pill-boxes had been by-passed and went with C.S.M. Hollis to see that they were clear. When they were twenty yards from the pill-box a machine-gun opened fire from the slit, and C.S.M. Hollis instantly rushed straight at the pill-box, firing his Sten gun. He jumped on top of the pill-box, re-charged his magazine, threw a grenade in through the door and fired his Sten gun into it, killing two Germans and making the remainder prisoner.
>
> 'Later the same day, in the village of Crepon, the Company encountered a field gun and crew armed with Spandaus, at a hundred yards range. C.S.M. Hollis was put in command of a party to cover an attack on the gun, but the movement was held up. Seeing this, C.S.M. Hollis pushed right forward to engage the gun with a P.I.A.T. from a house at fifty yards range. He was observed by a sniper who fired and grazed his right cheek, and at the same moment the gun swung round and fired at point blank range into the house. To avoid the falling masonry C.S.M. Hollis moved his party to an alternative position. Two of the enemy gun crew had by this time been killed, and the gun was destroyed shortly afterwards. He later found that two of his men had stayed behind in the house, and immediately volunteered to get them out. In full view of the enemy, who were continually firing at him, he went forward alone using a Bren gun to distract their attention from the other men. Under cover of his diversion, the two men were able to get back.
>
> 'Wherever fighting was heaviest C.S.M. Hollis appeared, and in the course of a magnificent day's work he displayed the utmost gallantry and on two separate occasions his courage and initiative prevented the enemy from holding up the advance at critical stages. It was largely through his heroism and resource that the Company's objectives were gained and casualties were not heavier, and by his own bravery he saved the lives of many of his men.'

Returning to the East Yorkshire Regiment, as 'D' Company came ashore it met heavy small arms and mortar fire from the sea wall fronting La Rivière, and machine-gun posts in houses behind. Aerial photography had revealed an 88-mm heavy anti-aircraft gun, converted into an anti-tank gun placed in a casemate which had a field of fire straight down the beach. It had been expected that it would have been put out of action by bombing or naval shell fire before the enemy landed. This had not happened and as the company landed this fire was directed on the landing craft. Three of the amphibious tanks were knocked out by the gun. A Churchill AVRE fitted with a 6" Petard Mortar from 280th Field Coy, 6th Assault Regiment, R.E., which was to have destroyed the gun, was itself hit by a shell from this gun causing it to blow up and disintegrate, killing all the crew, while the flying metal caused casualties amongst the infantry. Lieutenant W. H. J. McIlroy was killed, and Lieut. R. Appleton died of wounds while advancing up the beach. The company Commander, Major K. C. Harrison was wounded and Captain A. Consitt took over command. Another casualty was Capt. W. Sugarman, wounded for the third time in the war.

The gun having been put out of action, the company moved forward to the sea wall and set about clearing a group of houses with ten-foot high brick walls which separated each house from the next. When the men scaled the walls they were shot at. Captain Consitt then arranged for the commander of an amphibious tank to put his tank through the walls, fire at anything in the next garden, to enable a platoon to follow up and clear the enemy away. But just before 'D' Company arrived to give support. thirty to forty Germans came out and surrendered.

Following up on 'D' Company, 'C' Company suffered casualties from the 88-mm gun and small arms fire, and on reaching the top of the beach could not go forward to its further objective, the cross-roads east of La Rivière, as 'D' Company had not cleared the houses. The C.O., Lieut.-Colonel G. W. White, finding 'D' Company held up, took a platoon of 'C' Company along the sea-wall, arriving at 'D' Company's objective just as the tank crashed through the last brick wall. The enemy suffered many casualties and by 0900 La Rivière had been cleared.

Around midday, just before 'D' Company had cleared its objective, the 6th Green Howards with some of the 7th Green Howards in front supported by a few tanks from the 4th/7th Dragoon Guards and 68th Field Battery, R.A., passed through, and by 1000 hours had reached and captured Meuvaines Ridge, a mile inland, and continued to advance southward through Crepon to Villers-le-Sec, to the north-west of Creully.

The 7th Green Howards, the reserve battalion, had landed at 0815 hours, captured the battery at Ver-sur-Mer and continued along the road to Crepon which was reached at 1230 hours. Around 1500 hours they had captured the bridge over the River Seulles at Creully. They were followed by 'A' and 'B' Companies of the 5th East Yorkshires and a Composite Company formed from 'C' and 'D' Companies, which, had suffered heavy casualties.

On their way to Villers-le-Sec the 5th East Yorkshires passed through the 6th Green Howards and on the northern outskirts of the village became engaged in scattered opposition. Soon after 1500 hours the 6th Green Howards arrived and the C.O., Lieut.-Colonel R. W. H. S. Hastings, sent 'B' Company in to attack on the right side of the village and 'D' Company on the left. Accompanied by tanks of the 4th/7th Dragoon Guards, the companies of the 5th East Yorkshires in extended order on either side, advanced across open cornfields, clearing the Germans as they went forward. Most of the Germans ran and were shot; one was literally kicked from his Spandau (machine-gun) by the 2nd in Command of 'B' Company. Lieutenant-Colonel G. W. White, up with the forward troops received wounds from a mortar bomb and later died. Major J. H. F. Dixon, the 2nd in Command, took over command.

The Battalion now advanced along the road to the village of St. Gabriel, where they met a company of German infantry with two guns. These were disposed of and the village occupied. They were then ordered to occupy Brecy, north-west of Coulombs but soon after leaving St. Gabriel they met heavy automatic fire from a wood to the south of the village. The Brigade Commander ordered the 6th Green Howards to attack round the right flank. The attack with support by self-propelled guns of the 86th Field Regiment R.A, and machine-guns and mortars of the 2nd Battalion The Cheshire Regiment, commenced at 2130 hours and was successful, the enemy driven out, and the village of Brecy occupied. By 2300 hours the 69th Brigade had advanced some seven miles from the beaches. Brigade H.Q. was established at Coulombs, the 7th Green Howards to the north of the town, the 6th Green Howards just south of St. Gabriel, and the 5th East Yorkshires at Brecy.

Although some two thousand yards short of its original planned objective in the St. Leger area 69th Brigade had advanced seven miles inland but suffered heavily The 5th East Yorkshires suffered ten officer casualties, and some 85 other ranks were killed on the beaches alone.

The 50th Division had been held up at other places on the front, particularly at Le Hammel, but was some six miles inland; considering that the weather had hampered the naval and aerial bombardments, much credit must go to the infantry in the way that most of the objectives had been attained.

The follow-up brigades had landed at 1130 hours. The 151st Brigade following in the path of the 69th Brigade reached Esquay-sur-Selles at 2200 hours, just short of their planned objective for the day – the Bayer-St. Leger section of the main Caen-Cherbourg road. Tanks of the 4th/7th Dragoon Guards reporting little in front of them, they dug in for the night.

The 231st Brigade, 1st Hampshire Regiment and 1st Dorsetshire Regiment, covered by DDs of the 4th/7th Dragoon Guards, together with Flail tanks of 82nd Assault Squadron, Royal Engineers, had encountered strong opposition around Le Hamel and Ryes. Three of the Flail tanks were destroyed, but the remaining one pushed on through Le Hamel blowing up mines as it went, demolishing the sea defences, thus enabling the two companies of the Hampshires to attack Asnelles, south of Le Hamel, from the rear. By 1200 hours the town had fallen.

Le Hamel was defended by units of the 352nd (Richter) Infantry Division. Cut off and surrounded, they fought almost to the last man. But by 1700 hours Le Hamel was cleared of the enemy. The 231st Brigade then pushed on to Arromanches, defended by further units of 352nd Division. A full-scale assault resulted in the heights above Arromanches being cleared by 1700 hours and the town captured by 1830 hours. Just north of the town, 231st Brigade dug in for the night. The 56th Brigade by-passed the fighting area of 231st Brigade, and in the evening reached the northern outskirts of Bayeux, the 2nd Essex sending patrols into the city.

Meanwhile three of the five L.C.A.'s bringing the 47th Royal Marine Commando ashore struck mines and were sunk. When they regrouped on landing at 1000 hours on 'Item Red Beach' in the area behind Le Hamel and St. Come, forty-six men and almost every wireless set in the unit had been lost. At Le Hamel they found the 1st Hampshires still fighting and were forced to make a detour and fight their way through nine miles of enemy occupied territory to Port-en-Bessin on the extreme west of 'Gold' Beach, losing a further forty men. Those remaining reached the heights of the village of Ecures to the south of Port-en-Bessin and had captured it by nightfall on the 6th June. The next day they attacked the port from the landward side and, after fierce fighting throughout the day and night, 7th/8th June, the port was captured, and they linked up with the U.S. 1st Infantry Division on 'Omaha' Beach. In all the 47th Commando sustained some two hundred casualties, captured more than three hundred prisoners and, while those killed is not known, the number was considerable

Owing to the bad weather, mist and heavy seas the Germans had not expected an assault. Ships which would normally have been patrolling had gone into port and troops manning the defences were quite unprepared. The landings had achieved surprise.

The Allied Armies were firmly established on French soil, with a beachhead twelve miles long and six miles deep; casualties were much less than anticipated. But the 3rd British (Iron) Division and 3rd Canadian Division had failed to capture Caen, the ancient city on the River Orne, which was their prime objective for the first day, owing to the presence of the 125th Panzer Grenadiers of 21st Panzer Division (to which the 4th Battalion East Yorkshires had fallen in north Africa) around the city.

The American forces on 'Omaha' beach had, after a very hazardous landing, established a foothold, whilst those on 'Utah' beach, having secured the exits, had cut the lateral road (N13), thus preventing the enemy from concentrating in the sector and thus guaranteeing the success of the landing. The 6th British Airborne Division had captured bridges over the Caen Canal and secured the high ground to the east of the River Orne.

The Germans had all along expected the main landings to be made in the Pas de Calais and believed that the landings in Normandy were a feint for the real attack. Now, realising the strength of the forces ashore, they began to move reinforcements in order to contain the landings and counter-attack and drive the invaders back to the beaches.

But the Allied Air Forces – aided by the Resistance – had destroyed all but one of the bridges across the Seine between Paris and the river mouth, and many of those across the Loire; consequently it was necessary to make a long journey before coming into action, but there was an immediate move which would bring strong armoured forces into the battle during the next few days.

A Battle Honour, **Normandy Landing,** was awarded for the landings on the 6th June, and gained for the East Yorkshire Regiment by the 2nd and 5th Battalions.

CHAPTER XVI

THE ENLARGEMENT OF THE BRIDGEHEAD

The assault on the beaches of Normandy on the 6th June had been successful and, while the next day the Allied armies were firmly established on French soil, the situation still remained anxious. To the west of Port-en-Bessin and on Omaha Beach the United States had recovered from the precarious foothold of the previous day. In the centre during the morning of the 7th June, the 50th Division cleared Bayeux – its objective of the previous day. To the left, Caen, the 'D' Day objective of I Corps, had not been captured. It was held by the 21st Panzer Division, the one German Armoured Division in Normandy, part of which during 'D' Day had counter-attacked and penetrated almost to the coast at Douvre, driving a wedge between the 3rd British Division and the 3rd Canadian Division. It was joined on the evening of the 9th June by 12th SS (Hitler Jugend) Panzer Division, after a 90-mile dash from Chartres, and took up a position farther west and south of the front of the 50th Division. This division was made up of young Nazis brought up through the Hitler youth movement, devoted to the Fuhrer and the Nazi cause and prepared to die rather than surrender. It would take six weeks before these divisions were ejected.

From Loire the 17th S.S. Panzer Grenadier Division left for the battle area as did the 2nd Panzer Division from the other side of the Seine. The 130th Panzer (Lehr) Division (its literal translation, 'a demonstration') division was rushed to the front of the 50th (Northumbrian) Division, arriving on the 10th June. On the extreme left parachutists and gliderborne troops of the 6th Airborne Division had secured a bridgehead over the Orne and taken a number of villages to the east of the river.

The 5th East Yorkshires, having spent a quiet night at Brecy, were joined on the morning of 7th June by the unit's carriers and ammunition. The 69th Brigade moved forward early on the morning of 7th June, the 5th East Yorkshires in rear of the 6th Green Howards, reaching and occupying the village of St. Leger by mid-day. This had been the objective for the night of 6th June. The 6th Green Howards halted for the night just north of Duoy Ste Marguerite. The 7th Green Howards having successfully attacked and cleared a wireless station to the west of the Columbs-Loucelles road, established itself in positions between Ste Croix Grand Tonne and St. Leger.

At St. Leger reinforcements and officers arrived, enabling the reconstitution of 'C' and 'D' Companies of the 5th East Yorkshires, the Battalion refitted and rested, but there was some patrolling, and holding off small attacks by the enemy, while snipers harassed the positions. The 69th Brigade remained in these positions until the 11th June.

The 56th Brigade occupied Bayeux, which the Germans had evacuated on the previous day, then pushed forward some three miles towards Tilly-sur-Seulles, Sully and Longues.

THE FIRST BATTLE FOR VILLERS BOCAGE

The 50th Division was now entering the *bocage* (grove/copse) country, small stone-walled fields, others with high hedgerows, deep ditches and sunken lanes, most with standing corn, orchards which at this time of the year were in full foliage, and small woods, high hills and deep valleys. The roads were enclosed by steep banks and hedges. Houses and farm buildings were also made of stone. These and the stone walls were ideal for concealing German snipers, and a natural fortification. The country was quite unsuitable for tank operations, only for small units of infantry in companies and platoons with individual tank support.

In the plan for 'Overlord,' Second Army was ordered to push ahead to Villers Bocage and Evrecy, then south-east towards Falaise. The town of Villers Bocage, lying twenty miles from the beaches situated on high ground surrounded by hills, was at a junction of five roads and a centre of communications. Its capture was of prime importance. It had been planned to assemble on 'D' Day a mobile column from the 8th Armoured Brigade with the 1st Battalion, Dorsetshire Regiment, and supporting troops, for its early capture, but, with these troops still engaged on their first objectives, it was not until 2300 hours on the 7th June that orders for the operations were issued.

The column was formed from all units of the 8th Armoured Brigade, and from the 50th Division, the 1st Dorsetshire Regiment of the 231st Brigade (in vehicles), the 147th (Essex Yeomanry) Field Regiment, R.A., with self-propelled guns, a troop of the Northumberland Hussars (anti-tank gunners), tanks of the 24th Lancers, the 61st Reconnaissance Regiment (armoured cars and carriers), a company of the 2nd Cheshire Regiment (machine-guns and mortars) and 168th Light Field Ambulance. It assembled at daylight on the 8th June at Brecy under command of Brigadier R.G. Cracroft (Royal Tank Corps).

At 1000 hours the column prepared to move off, to cross the Bayeux to Caen railway, then advance through Point 103 on to St. Pierre, seize and hold a feature at Tessel-Bretteville some six miles south which threatened the road south, cross the River Seulles to Tilly-sur-Seulles then south along the road to Villers Bocage, and create one part of a pincer movement on Caen.

The start was delayed by anti-tank fire from a village to the east which in the afternoon was overcome by the 1st Dorsetshires. The column then moved on and by nightfall forward troops of the 1st Dorsetshires had established themselves on bridges between St. Pierre and Tilly-sur-Selles and on Point 103, south of Adrieu.

During the night the enemy attacked. This caused new dispositions to be taken. The 1st Dorsetshires, supported by the 4th/7th Dragoon Guards, assembled round Audrieu, the Sherwood Rangers a few miles south between Point 103 and Le Haut Audrieu.

During the afternoon of the 8th June, the 8th Durham Light Infantry from 151st Brigade was added to the column. At 0650 hours the next morning it left Sommervieu and moved along the Bayeux-Caen road to a point one mile beyond St. Leger where it joined up with the column and took up a position to the right of the 1st Dorsets. At 0930 hours, having advanced some two miles, the reconnaissance troop of ten armoured cars reported that the village of Audrieu was held by the enemy. It was decided to by-pass the village and move on to Point 103, a feature overlooking the village of St. Pierre, held by troops of the 12th S.S. (Hitler Jugend) Division and the 130th Panzer Lehr Division The village must be taken to enable an advance to be made on Tessel-Bretteville.

At 1730 hours the 147th (Essex Yeomanry) Field Regiment R.A. laid down concentrated fire on the village and fifteen minutes later the 8th Durham Light Infantry went into the attack, protected on the left flank by tanks of the 24th Lancers. The Durhams got into the village where they met fire from Spandaus and mortars. Despite heavy casualties they pressed forward and after fierce close quarter fighting in the streets and gardens of cottages the Germans were driven from the village. The Durhams dug in but the Germans on the outskirts kept up accurate fire from mortars while their machine guns ranged over the area, and long range anti-tanks guns hit and set on fire two of the tanks.

At 0615 hours the next morning (the 9th June) the Germans bombarded the area with a heavy concentration of fire from artillery and mortars in preparation for a counter-attack by tanks and infantry. When the barrage stopped the Germans attacked the area held by the 8th Durham Light Infantry. A fierce battle ensued against enemy tanks and infantry. Sherman tanks of the 24th Lancers were called from Point 103 to give assistance. The first to enter St. Pierre was hit and set on fire, completely blocking the road; others in the surrounding countryside came under fire from anti-tanks guns, two being knocked out. Around mid-day fighting died down and the Germans withdrew. Apart from some shelling the night passed uneventfully. Throughout the next day the 8th Durham Light Infantry reorganised and consolidated their defences.

At 1900 hours a further attack was launched on St. Pierre. Preceded as yesterday by artillery and mortar fire, German armour attacked from the east and south-east. A number of the tanks of the Sherwood Rangers, which had that morning relieved the 24th Lancers, were set on fire and put out of action. Casualties amongst the Durhams were high and only half the numbers of the attacking force of the days previous were still able to fight. Part of the attacking force by-passed the village to launch a ferocious attack on the 1st Dorsetshires and for a time the 8th Durham Light Infantry were completely surrounded. The Dorsetshires fought on until 2230 hours when the Germans withdrew. Realising that the Tessel Bretteville feature could not be captured other than with a much larger force, on the 12th June the Corps Commander gave orders for a withdrawal, but the ground gained must be held.

At 2315 hours St. Pierre was evacuated and the 8th Durham Light Infantry moved back to Point 103, now held by the 5th East Yorkshires of the 69th Brigade (an account of which follows) who had arrived to relieve the 1st Dorsetshires. On Sunday the 11th June, while 7th Armoured Division was slowly moving south, on its left flank the 69th Brigade received orders to cross the main Bayeux-Caen railway line, secure the left flank of 8th Armoured Brigade and link up with troops of the Canadian 3rd Division at Putot-en-Bessin and exploit another reported gap in the German line around Oristot, north of the Caen-Bayeux-Cherbourg road. Support would be given by tanks of the 4th/7th Dragoon Guards, self-propelled guns of the 147th (Essex Yeomanry) Field Regiment R.A. and 90th Field Regiment R.A.

The 5th East Yorkshires at St. Leger received orders at around 1000 hours on the 11th June to advance to Oristot, and at around 1430 followed the 6th Green Howards through Duoy St.Marguerite, coming under shellfire. Audrieu was reached at 1600 hours and the 5th East Yorkshires established a firm base for an attack by the armour. The tanks, having passed through Audrieu, the Green Howards followed on. At 1800 hours, as they approached Les Hauts Verts, the Green Howards came under heavy fire from small arms and Spandaus from Oristot. A fierce battle ensued. The Germans launched a counter-attack with tanks and the 5th East Yorkshires were called in, sustaining casualties; Major J. H. F. Dixon, the acting Commanding Officer, died of wounds; Major H. C. Cocking and Lieutenant J. L. Sykes were missing, (later found to have been killed in action), while ten O.R.s were missing; twenty-five were wounded.

The 6th Green Howards had also suffered heavily – some two hundred and fifty casualties. The support weapons were called for, but then information was received that German tanks had broken through the 8th Armoured Brigade positions on the right and were approaching the line of advance of the Green Howards. The Commanding Officer of the 6th Green Howards ordered his Battalion to withdraw and, after consultation with the Officer Commanding 5th East Yorkshires and the Brigade Commander, fell back to a position between Audrieu and Point 103.

In this action Lieutenant P. C. Bawcombe of the East Yorkshire Regiment, attached to 'B' Company of the 6th Green Howards, commanding the right forward platoon, came under fire from Spandaus. Although the left-hand platoon was pinned down he handled his men so ably that he advanced three hundred yards and captured the immediate objective with three casualties. Learning that the Company Commander and second-in-command had become casualties, he took command of the company, rallied the other two platoons, who were temporarily disorganised, and led them forward to join up with 'A' Company, and so distinguished himself by his leadership that he was awarded the Military Cross.

Although the battle continued for the next two days the 5th East Yorkshires were not involved in any of the fighting, sending out patrols while holding on to its base, then on the 12th June moving to Point 103 to relieve the 1st Dorsetshires. On the night of the 13th June they were relieved by a battalion of the 49th (West Riding) Division, and moved to a rest area near Condé-sur-Selles, where the next day was spent with visits to Bayeux – the first French town to be captured – where the men were able to avail themselves of baths, see the sites and enjoy a day of relaxation.

* * * * *

At first light on the 10th June, the 7th Armoured Division – the Desert Rats of North Africa fame – under command of Major-General W. R. J. 'Bobby' Erskine, together with the 56th Brigade, moved through 50th Division's positions from roads to the west of Caen, to advance through Tilly-sur-Seulles and Hottot to the south-west in an attempt to capture Villers-Bocage and threaten the supply lines of enemy forces attacking the 50th Division to the north. Hottot lies on a road from Caen to Caumont, one of the enemy's main lateral routes. Throughout the day, small parties of the enemy armed with anti-tank weapons, together with armoured fighting vehicles and tanks, hindered progress, as did the *bocage* country which slowed the speed of tanks. Little advantage was gained that day or the next.

On the 12th June, the XXX Corps Commander (Bucknall) seeing a gap in the enemy line between Caumont and Villers Bocage, ordered the division to move farther to the right between the 50th Division and the 1st U.S. Division and, passing north-east of Caumont, move on to Villers Bocage. The 22nd Armoured Brigade led off and advanced against negligible opposition, reaching a point some six miles from the town where it halted. Early next morning the leading regiments entered the town and halted, being given an enthusiastic welcome by the occupants.

Then at 1000 hours, Hauptman Michael Wittman, leading a group of five tanks from 501 SS Heavy Tank Battalion, seeing the stationary British column, charged down the line firing shell after shell into tanks and vehicles, destroying four tanks of the 4th County of London Yeomanry (Sharpshooters) (under command of Viscount Cranleigh) in five minutes, before making away from the devastated spearhead of the division.

Having refuelled and re-armed, he joined four other Tiger tanks and returned to Villers with the leading elements of 2nd Panzer Lehr Division where he came on British armour which destroyed his tank and three others. Wittman escaped but most of the crews were taken prisoner.* The 7th Armoured Division held on against enemy counter-attacks until, at 1700 hours, the division was forced to evacuate the town and withdraw to

*Wittman and his tank crew of five were killed on the 8th August, 1944, when their tank was destroyed by gun-fire of the Northampton Yeomanry on the Caen – Falaise road. Their bodies were found in a roadside grave on the Caen-Falaise road in 1982 and buried at the La Cambes Military Cemetery.

Prinz William von Schonburg Waldenburg, Commander of the 2nd Tank Battalion, 2nd Panzer Lehr Division, was killed and buried with two of his tank crew at the village churchyard at Parfoure-sur-Odon.

Tracy-Bocage some two miles west. Owing to the failure of the 50th Division to break through at Tilly-sur-Seulles, the first part of the pincer on Villers Bocage had failed.

The failure of the attack by 7th Armoured Division was the beginning of a lack of confidence in Erskine and Bucknall by both Dempsey, the 2nd Army Commander, and General Montgomery.

* * * * *

On 14th June, the 49th (West Riding) Division, which had recently landed, took over that part of the front of the 50th Division held by the 69th Brigade, enabling the 50th Division to turn its intentions on Tilly-sur-Seulles and the surrounding area, in the second part of the pincer movement on Caen. Here it was destined to fight for the next five weeks in an attempt to gain ground held by the 130th Panzer Lehr Division which had been reinforced and strengthened. During the next five days there was hard fighting along the whole line – La Belle Epine – Longraye – Hottet – Tilly.

The action began on the 14th June with an attack by the 151st and 231st Brigades supported by armour. Early in the morning of the 14th June the R.A.F. bombed the road between Tilly and Lingèvre and the area around Verrières. This was followed at 1000 hours by a creeping barrage from the guns of the divisional artillery, and fifteen minutes later the infantry crossed the start line.

The 151st Brigade launched its attack with the 9th D.L.I. advancing towards the village of Lingèvres on the Tilly-Balleroy road three miles west of Tilly and the 6th D.L.I., the village of Verrières to the north-east of Lingevres. Supported by a squadron of tanks from the 4th/7th Dragoon Guards, the 6th D.L.I. moved off. After advancing for a mile, the forward companies came upon enemy forces dug in to the front of an orchard. As they closed on them they met intense machine-gun fire. It was not until 1600 hours that the orchard was cleared. There had been many casualties, two company commanders and one other officer, and one hundred and two other ranks, including twenty-five killed. After re-organising the battalion went on to take Verrieres.

The 9th D.L.I., also supported by a squadron of tanks of the 4th/7th Dragoon Guards, crossed the start line at 1015 hours and by 1330 hours, after tanks of the Dragoons had knocked out six enemy Tiger tanks, the Tilly-Balleroy road was reached. In the evening the 2nd Panzer Lehr Division held on against a strong counter-attack by tanks, stabilising its positions from Lingèvres towards Verrières.

As the 1st Dorsetshire Regiment and the 1st Hampshire Regiment of the 231st Brigade advanced they met heavy mortar, machine-gun and sniper fire. Throughout the day there was hard fighting with attack and counter-attack by infantry and tanks, but by nightfall the 231st Brigade had forced its way through La Belle Epine and La Senaudière and linked up with the 151st Brigade just west of Lingèvres.

On 14th June the 69th Brigade received orders to prepare to move the next day and advance some two miles to a point south of the Tilly-sur-Seulles/Lingèvres/La Belle Epine road and launch attacks.

In the afternoon of 15th June, the 69th Brigade moved forward from Condé-sur-Seulles through Jerusalem and Folliot, halting at Bernières Bocage where it bivouacked for the night. Early next morning the Brigade passed behind 151st Brigade through La Senaudière and reached Les Orailles. The 7th Green Howards then advanced south-eastwards along the road towards La Vardière and La Paterie. Almost at once strong opposition was met. An 88-mm gun firing down the road prevented any movement of vehicles. The forward companies came under machine-gun and mortar fire. Both company commanders were killed. Having gained no more than half a mile the advance came to a halt, and positions were taken up for the night.

At Les Orailles on the morning of the 16th, the 5th East Yorkshires relieved the 6th Green Howards and the latter, supported by a squadron of tanks, moved north-eastwards to Point 113, then southwards along the Lingevrès/Longraye road with the cross roads at La Taille as the objective. As they advanced they met fire from mortars and Spandaus, and by 1600 hours were held up around Point 113 about a mile from the objective. Although further attempts were made to capture La Taille, it was not until 27th June, when supported by tanks of 'C' Squadron of the Northamptonshire Yeomanry commanded by Major D. G. Bevan, and under cover of an artillery barrage and a concentration of machine-gun fire, that La Taille was reached.

On the morning of 17th June the 7th Green Howards moved a short distance to the north-east and took over from the 5th East Yorkshires and in the afternoon advanced to within a half-mile of Longraye and the Longraye-Granville road. Coming under machine-gun fire they halted for the night.

On 19th June the 5th East Yorkshires at La Butte were ordered to take over the positions of the 1st Hampshires and put in an attack on the village of Longraye. 'B' Company, supported by mortar and shell fire, advanced and the village was occupied. Shortly afterwards, following a heavy counterattack, it withdrew to its original position. Lieutenant J. R. Welsh and thirty other ranks were missing.

These attacks by the 69th Brigade led to a heavy counter-attack by the enemy and on 18th June the 7th Green Howards withdrew and took up positions a mile to the rear to the area held by the 5th East Yorkshires. A few days later these battalions moved to La Butte, just east of Les Orailles where they remained until the 28th June.

On the following day the former Commanding Officer of the 5th East Yorkshires, Lieutenant-Colonel R. B. James, D.S.O., who had left the Battalion to take up a staff appointment at the end of the campaign in Sicily, voluntarily relinquished his staff appointment in order to return to the Battalion.

The 69th Brigade remained in the area of La Taille/La Butte for the next ten days under intermittent shelling and mortaring, resulting in casualties. The 5th East Yorkshires along with the other battalions took part in continuous patrol activity, waiting for the outcome of the battle for the key point of Tilly-sur Seulles.

In the meantime, with the concentrated attacks on the 69th Brigade, the 2nd Essex Regiment of the 56th Brigade and the 6th D.L.I. of 151st Brigade on the left flank of 50th Division attacked in the Tilly-sur-Seulles sector. A fierce battle followed. Tilly fell on 19th June, completing one half of the pincer movement. But Hottot just further south was strongly held by the Germans.

In the afternoon of 19th June the 231st Brigade launched an attack south from the Parc de la Mare to capture the village of Hottot on the Caumont-Fontenoy-le Pesnel road. Hottot was held in strength by the enemy. Under a heavy barrage the 1st Hampshires moved forward and reached the village. They were met by fire from mortars and Spandaus. The Germans counter-attacked with tanks and forced a retirement. The 2nd Devonshire Regiment then fought their way into the town and held off several counter attacks, but were driven out. During the night the 231st Brigade was forced to retire and took up positions just north of the town. Hottot remained in enemy hands.

A Battle Honour, **Tilly-sur-Seulles,** covering all actions between 14th and 19th June and the thrust to Hottot was awarded to the East Yorkshire Regiment.

The 50th Division now settled down to a static role, but still in close contact with the enemy, the 69th Brigade patrolling the enemy around Longraye and La Taille.

Having been set the task of capturing Villers Bocage and an advance to Condé-sur-Noireau, brigades were arranged in readiness. The 151st Brigade occupied an area around Tilly; the 231st Brigade north of Hottot; the 69th Brigade south of La Belle Epine and Senaudière; the 56th Brigade to the right.

On 8th July the 56th Brigade moved forward to the road to the west of Hottot where tanks and infantry were concentrated. Soon after setting off they met with heavy mortar and machine-gun fire. Although the village was reached in the afternoon, the Germans launched a counter-attack forcing the Brigade to retire a short distance. The next morning enemy tanks and infantry attacked the 2nd Essex Regiment. A stiff battle followed, a number of enemy tanks were knocked out and heavy casualties inflicted on the infantry. It now fell to the 231st Brigade to capture Hottot.

At 0700 hours on the 11th July the 2nd Devonshires on the left and the 1st Hampshires on the right, supported by Shermans of the Sherwood Rangers from the 8th Armoured Brigade, together with Churchill Crocodile flame-throwing A.V.R.E.'s of 82nd Assault Squadron R.E. and mortars and medium machine-guns, launched a further attack, the infantry moving forward under a creeping barrage of fifty yards in two minutes. The enemy resisted with determination, letting loose with 88-mm guns and mortars. Casualties were heavy. By 1530 hours the surrounds of the village had been reached. Then shells from our own guns fell on the troops as they dug in. Half an hour later Typhoons of the R.A.F. swept down, mistaking the British troops for the enemy. At the end of a day of bitter fighting the 231st Brigade held a line some one hundred yards north of Hottot. The Germans still held the village. A week later the enemy withdrew, leaving mines and booby traps for the oncoming troops of the 50th Division.

THE FALL OF CAEN

In order to follow the progress of the war it is now necessary to turn to the British and Canadian forces to the east.

On 8th July, I Corps launched its full scale attack on the city of Caen which at this time was the focal point of the enemy's defence line. It was preceded on the night of the 7th July by an attack by 450 heavy bombers of the R.A.F. unleashing thousands of tons of high explosives. Guns of *H.M.S.s Rodney, Belfast* and *Roberts* gave supporting fire. Eighty per cent of the city was destroyed. By the afternoon all Caen north and west of the Orne was in British hands. That night, cut off from supplies and short of ammunition and rations, the Germans evacuated the city, but still held the suburbs of Faubourg-de-Vaucelles across the river. Caen was not captured until 10th July, the eastern suburbs not finally cleared until the 20th July.

On 10th July the attack was switched to the area west of the city between the Rivers Odon and Orne to extend the Odon bridge head. An attack was made on Hill 112 and the neighbouring village of Maltot by the 43rd (Wessex) Division and supporting armour. Although the hill was captured in bitter fighting, German 'Tiger' tanks succeeded in reaching the summit on the 11th July, driving the infantry off and out of Maltot

The 59th (Staffordshire) Division surrounded Noyers, a village west of the River Odon, on 15th July, and entered Bougy and Esquay against heavy opposition. Evrecy was attacked by British forces on 16th. Enemy armour which had been moving westwards to oppose the Americans was brought back into the battle, but withdrew the next day.

Soon after landing, the 50th Division began to produce its own news-sheet, 'The T.T. Times', and also a Situation Report giving news of the campaign, enabling the troops to find out what was happening other than in their own sector.

From 14th July the 5th East Yorkshires were placed in Brigade Reserve. Rations were cooked in the rear of the forward positions on petrol-burning stoves which gave no smoke, and were then regularly sent to the front lines. The standard of food was good and much enjoyed. A mobile canteen arrived and was most welcome. The unit established a bathhouse where hot baths were available and there were facilities for the washing of clothes.

Reinforcements arrived, and platoons were withdrawn one at a time during quiet periods so that they might go back to the Divisional Rest Centre where they could attend an Army Mobile Cinema and concerts arranged by ENSA (Entertainments National Service Association).

Awards for gallantry were announced on 14th July. The Military Cross was awarded to Major A. M. N. Rice (Northamptonshire Regt attached 5th East Yorkshires), Captain W. Sugarman, Major Woodruffe, and the Battalion's Medical Officer, Captain W. R. Lunt, R.A.M.C. The Military Medal was awarded to R.S.M. F. Gibson, C.S.M. W. E. McDougal, Sergeant F. Webber, Lance Sergeant E. P. Smith, Lance Corporal T. Mills, Privates R. Clare and A. Emson. These awards were presented to them the next day by the C-in-C, General Sir Bernard Montogomery.

On 19th July, the 5th East Yorkshires were taken out of Brigade Reserve, joining the 6th and 7th Green Howards occupying positions along the road between Le Lion Vert and La Croix des Landes. The Battalion advanced to maintain contact with the enemy who were withdrawing from the front of the 50th Division as a result of pressure all along the line.

OPERATION GOODWOOD

At 0615 hours on 18th July, 1,100 heavy bombers from R.A.F. Bomber Command, 1,600 American Fortresses and Liberators from the U.S. 8th and 9th Army Air Forces, together with 600 British and U.S. medium bombers and 1,200 fighter-bombers, saturated the German front with over 7,000 tons of high explosive bombs in two hours. Guns from the ships of the Royal Navy off the Normandy coast also played a part in the bombardment.

At 0745 hours on a bright sunny morning, the VIII Armoured Corps (Lieut.-General Sir Richard O'Connor, captured on 6th April, 1941, when commanding the Western Desert Force, escaping from Italy in December, 1943) began 'Operation Goodwood'. This attack was designed to pass through the Orne bridgehead, thrust south from the eastern side of Caen, capture the Bourgebous Ridge and hopefully reach Falaise.

The advance began with the 11th Armoured Division (Major-General G. P. B. 'Pip' Roberts) as the spearhead. After making speedy progress in the first two hours, strong resistance was met. General O'Connor then ordered a two-pronged attack with the 11th Armoured Division on the right, the 7th Armoured Division on the left. By the afternoon the 11th Armoured Division had reached the village of Cagny; here it met heavy fire from 88-mm anti-aircraft guns of the 16th Luftwaffe Field Division which had escaped destruction by the air bombardment. Sixteen Sherman tanks were destroyed. Further determined resistance delayed the advance and it was not till 1600 hours that Cagny was entered by the

Guards Armoured Division and Faubourg de Vaucelles captured by the 3rd Canadian Division. During the night the Germans reinforced Bourgebous Ridge which halted the advance, and, with heavy rain turning the low lying area into a sea of mud, the operation was brought to a halt.

* * * * *

Meanwhile on the U.S. front Carentan had fallen on 12th June, effectively joining the two beachheads, and the 9th Infantry and 82nd Airborne Divisions struck out to the west towards St. Sauveur-le-Vicomte to isolate Cherbourg. St. Sauveur was evacuated by the enemy on the 16th June, and the next day the 9th Infantry Division reached the coast around Barneville. At the same time U.S. forces were attacking north towards Cherbourg. Montebourg fell on 19th June, Valognes the next day. The attack on Cherbourg opened on 22nd June, and three days later the outer defences had been penetrated and troops were engaged in street fighting in the city. At 1500 hours on the 26th the joint Naval and Army commanders surrendered. By the 1st July all resistance had ceased on the northern part of the Cotentin peninsular which was now cut off from the rest of France.

It was now hoped that it would be possible to drive southwards, but the U.S. First Army advance was held up by atrocious weather. The marshes south of Carentan became flooded, the close *bocage* country north of St. Lo hindered progress, and the enemy fought strongly along the whole front. For seven days a violent battle was fought, but on the 11th, having broken an enemy counter attack, the advance moved towards St. Lo.

The enemy. aware that command of the road junction through this small market town was essential to any American breakthrough, decided to make his main stand here, and, as the U.S. First Army gradually drove forward, established a front on the Lessay-Periers-St. Lo road. Every inch of ground was fiercely contested, the Americans suffering some 11,000 casualties, but, on 18th July, U. S. forces captured the town. The U.S. VII Corps reached the heights from which the drive southwards out of Normandy and into Brittany could begin.

Three days were required to re-form, but there was now a break in the weather and for six days the U.S. forces waited in their foxholes in miserable conditions.

THE BREAK-OUT

OPERATION COBRA

On the morning of 25th July, 'Operation Cobra', the great break-out was launched. It was preceded by a massive air attack by 1,495 bombers of the U.S. Eighth Air Force and 388 aircraft Allied Expeditionary Air Force dropping 4,700 tons of bombs on an area five-miles long and one-mile wide, south of the 20-mile straight stretch of road that runs from St. Lo to Periers. General Bradley had expected the aircraft to fly in, parallel to the road, and thus they would not pass over the troops who were close up to the road waiting to make an immediate attack. The air commanders decided to approach the target area by flying in at right-angles to the road. Unfortunately some bombs fell short of the target resulting in 558 casualties, including Lieut.-General Lesley J. McNair

The ground battle began at midday, the U.S. VII Corps positioned west of St. Lo meeting strong resistance, but by midnight the Periers-St. Lo road had been crossed. VIII Corps in the Periers-Lessay area joined in the offensive crossing the road to the west of VII Corps. The next day Periers and Lessay fell. Coutances was captured on the 28th July and, as the Germans retreated, some 4,500 prisoners were taken. The U.S. VIII Corps Armour crossed the Seine River south of Coutances on 29th July. Two days later Avranches fell to the U.S. 4th Division. Granville was cleared of the enemy on 31st July by the U.S. 6th Armoured Division.

* * * * *

On 23rd July, the Canadian First Army under General H. D. G. Crerar became operational, having under command initially the British I Corps (Lieut.-General J. T. C. Crocker, D.S.O., M.C.) of three divisions, to which was joined on the 31st July the Canadian 2nd Corps (Lieut.-General Guy Simonds) of three Canadian divisions and the 1st Polish Armoured Division. This army took over the easternmost coastal sector of the whole front. With the British Second Army (General Miles Dempsey) it formed the 21st Army Group..

It had been agreed in the planning that when the Americans had sufficient troops in action a separate Army Group should be formed. On the 1st August the U.S. Third Army was formed under General George Patton, taking under command VIII Corps (Major-General Troy H. Middleton), XII Corps (Major-General Gilbert R. Cook), XV Corps (Major-General Wade H. Haislip) and XX Corps (Major-General Walton H. Walker). The First U.S. Army retained V Corps (Major-General Leonard T. Gerow), VII Corps (Major-General J. Lawson Collins) and XIX Corps (Major-General Charles H. Corlett). The U.S. First and Third Armies formed the 12th Army Group under General Omar Bradley. Lieut.-General C. H. Hodges succeeded Bradley in command of the U.S. First Army.

General Montgomery, who had been in overall command of the British and U.S. Forces, was relieved of this role, taking over command of 21st Army Group, but throughout August was responsible for co-ordination between the U.S. 12th and 21st Army Groups.

* * * * *

On 1st August Patton's highly mobile U.S. Third Army began to exploit the break-out. Against negligible opposition the army swept southwards and by 4th August had reached Rennes, the capital of Brittany.

With supplies having to be brought to the corridor at Avranches from the Mulberry artificial harbour at Arromanches (which would be unusable when the weather deteriorated in the autumn) and the port of Cherbourg, Patton detached the U.S. VIII Corps to move through Brittany to capture the vital ports through which necessary supplies could be brought. The Germans offered little resistance, falling back to defend the ports at St. Malo, Brest, Lorient, and St. Nazaire. Little was gained: Brest held out until 19th September, Lorient and St. Nazaire were held by German forces until the end of the war.

The German western front having collapsed, an opportunity arose to effect an encirclement. Those corps of the U.S. Third Army not fighting in Brittany struck south and occupied the towns of Mayenne and Laval on 6th August. They would then advance south-east to capture Le Mans on 9th August and turn northwards on Alencon to Argentan, to threaten the rear of the German forces fighting at Mortain, while Hodges U.S. 1st Army advanced south to widen the gap in the Vire-Mortain area.

Montgomery, seeing an opportunity to join in the drive, switched the greater part of the British Second Army across to the Caumont sector on the left of the western front to close in through Vire, Vassy, Condé-sur-Noireau on Falaise, then attack the flank of the German thrust, and join up with the U.S. Third and First Armies in a three-pronged attack: while the 1st Canadian Army with supporting British and Polish troops thrust from a position just south of Caen to Falaise. If successful, the main body of the German army would be contained and annihilated in what was to become known as the Falaise pocket. The Second Army part was designated Operation Bluecoat.

The German High Command realised that the situation was critical, and only a withdrawal to the line of the lower Seine could save the army, but Hitler, away in his Headquarters in East Prussia now intervened. Studying the maps he saw that at the base of the Cotentin peninsular Patton's army was held in a twelve-mile narrow corridor between the Germans and the sea, The vital road south out of Avranches crossed only a single bridge. This was a place where the U.S. forces might be cut off, thus isolating Patton from his communications and supply base. Ignoring the advice of his generals, Hitler gave orders to Field Marshal Gunther Hans von Kluge that all available Panzer divisions be disengaged and concentrated east of Mortain, in a counter-offensive on Avranches only twenty-five miles distant.

Von Kluge assembled some 185 tanks of the 1st and 2nd SS Panzer Divisions and the 2nd and 116th Panzer Divisions, together with part of the 17th SS Panzer Grenadier Division and supporting infantry to form Panzer Group Eberbach, and on the morning of 7th August launched a counter-offensive.

In heavy fighting, early gains of a few miles were made. The 2nd SS Panzer Division went on to recapture Mortain but the counter-attack ground to a halt when air attacks by rocket-firing Typhoons strafed and bombed advancing German armour, destroying more than one hundred tanks and many vehicles. By 14th it was obvious to the enemy that it was impossible to achieve the objective and the force must fall back.

On 15th contact was lost with von Kluge, when having gone forward to visit the forward troops, he suffered the destruction of his radio from a low-flying air attack. When he got back the following day he communicated with the German High Command saying that only a withdrawal to the line of the Seine could save the German Army. When told, Hitler angrily dismissed him and appointed Field Marshal Walther Model as western front commander. The previous day the Allies had landed in southern France. Ordered back home, von Kluge, aware of the what might happen to him following the attempt on Hitler's life on 20th July, in which he may have been associated, committed suicide by poisoning himself.

Model found the situation to be chaotic. For some days there had been a general retreat, but, as the enemy forces headed towards Falaise-Argentan, this had turned into a rout. For several days there was a steady escape through the gap, but by the 22nd the enemy was sealed off in the Falaise Pocket.

OPERATION BLUECOAT

To co-operate with the advance of the U.S. 1st Army on Vire-Mortain, a thrust on its flank was launched on 30th July by the British Second Army, south-east from the Caumont area, the first objective to capture Mont Pinçon on the road running from Vire through Vassy to Condé-sur-Noireau: VIII (British) Armoured Corps towards Le Beny Bocage and Vire along the boundary with the U.S. XIX Corps, while on their left XXX Corps (consisting of the 50th (Northumbrian) Division, the 43rd (Wessex) Division and the 7th Armoured Division plus the 8th Armoured Brigade) would head for the heavily fortified and steep-sided Mont Pincon, eight miles south of Villers Bocage, which commanded the approaches to the River Orne. Continuing the line eastwards were the XII Corps, the I Corps and 2nd Canadian Corps.

The 50th Division's task was to capture the Amaye feature and advance to Villers Bocage and secondly to advance to Condé-sur-Noireau. In the early morning the 56th and 231st Brigades moved off and, finding only small opposition, reached the high ground in the area of Anctoville and Feuguerolles-sur-Seulles, and by 1st August had dug in. It was not until 1st August that 69th Brigade became fully active, receiving orders to take over from the 130th Brigade of the 43rd (Wessex) Division in the Caumont area.

On 2nd August an attack was launched by the 69th Brigade to the north-east of Amaye-sur-Seulles where the strong hill feature to the west of Villers Bocage was attacked against small arms fire and on 3rd August, after considerable resistance, captured. In the face of small arms opposition the 5th East Yorkshires went on to occupy the town of Amaye. There was some shelling afterwards and at 1530 hours a shell hit Lieut.-Colonel Robert Brian James, D.S.O., a much respected commanding officer, who was killed outright. The shelling continued at intervals during the night, the afternoon and evening of the next day. Major C. G. Percy Hardman took temporary command until a few days later when Lieut.-Colonel T. L. G. Charles, an officer of the Essex Regiment, took command.

On 4th August the 69th Brigade went forward, meeting little opposition and advanced to Point 174 north of Tracey Bocage just outside Villers Bocage, and late in the evening the 7th Green Howards sent a patrol into Villers Bocage, but found the 1st Dorsetshire Regiment already in the town which was deserted and ruined by the massive air attack of the 18th July. This was some six weeks after it was scheduled to fall.

In this close country the enemy made much use of mortars, machine guns and camouflaged Teller (plate) mines packed with 30lb of TNT which had a devastating effect not only on personnel but on tanks and wheeled vehicles and self-propelled guns; the 5th East Yorkshires suffering many casualties.

The next day the 50th Division was relieved, the first time it had been out of the front line since landing on 'D' Day. The men were tired and weary. For the past six weeks they fought and marched; now they could relax, weapons could be serviced and maintained and welcome reinforcements would arrive.

In the meantime the 11th Armoured Division had seized the high ground of Le Beny Bocage and on the 1st August the town was captured. It should have pushed on to Vire which was virtually undefended, but owing to the boundaries laid down this was left to the U.S. XIX Corps. Vire was entered on the 1st August, but the Germans rushed in the 2nd Panzer Division and mounted counter-attacks, recapturing the town the next day. There was hard fighting and as a result Vire was not taken until the night of the 6th August. The forward divisions had now reached the reverse slops of the ridge overlooking the Vire-Vasssy-Condé road.

The XXXth Corps advance during the days of Operation Bluecoat had been slow, and 7th Armoured Division had failed to show the drive that was expected. Bucknall, the Corps Commander, had failed to reach Aunay-sur-Odon on the 1st August as ordered, being five miles distant. Thoroughly dissatisfied, Montgomery relieved Bucknall of command; Erskine, the G.O.C. 7th Armoured Division, likewise.

Montgomery asked the C.I.G.S. to send out Lieut.-General Brian G. Horrocks in whom he had confidence, Horrocks having commanded XIII Corps and X Corps in north Africa. Wounded in June, 1943, he had spent the past four months in hospital. So anxious was Montgomery to have his presence that he sent his personal Dakota to transport him from Northolt and he arrived on the 3rd August. Horrocks was given command of XXX

Corps and Major-General G. L. Verney, 7th Armoured Division.

* * * * *

The dominant Mont Pinçon, a steep-sided heavily fortified hill some eight miles south of Villers Bocage running from east to west for 3,000 yards, commanded the approaches to the River Orne where the main part of the Second Army had been fighting, and was astride a number of roads running from Vire through Vassy to Condé-sur-Noireau, essential for the advance to join up with U.S. Third Army at Argentan to form the Falaise pocket.

The attack was launched on the 6th August by the 43rd (Wessex) Division (Major-General G. I. Thomas who by this time had earned the soubriquet 'Butcher' for his ruthless drive and apparent insensitivity to casualties, and the 8th Armoured Brigade of the 7th Armoured Division. At the foot of the mountain there was heavy enemy resistance; the 5th Wiltshires were reduced to a strength of 60. In the thick of the battle Captain Denny of the 13th/18th Hussars commanding the leading tanks found an unguarded narrow track leading to the top of the mountain. His C.O., Lieut. Colonel Dunkerley, gave permission to lead two troops up the track under cover of a smokescreen. The track was so narrow that one tank overturned, while another had its tracks blown off. Only seven reached the summit. A blanket of fog came down and they could hear German voices all round them. In a radio message he complained that they were feeling rather lonely. The 4th Wiltshires were led up the mountain by their Commanding Officer, Lieut.-Colonel Luce, reaching the summit under cover of darkness, and the next day repulsed a German counter-attack, after which the enemy retired. Mont Pinçon was now in British hands, The way was now open for the advance southwards on Condé-sur-Noireau, a vital point on the German line of escape to the Falaise pocket.

On 7th August the 7th Armoured Division was ordered to move forward at once to capture Condé-sur-Noireau, the 50th Division to follow on and mop up. The enclosed country was soon found to be not suitable for a quick advance by armour, and on 9th August the lead was taken over by the 50th Division.

At midday on 9th of August, the 151st Brigade, supported by tanks of the 13th/18th Hussars, moved down through Le Plessis Grimoult on the southward slopes of Mont Pinçon, to advance four miles along the high ground to the south-east of the village of St. Pierre-la-Vielle, their objective being a road some two and a half miles north of St. Pierre. When two miles from the village, stiff opposition was met from artillery, machine-gun, and mortar fire, and soon the leading infantry were pinned down, but after hard fighting the enemy was dislodged.

Meanwhile on the 8th August the 69th Brigade had moved to an assembly area near Ondefontaine, six miles south of Villers Bocage. The next morning it moved on to Posty on the northern slopes of Mont Pincon, and at 1400 hours the 6th and 7th Green Howards passed through the 151st Brigade to take up the attack. The Germans fought desperately but they moved forward another mile until at 2000 hours the advance came to a halt and the positions stabilised, although under fire from heavy artillery. It was then decided that the 5th East Yorkshires would attack the next day to capture St. Pierre-La-Vielle and Point 229, a hill feature to its western side.

All night long the Battalion suffered heavy shelling and it was expected that the forming-up place, under direct enemy observation, and shelled throughout the day would be shelled again as they formed up, and possibly suffer heavy casualties. The next morning the Battalion moved to its forming-up place, but at daylight, as they prepared to move off, fog descended over the area enshrouding tanks and infantry.

Several attacks were put in. At first the opposition was light, 30 prisoners taken and many Germans killed, but, when two companies tried to storm Point 229, they came under heavy fire from enemy tanks and self-propelled guns on the crest. An attack at Battalion strength, supported by artillery, was made, but the enemy put up a stubborn defence, with heavy mortaring and shelling to a degree not previously experienced in the campaign and the attack was halted short of both objectives. Losses were heavy. In one case, the only section commander left in his platoon was Corporal J. Grace, who showed exemplary leadership and bravery. Disregarding his own safety he dashed across open ground under enemy sniper fire and rescued a wounded comrade. This act of gallantry brought him the award of the Military Medal. Major A. M. N. Rice, who had received the award of the Military Cross only four weeks earlier, was killed. The 69th Brigade was then held up just short of St. Pierre-la-Vielle and Point 229 and together with the 151st Brigade stayed there for the night.

At 0830 hours on the 11th August, the 231st Brigade was ordered up to renew the attack and capture Condé-sur-Noireau. After hard fighting throughout the day against determined opposition on both the village and the high ground the enemy was forced back. The next morning the leading infantry were well south of the town, while other units were fighting there.

While the 231st Brigade was carrying out this action, the 151st Brigade, supported by tanks of the 13th/18th Hussars, attacked on the high ground at Points 249 and 262 and cleared the enemy away. During the night of the 12th/13th the 7th Green Howards cleared the Germans out of St. Pierre-la-Vielle, and the way to Condé-sur-Noireau was open.

All brigades of the 50th Division took part in the action which opened up the road to Condé-sur-Noireau. The advance on Condé-sur-Noireau was the 50th Division's contribution to the closing of the gap to trap the German Seventh Army, when the 1st Polish Armoured Division operating southwards from Falaise under command of the First Canadian Army met the Americans coming north at Chambois the story of which follows later.

On 13th August the 50th Division was withdrawn. Its place was taken by the 11th Armoured Division which entered Condé-sur-Noireau on 16th.

The Battle Honour, **Mont Pinçon** (30th July-9th August, 1944), was gained for The East Yorkshire Regiment by the actions of the 5th Battalion and **St. Pierre-la-Vielle** (9th-16th August, 1944) was recognised as a Battle Honour and also gained for The East Yorkshire Regiment by the 5th Battalion.

The Commander XXX Corps, Lieutenant-General B. G. Horrocks, sent the following message to Major-General Graham commanding 50th Division.

Main HQ 30Corps
DO/915
Aug 44

Commander, 50 (Northumbrian) Division

I would like all ranks of 50 (N) Division to realise how much their efforts of the last few days have contributed to the general plan for the encirclement and destruction of the German Army.

The road VIRE – CONDE and to the east has been one of the main German supply routes, and recently the enemy has done his best to use it for the withdrawal of the large forces west of our present area.

It was vital that this escape route should be closed, and the task was initially given to 50 (N) Division.

During the past week the Division had been fighting its way down towards CONDE SUR NOIREAU from Mont Pincon. Although the country was well suited for defence, and although enemy was fighting stubbornly, all the attacks launched by 50 (N) Division have been successful, and many prisoners have been taken.

Owing to the scarcity of roads deployment was difficult, yet the Division never faltered, and we can now say that the escape route through CONDE is closed to the Germans.

I cannot give you higher praise than by saying that the most experienced battle-fighting Division in the British Army has once more lived up to its reputation.

Well done, 50 Div.

(Sgd) B. G. Horrocks,
Lieutenant-General,
Commander 30 Corps.

From 14th August the 50th Division was out of touch with the enemy. The 69th Brigade made a short move to Posty where they enjoyed four days of rest and reorganisation. A further move was made on 18th August to Athis. This brought the 5th East Yorkshires close to the area of the 2nd Battalion. That evening the 5th had the pleasure of a visit from Officers, W.O.s and N.C.O.s of the 2nd Battalion. In Northern France in 1940 there had been a similar exchange of visits between the 4th Battalion – now in German and Italian prison camps – and the 2nd Battalion.

OPERATION TOTALISE

Following the formation of the 1st Canadian Army on the 23rd July, the eastern-most part of the line was placed under its command. Montgomery having moved a large part of I Corps over to the British Second Army, most of the troops were Canadian together with the 1st Polish Armoured Division (General S. Maczec). On the other flank the U.S. Third Army, having thrust southwards, was swinging round in an easterly direction on Le Mans with the aim of moving on to Argentan to get behind the retreating German forces. During the past weeks it had fought its way south from the suburbs of Caen in a series of bitter battles. Twenty miles to the south lay Falaise, the capture of which was the task of the Canadians. If the two prongs of the U.S. and Canadians could be brought together, the bulk of the enemy forces in Normandy, driven eastward from the Mortain salient by the 1st American and 2nd British Armies, would be surrounded, and, should this bring about their surrender, the war might well quickly end.

At 2330 hours on the 7th August, Lieut.-General Guy Simmonds, the 41-year-old commander of the Canadian II Corps, launched an offensive southwards towards Falaise. It was preceded thirty minutes earlier by a heavy aerial bombardment, 700

R.A.F. heavy bombers supported by 500 Allied Expeditionary light aircraft dropped 300 tons of bombs on the flanks of the axis advance, the main road from Caen to Falaise. The advance began with two columns of vehicles, each of four abreast, led by navigating and 'flail' Sherman tanks with Bren carriers and 'Kangaroos' in the middle, the latter being armoured carriers, improvised from chassis of American self-propelled guns, carrying the infantry. By first light, against little opposition, the columns had advanced three miles.

The second phase of the advance began on the afternoon of the 8th August. Everything was to go wrong. Two untried armoured divisions, the 1st Polish and the 4th Canadian Armoured Divisions, took over to continue the advance. Some six miles from the forming-up positions the attack ran into considerable resistance from enemy mortaring and shelling, and by nightfall the advance was bogged down. A call for support was sent out to the supporting U.S. Air Force. Some twenty heavy bombers answered the call, but dropped their loads on to the columns that were held up near Caen, causing considerable confusion. Many of the tanks of the 1st Polish Armoured Division were destroyed or put out of action, while 65 Poles and Canadians were killed and 250 wounded.

When the attack was resumed on the 9th August it was quickly broken up, the Polish Armoured Division lost 26 of its 36 tanks, and the Canadians went in with no armoured support. The British Columbia Dragoons armoured regiment and the infantry of the Algonquin regiment did break out but lost their way and were cut off, most of the troops being killed, wounded or captured.

During the next forty-eight hours 150 Allied tanks were destroyed. Although the break-out had failed and the advance stalled, nine miles of ground had been gained and II Canadian Corps was more than half-way from Caen to Falaise. Bogged down, on the 11th August General Simmonds withdrew the armour of II Corps, replacing it with infantry divisions.

OPERATION TRACTABLE

By 13th August General Patton's Third Army had reached Argentan, 15 miles from Falaise. It was his intention to drive north and join with the Canadians, now eight miles from Falaise, cutting off the enemy withdrawing eastward from Mortain. Only 23 miles separated the two armies. At this point General Bradley, commanding the 12th Army Group, ordered Patton to halt, believing that the Canadian offensive, due to start the next day, would get there before the Americans.

At 1142 hours on 14th August, the II Canadian Corps opened a large set-piece attack on Falaise. After its capture it was planned to move on to Argentan and link up with Patton's Third Army. Both sides of the Caen-Falaise road being impassable, including Quesnay Wood which the Germans had turned into a fortress, Simmonds set his axis ten miles to the east of the road.

Following the laying of an artillery smoke-screen designed to conceal the direction of the advance, R.A.F. Bomber Command sent in a strong force of Halifax and Lancaster bombers. The first wave successfully dropped their loads on the assigned targets, particularly on Quesnay Wood, but the second wave brought tragedy. Yellow flares had been lit to indicate the area was occupied by friendly formations, but through a lack of communication the R.A.F. had not been properly informed and thought the flares were to indicate target areas. Four hundred casualties were caused amongst Canadians and Poles, 150 lives lost and 250 wounded.

There was to be another catastrophe. The previous day a Canadian officer in an armoured car had driven into the German lines and lost his way and was killed. Contrary to standing orders, he had with him the plans for Tractable. Thus the Germans were able to adjust their defences.

Despite these setbacks the advance began. At first the Canadians were concealed by the smoke-screen but after some four miles they met with the 12th SS Panzer Division which counter-attacked. Slow progress was made, but on the evening of the 15th the 2nd Canadian Division reached a position a mile from Falaise, entering the devastated town on the 16th and finally clearing it on the 17th. A pocket had been created by the pincer movement of the Americans in the north at Argentan and the Canadians in the south.

Patton, having been halted at Argentan on the 13th, went on to Dreux and Chartres leaving some depleted divisions behind. They were transferred to the U.S. First Army which had swept round on the south.

THE CLOSING OF THE FALAISE POCKET

In order to close the gap, Montgomery, on the 16th, ordered the Americans to move on to Chambois, while General Crerar was to send Simmonds with II Canadian Corps through Trun to meet them, and narrow the neck of the Falaise Pocket.

Owing to difficulties in transferring divisions from the Third to the First Army there was delay and it was not until the 18th that they began the move. By this time the Canadians had captured Trun. Owing to determined and violent fighting of the enemy between Trun and Chambois, the Canadians made little progress during the next two days. Gradually the gap was shrunk to a strip seven miles long and six miles wide, which, for a time, the Germans fighting frantically, kept open, allowing some of their forces to extricate themselves. But by the 20th the 1st Polish Armoured Division linked up with the Americans at Chambois, and were soon joined by the Canadians. The gap was closed and by the 22nd the pocket eliminated.

Until 17th August the Germans had been fleeing eastwards through the gap; II SS Panzer Corps had broken out and attacked outside the 'Pocket' to assist those trapped to escape. As the gap narrowed they were compelled to look to their own safety and keep a gap open through the Allied troops to prevent being trapped by Patton's Third Army in its advance to the Seine. Two days later the 'Pocket' was divided into zones: one for the artillery of XII Corps; one for the guns of an armoured division and one for the air forces. Three thousand guns were moved within range of the enemy and a systematic destruction began of all within. High explosive shells fell on the trapped German forces which were tightly compressed and inextricably mixed up. Terrible slaughter was inflicted; tanks, columns of motor vehicles and horse drawn transport were blown apart and the scene was reminiscent of the First World War: Typhoons and Spitfires of the Allied Tactical Air Forces swept down over a wide area in and outside the 'Pocket' strafing the enemy day and night with a hail of bombs, machine-guns, rockets and cannon shells; the overall scale of destruction was incomprehensible.

It was impossible to count the dead; they were closely packed and piled on one another, intermixed with dead and wounded horses. The stench of decaying bodies was unbearable. It was later estimated that 10,000 had been killed and 40,000 taken as prisoners. This was the greatest disaster the enemy had suffered in Europe since Stalingrad.

The German Seventh and Fifteenth Armies had been destroyed as coherent fighting forces, while the Fifth Panzer Army had been severely mauled, but caution among the Allied field commanders (notably Montgomery, and Bradley's halting of Patton) had slowed things up, allowing some 35,000 of the Seventh Army to escape before the pincers finally closed.

The Battle for Normandy was over. Since the landings on 6th June, the enemy's losses had been enormous, five panzer divisions had been destroyed and a further six broken. The equivalent of 20 infantry divisions had been eliminated, and 12 more (including three parachute divisions) had been badly mauled. By 25th August the enemy had lost some 400,000 killed, wounded or captured, of which some 200,000 were prisoners of war. One hundred and thirty-five thousand of these prisoners had been taken between the breakthrough on 25th July and the end of August. Thirteen hundred tanks, 20,000 vehicles, 500 assault guns, 1,500 field and heavier guns had been captured or destroyed.

The battle for Normandy cost the Allied ground forces 209,762 (including 36,976 killed).

OPERATION DRAGOON/ANVIL

Meanwhile, on 15th August the 6th Army Group (the First French Army and the U.S. Seventh Army) under Lieut.-General Jacob L. Devers landed with little opposition on the Mediterranean coast of France, between Toulon and Cannes (Operation Dragoon/Anvil). Advancing rapidly northward with little opposition, they first made contact with patrols of Eisenhower's forces at Dijon. Harried by the French resistance, the Germans hastened to withdraw from France.

Those who had escaped from the pocket were in total disarray, fleeing towards the rivers Seine and Somme and on to the Low Countries. It was essential that they be pursued with all speed. High priority was given to an advance in order to open up the Channel ports at Dieppe and Le Havre and lessen the distance from which supplies had to be brought up, thus reducing the demands on the port of Cherbourg and the bases on the Normandy coast. London and the Home Counties had been subjected to attack by V1 Flying Bombs (*Doodlebugs*) since June, launched from sites in Belgium around L'Isle Adam near Pontoise, and it was necessary that these should be eliminated.

CHAPTER XIII

THE ADVANCE TO THE SEINE AND THE LOW COUNTRIES

With signs of enemy resistance collapsing along the whole front, during the first two weeks of August the Supreme Allied Commander conducted a series of staff meetings with his commanders to plan strategy for the future conduct of the war, principally the development of the allied offensive once the Seine had been crossed. Eisenhower favoured an advance on a broad front up to the Rhine, then a set-piece crossing, with 21st Army Group advancing through Belgium and Holland north of the Ardennes, while Central Army Group and Southern Army Group attacked between the Ardennes and Switzerland, all battle formations in line and fighting all the time.

Montgomery argued that, having drawn in and defeated most of the German Divisions into the Normandy battle, all resources should be concentrated on an overwhelming thrust up the less well-fortified Belgian coastal plain, giving the disorganised Germans no time to make a stand; break across the Rhine north of the Ruhr, then press on to Berlin. There was also the possibility that, having encircled the Ruhr and captured important industrial cities, the war might be over before autumn 1944, particularly important to the British as the manpower situation was becoming critical. He also stressed that Eisenhower as Supreme Commander should not become the commander of the land battle, his responsibilities being on a higher plain, viz. overall supervision and direction of land, sea and air, civil control, politics, etc.

Montgomery's scheme would mean that 21st Army Group would take on the major part of the battle. Eisenhower's 'broad front' policy would bring more American troops into the battle. With the Americans the dominant partner in the Alliance, public opinion in the United States would have expected the American armies to have borne the brunt of the fighting.

Eisenhower would not give way. The 'broad front' was adopted, but, after much controversy and no little ill-feeling, a compromise was reached. While not departing from the 'broad front' strategy, Eisenhower accepted that the mountainous and forested terrain in the southern part of the country was unsuitable for a rapid advance. He agreed to employ the greatest strength in the north. Twenty-first Army Group to advance through Belgium and Holland north of the Ardennes to attain flanking bridgeheads across the Lower Rhine and seize the bridges there: south of the Ardennes the U.S. Twelfth Army Group and the French First Army. Eisenhower also accepted Montgomery's plan to the extent that the 12th Army Group, whilst directing its main effort towards Metz and the Saar, would give support on Montgomery's right with U.S. 1st Army to strengthen the advance of 21st Army Group. Thus the 'broad front' strategy was maintained, as was Montgomery's plan to secure the industrial area of the Ruhr in preparation for the advance on Berlin.

Montgomery's proposal and Eisenhower's rejection of it would cause considerable ill-feeling between Americans and Montgomery, both during and after the war.

* * * * *

On 20th August Montgomery issued orders for an advance to clear all enemy forces in the Pas de Calais and north-west France, then to destroy all enemy forces in north-east France. Twenty-first Army Group would then move into Flanders, capture Antwerp and the Belgian airfields in preparation for an eastward advance on the Ruhr. Speed was the essence of advance, the capture of Antwerp being of prime importance; the strain on the supply services of 21st Army Group was considerable as long as it was necessary to depend on the artificial port of Mulberry at Arromanches on the Normandy coastline and the heavily damaged ports at St. Malo and Cherbourg. The capture of Antwerp would allow a shorter and easier route of supplies than the long one from Normandy.

Already the resources of 21st Army Group were so strained that it became necessary to ground VIII Corps in the Vire area and allocate most of its transport to XXX and XII Corps. XXX Corps was ordered to move on to the Seine and make the right-hand crossing at Vernon; XII Corps would later cross at Louviers.

On the 14th August the 11th Armoured Division was placed under command of XXX Corps with orders to begin the advance on the Seine as soon as the Falaise Pocket had been liquidated. The Corps now consisted of the Guards Armoured Division, the 11th Armoured Division, 8th Armoured Brigade, the 43rd (Wessex) Division and the 50th (Northumbrian) Division. The Guards Armoured Division was to lead on the right with the 11th Armoured Division on the left and the 8th Armoured Brigade positioned between them. Their orders were to advance at maximum speed, keeping the Germans on the run with no time to draw breath, without regard for the units on the flanks, and by-pass local resistance. The 50th (Northumbrian Division was to follow on, with the 231st Brigade behind the Guards Armoured Division, the 151st Brigade behind the 11th Armoured Division, the 69th Brigade in reserve behind the 8th Armoured Brigade. The task of the infantry was to mop up the enemy left by the armour, clear areas bypassed by the armour and give flank protection to the XXX Corps.

The initial crossing was to be made by the 43rd (Wessex) Division. General Horrocks had selected this Division as its commander, Major-General G. I. Thomas, had spent two and a half years prior to 'D' Day training his troops in this type of operation on the Medway and the Rother rivers. The Corps Commander's orders for Thomas were 'To force the crossing of the Seine at Vernon, on or about the 25th August – to cover the construction of a Class 9, and a Class 40 bridge – to form a bridgehead of sufficient depth to allow the passage through of the remainder of the Corps.'

Between the 25th and 27th August the crossing was forced at Vernon, and a bridgehead established on the far bank; Royal Engineers had completed a light bridge 650 ft long over the river and by 1715 hours on the 27th a Class 40 bridge which would take tanks had also been completed.

On the afternoon of 28th, the 8th Armoured Brigade led the crossing of the armour, followed the next day by the Guards Armoured Division and the 11th Armoured Division. The advance began at first light on 29th August. The next day the 11th Armoured Division advanced. With vehicles and tanks nose to tail they went on throughout the day and night meeting with slight opposition. But the Guards Armoured Division met with considerable resistance from enemy rearguards, counter-attacking to hold the line of the river to enable their own troops, guns and transport to be ferried across; the bridges had been systematically demolished by the British and American Air Forces.

Having crossed, they broke out of the bridgehead and pushed on some 70 miles to capture the town of Amiens (and the commander of the German Seventh Army – General Ederbach) on the 31st August. The 11th Armoured Division then seized two intact bridges, crossing the River Somme at Amiens, and against considerable opposition the Guards Armoured Division captured two more against little opposition. All had been prepared for demolition, but engineers moved up swiftly and removed the charges. The next day the Division crossed and established a bridgehead four-and-a-half miles deep.

On 19th August, the 50th Division, after four days rest, began to move forward. The advance through Argentan and Laigle encountered little opposition. The town of Rugles, near which the last of the battles of the Falaise Pocket were fought, was entered by the 5th East Yorkshires and 6th Green Howards on the 23rd. They were the first troops to enter the town, and the inhabitants gave them a rousing welcome. The 5th East Yorkshires were given the task of searching the Foret de Breteuil for Germans or their war material: a good deal of material was found but no Germans.

On the 24th August the 50th (Northumbrian) Division now situated around Rugles and Conches began its move towards the Seine. The 5th East Yorkshires as part of the 69th Brigade in reserve, moved off from Rugles on the 26th, and that night was established tactically on the banks of the Seine at Notre-Dame-de-la-Mer, south-east of Vernon. In front of the unit was a partially demolished weir, the far bank in enemy hands.

On the night of 27th August, 'C' Company was ordered to establish itself on the far bank, but as no assault boats were available a patrol of one officer and three men were first sent. Climbing across the broken weir the patrol was ambushed by Germans using grenades. In consequence of this and the fact that the lightning from a heavy thunderstorm provided the enemy with continuous illuminations, the operation was postponed. The next day, two power-driven assault boats became available, and with the withdrawal of the enemy, 'D' Company crossed, bringing back four prisoners. During the days spent in Notre-Dame-de-la-Mer 'D' and 'S' companies played a game of cricket in a stubble field but the game was interrupted by a call to duty.

On 29th August the 69th Brigade moved to Vernon where the 43rd (Wessex) Division had forced a crossing between the 26th and 28th August, and thrown over a bridge. The 50th Division began crossing the River Seine on the night of 29th/30th August following up the Armour; the 69th Brigade crossing soon after midnight in artificial light created by batteries of searchlights. There was little opposition, the German forces were hurrying back.

Across the Seine, the 69th Brigade headed for Beaugrenier, where the remainder of the night of the 29th/30th was spent. Here, local people reported that at nearby Nucourt there was a depot for the storage and assembling of flying bombs which were launched from a site at L'Isle Adam. The village was visited but found to be deserted. There did seem to be evidence that this could be so as there were tunnels with overhead roofing of concrete up to 12 feet thick with railway lines entering them.

On the 31st the Brigade moved on, the 5th East Yorkshires to Villotran, and Annueuil. then Petit Cagny, just south of Amiens. That evening General Montgomery received the following message from the Prime Minister:

> 'It gives me great pleasure to tell you that on my submission His Majesty has been greatly pleased to approve your promotion to the rank of Field-Marshal with the date of September 1st, thus recognising your outstanding service in the memorable and possibly decisive battle which you have personally conducted in France.'

On 1st September SHAEF (Supreme Headquarters Allied Expeditionary Force) opened in Normandy, Montgomery's responsibility for co-ordinating Twenty-First Army Group and Twelfth Army Group ended, but Montgomery retained command of Twenty-First Army Group. Eisenhower would now be in personal control of the battle. Twenty-First Army Group, also designated the Northern Army Group, consisted of First Canadian Army and Second British Army; General Omar Bradley's Twelfth Army Group, now to be known as the Central Group of Armies, consisted of United States First Army under General Courtney Hicks Hodges, Third Army under General George Patton and Ninth Army under General Simpson.

Although in late August there had been initial contact between Sixth Army Group and Eisenhower's forces, this Army Group was not to come under control of Eisenhower until 15th September when it would become established with the Central Group of Armies.

Sixth Army Group under Lieut.-General Jacob L. Devers, designated Southern Group of Armies, consisted of the French First Army under General de Lattre de Tassigny and the United States Seventh Army under Lieut.-General Alexander E. Patch. There was also the First Allied Airborne Army under the United States commander, General Lewis H. Brereton.

The Order of Battle for the drive north-eastward read from left to right: General Crerar's First Canadian Army which included the British I Corps (49th and 51st Divisions) on the Channel coast to capture the ports of Le Havre and Dieppe and clear the sites of the V1 Flying Bombs (*Doodlebugs*) which had been launched against London and the Home Counties since June. General Miles Dempsey's Second British Army inland on its right, on the axis of Brussels and Antwerp, with XII Corps to the left and XXX Corps on their right; the First U.S. Army with its XIX Corps on the immediate right of British Second Army; and the United States Third Army on the right flank directed on Verdun. The U.S. 6th Army Group (*Dragoon/Anvil*) coming up from the south heading for Nancy and the Saar.

* * * * *

On 1st September the 11th Armoured Division crossed the River Somme in the region of Amiens, one column pushing on some 12 miles north-east to take Albert, another, 28 miles to Bapaume. Meanwhile a column of the Guards Armoured Division captured Arras, while another took Doullens some 23 miles east of Abbeville, going on the next morning to capture Douai. During the next 36 hours the armour advanced 60 miles, crossing the border east of Lille: and on 3rd September the Guards Armoured Division together with the 1st Belgian Brigade commanded by General Piron attached to XXX Corps entered the capital, Brussels, which the Germans had evacuated. The 151st Brigade temporarily placed under Second Army garrisoned the city.

It was five years since the outbreak of the war and an ecstatic welcome was given by cheering crowds, who surrounded the vehicles. plying the troops with champagne, beer, flowers and other gifts, making it difficult for transport to move. On 4th September the 231st Brigade turned east to capture Louvain, while the remainder continued north to join up with the 11th Armoured Division. The next day they captured the vital port of Antwerp with the dock installations intact, but failed to clear the Germans from its approaches along the Scheldt.

Antwerp is approached by waterways from the distant sea, principally the River Scheldt, the approaches of which the 11th Armoured Division had failed to clear when capturing the city rendering the port unusable In order to deny the use of the port, the Germans had not only heavily mined the river but covered it with artillery from the islands of Walcheren and South Beveland. It was to take five weeks of intense amphibious operations by the Canadian Army and naval forces before the estuary was finally cleared on the 4th November. Meanwhile the small port at Ostend had been opened, lessening the strain on the supply lines from Normandy.

* * * * *

The 50th (Northumbrian) Division crossed the Somme on the 1st September, troops of the 151st Brigade following the 11th Armoured Division to mount a guard over the main road bridge, others to secure the bridge over the river at Picquigny a few miles down river north of Amiens, and began clearing the area to the north.

The next day the 69th Brigade went on to reach the neighbourhood of Arras, the scene of decisive battles of the First World War, and of 21st May, 1940, where the 5th East Yorkshires, and the 6th and 7th Green Howards as part of the 23rd Division, had fought their first major action.

A great stride forward into Belgium was made on 4th September, the 5th East Yorkshires and the 7th Green Howards going on some 50 miles to Tournai where the local inhabitants expressed their hospitality with gifts of plums. As advanced guard to 50th Division the 5th East Yorkshires went forward on the 5th September, through Ninove to Alost, which was reached that day, having covered some 90 miles since leaving Arras. At Ninove they were presented with locally made matches. At Alost they were joined by the 6th Green Howards where tumultuous and enthusiastic crowds lined the streets to welcome them with gifts of food, flowers, beer and wine.

From Alost 'C' and 'D' Companies of the 5th East Yorkshires advanced to occupy the bridges over the Scheldt at Termonde, while the occupation of that area was carried out. At Zele, just east of Ghent, Germans were met and engaged. Nearby, at Brugschen a carrier patrol came upon some 250 Germans at rest with horse transport. A sharp action was fought, the patrol suffering casualties, but four of the enemy were killed and over 300 prisoners were taken including five officers. Others were rounded up by the Resistance who found that one was a secret service agent with a collection of passports and identity documents, as well as a complete German officer's uniform.

The Battalion C.O., Lieutenant-Colonel Charles, became temporarily not only O.C. British troops, but O.C. Resistance, the Belgian Army, and the local police co-ordinating the work of all.

CHAPTER XIV

THE LAST PHASE OF THE CAMPAIGN OF THE 50th DIVISION IN EUROPE

The advance of XXX Corps required the opening of two routes across the Albert Canal, at Beeringen and further west near Gheel. The Guards Armoured Division to the right of the 50th Division set out from Louvain to capture the bridge over the canal at Gheel; the 11th Armoured Division at Antwerp to capture that at Beeringen. The main Gheel road bridge was found to have been blown up but the other at Beeringen had been only partly destroyed. The Royal Engineers threw a Bailey bridge across at Gheel and local bargees marshalled their barges and anchored them 200 yards to the north, one against another to secure an alternative means of crossing. The bridge was quickly completed, enabling tanks of the Welsh Guards to promptly cross over, and press on towards Helchteren and Hechtel where recently arrived German reinforcements were bringing down shell and mortar fire on the area of the bridge.

On 7th September the 50th (Northumbrian) Division was ordered to concentrate at Hersselt, give support to the Guards Armoured Division, force a crossing and make a bridgehead south-west of Gheel, 15 miles west of Beeringen. The 50th Division's detached brigades were called in, the 151st Brigade moving from Brussels to Hersselt on 8th September, the 231st from Antwerp; the 69th Brigade at Alost 50 miles from the canal was ordered to move to Hersselt, cross as quickly as possible and secure a bridgehead to cover the construction of a bridge by the side of the original road bridge near a hamlet called Het Punt. On reaching that point the Brigade would have advanced some 500 miles since leaving the Posty area on 18th August.

The leading Battalion, the 6th Green Howards, left Alost on the morning of the 7th September and, after a long day's march in the rain through Malines and Westerloo, arrived at the assembly area, Zammel, at 1500 hours.

Shortly after leaving Alost, Lieut.-Colonel Robert. K. Exham (an officer of the Duke of Wellington's Regiment), commanding the 6th Green Howards, was called to Brigade Headquarters to receive orders. Brigadier F. Y. C. Knox, D.S.O., the Brigade Commander, told him that the assault crossing was to be carried out by the 6th Battalion followed by the 7th Battalion. But first he must go forward and conduct a reconnaissance of the seven bridges which spanned the canal to find out whether any of the six bridges eastward of the main Gheel Road Bridge (Bridge A), which was known to have been destroyed, were still useable. If no bridges were left standing reconnaissance parties were to take possession of any boats they could find and use them to cross over; the crossing places would be decided as a result of the reconnaissance, but the bridgehead must include the village of Het Punt on the main Gheel road which was of significant importance to future movements. From Brigade Headquarters, Lieut.-Colonel Exham proceeded to Zammel. He made a quick reconnaissance, found that the main Gheel Road Bridge had been blown. He met with no enemy troops but was told by villagers that the enemy was dug in on the far side, and saw posts at likely crossing places and patrols between them. He also noted the steep bank which would make difficult the launching of assault boats.

On the arrival of the 6th Green Howards, 'A' and 'B' Companies were sent to reconnoitre the canal bank. The Brigade commander arrived at about 1630 hours, stressed the importance of a second crossing point over the canal and said that if it was found to be impossible to cross later in the afternoon then it would be necessary to cross during the night. As he did not expect the reconnaissance parties back for some time, Colonel Exham set off with the Battalion Intelligence Officer and the O.Cs 'C' and 'D' Companies to find a place where a night crossing could be made. They found that all bridges had been destroyed. Reporting back to the Brigade Commander to inform him that all the bridges were destroyed, Lieut.-Colonel Exham was told that a night crossing must be made by the Battalion at two points half-way between bridges 'B' and 'C'.

During the afternoon the 7th Green Howards left Tournai to make a long journey over unknown routes to join up with the 6th Battalion, arriving at Zammel at 2200 hours to find the latter battalion on the southern bank of the Albert Canal preparing for the crossing. The move to the Albert Canal had been so hurried that only two Mark II assault boats and twelve reconnaissance boats had been brought with them. The reconnaissance having been made by the officers commanding 'C' and 'D' Companies of the 6th Battalion, these companies were each given one Mark II assault boat and three reconnaissance boats with which to make the assault. They would be covered if necessary by fire from 'A' Company.

THE BATTLE OF THE GHEEL BRIDGEHEAD
8th-11th September, 1944

At 0130 hours on 8th September the two assault companies hauled their boats up the steep south bank of the canal, carried them over the top, pushed them into the water and in bright moonlight silently started the crossing as the spearhead of the 50th (Northumbrian) Division. Surprise was essential and therefore the assault must be made in silence with no artillery support. To their astonishment, undetected, they reached the far bank by 0230 hours. The boats returned, a cable was laid across the canal and the tedious process of ferrying over the Battalion, a section at a time, began. Owing to the shortage of boats the crossing proceeded slowly, but when daylight came at about 0430 hours all four companies were across. By 0800 hours the whole battalion was established north of the canal around Meulenberg with forward troops of 'D' Company reaching the main Gheel Road, 'C' Company in front of Meulenberg.

The situation now changed, and in the jargon of the time 'all hell was let loose'. Determined opposition was met, enemy heavy machine-gun and mortar fire falling on the forward companies from houses in Het Punt. For a time these companies were cut off but later secured a footing amongst the houses. Lieut.-Colonel Exham set off to find out what was happening and was wounded. Major C. M. Hull was called forward to assume command.

The 7th Green Howards, who had arrived at the south bank of the canal on the night of 7th, began to cross the canal to the east of the 6th Green Howards at 0400 hours on 8th September. With only two assault boats at their disposal, which were by this time leaking badly and under heavy fire, it was not until 0900 hours that the crossing was completed. They then moved off to reinforce the casualty-stricken 6th Battalion in the region of Meulenberg. Lieut.-Colonel W. R. Cox commanding the 7th Green Howards then took command of both battalions, and held the position throughout the day.

On 7th September the 5th East Yorkshires moved east from the Ghent area and concentrated just south of the canal at Westerloo in readiness to cross. In the afternoon of 9th September, the Brigade Commander ordered them to make an assault crossing that night to the west of Het Punt and 'A' Bridge to widen the bridgehead made by the Green Howards. The area in which the crossing was to be made had a high bank running about 400 yards in front of and parallel with the canal. To the south of the bank and up to the canal there was a stretch of flat land with little cover.

The plan was for an attack by two companies, 'B' Company on the left and 'D' Company on the right. The crossing was to be made in silence but, should the enemy offer resistance, then a call could be made for artillery support and machine-guns and mortars of the 2nd Cheshire Regiment.

At 2100 hours 'B' and 'D' Companies, each with three assault boats, moved forward across the flat, sandy stretch towards the canal bank. Night was coming down, it was bitterly cold and rain was falling as they reached the canal bank without having been observed. At 2130 hours they dragged the boats up the bank and silently crossed over. The crossing by the other companies was accomplished successfully, but, on landing, met strong enemy resistance from small arms fire. Battalion headquarters crossed safely together with its attached 288th Battery of the 124th Field Regiment but when they arrived they learnt that 'D' Company was held up by fire from buildings in Het Punt

At 0100 hours the buildings were assaulted by 'A' Company with supporting fire from four P.I.A.T.'S, three 2-inch mortars, Brens and rifles of 'D' Company. The buildings were set on fire and a party of ten men under Lieutenant D. J. Smith attacked. Two German officers and 48 other ranks were taken prisoner; ten men of the 6th Green Howards who had been taken prisoner on the 8th September were found in a cellar and released from captivity. By 0400 hours the whole of the 69th Brigade was in an established bridgehead, with little enemy opposition.

At 0830 hours on the 10th, the 6th Green Howards were relieved by the 7th Battalion, and they together with the 5th East Yorkshires moved to the area of the original bridgehead north of Steelen to give support to units of the 151st Brigade.

This brigade had on 8th September been brought to Steelen to the east of the 69th Brigade with orders to cross the canal and further expand the bridgehead and cover the construction of a folding boat bridge, then advance on Doornbloom, and capture Gheel. The task was formidable. The crossing of the leading troops of the 8th Durham Light Infantry at 1730 hours on the 8th September was met by machine-gun and mortar fire causing many casualties. Having crossed over, they dug in. Their positions were swept by enemy machine-gun fire, followed by a counter-attack which petered out. The rest of the night was quiet.

The next day at 0700 hours the 61st Reconnaissance Regiment crossed the folding bridge, moved through the 8th D.L.I. and held off attempted attacks. The crossing by the 6th D.L.I. was hampered when the bridge collapsed under fire. The infantry crossed in assault boats and, after the bridge was restored at 1100 hours, carriers and ant-tank guns crossed over. They then pressed on to Doornboom against light opposition. On the 10th September, the 9th D.L.I. crossed over.

The 151st Brigade soon met determined opposition, first from the German Luftwaffe Division, formed into regiments of infantry and supported by armour, and the 2nd Parachute Division which they had last met and defeated at the Primasole Bridge in Sicily in one of the bloodiest battles of the Second World War. At Doornbloom the Germans put up a strong and determined resistance but the 151st Brigade pressed on to Gheel. Throughout the morning of the 11th the battle raged, the enemy suffered heavily, with some units virtually wiped out. As Gheel was penetrated there was bitter hand-to-hand street-fighting. On the morning of the 11th September, the Germans counter-attacked the right of the 5th East Yorkshires. The attack was repulsed, but heavy enemy shelling caused casualties; Captain E. J. Crews was mortally wounded.

Throughout 11th and 12th the battle continued in all ferocity, resuming their attempts to break into the bridgehead, but with no success. In the evening of the 12th, the 69th and 151st Brigades were relieved by the 15th (Scottish) Division. When the Scots attacked on the 13th they found the enemy had pulled out and fallen back to the Escaut Canal.

The fighting between 8th and 11th September was recognised with the Battle Honour **Gheel** and gained by the 5th Battalion East Yorkshires.

* * * * *

On 13th September the 69th Brigade moved to sites around Beeringen where it was to remain for six days in close protection of the Escaut bridgehead.

At Beeringen, on the 13th September, the traditional Quebec Day was celebrated by the 5th East Yorkshires, the officers gathering at Battalion headquarters in the evening for a festive drink, whilst those men off duty attended a concert given by ENSA. In the middle of the officers' party there was an air-raid alarm, the officers having to repair to the slit-trenches for a quarter of an hour – drink in hand. During the next three days trips were made to Brussels. Every opportunity was taken for sports activities. A Rugby team of the 5th East Yorkshires beat that of the 6th Green Howards, 45 points to 6, the 7th Green Howards, 9 points to 8.

On the 18th, German aircraft flew over and the Brigade was subjected to its first direct air attack since landing in Normandy. Anti-personnel bombs were dropped, but there were no casualties.

Meanwhile the First Canadian Army had been moving up the coast. Nieuport and Ostend had been taken on 9th September, Le Havre fell on 12th September, Boulogne and Calais were cut off (to be freed at the end of the month). With the freeing of the Channel ports, supplies could be more easily brought up to the armies in the north, the supply lines having become so extended that the momentum of the advance was slowing.

OPERATION MARKET GARDEN

The German forces, having been decisively defeated in the Battle of Normandy, were now completely disorganised and fast falling back into Germany. Montgomery, with the approval of the Supreme Allied Commander, devised a bold plan for the Allied forces which if successful might bring a speedy end to the war in 1944.

The overall plan was divided into two parts, Operation Market, the largest airborne operation undertaken by the Allies up to this time, and a land advance, Operation Garden, by the British Second Army to Nunspeet on the shores of the Zuider Zee by way of Arnhem. If successful all German forces in western Holland would be cut off, the Siegfried Line turned from a flank and the British Second Army established beyond the Rhine to the north of the industrial Ruhr

In August, 1944, the American General Lewis Hyde Brereton had been appointed the first Commander of the 1st Allied Airborne Army. For Operation Market he allotted to Montgomery the 1st Allied Airborne Corps under command of Lieut.-General Sir Frederick (known to everyone as Boy) Browning. This was placed in the British Second Army (Lieut.-General Miles Dempsey). The Corps consisting of the 1st British Airborne Division, (1st Airlanding Brigade (glider-borne), 1st and 4th British Parachute and 1st Polish Parachute Brigades) under Major-General R. E. Urquart was to drop farthest north in the Arnhem area and secure Arnhem Bridge and establish a bridgehead to the north of the Neder Rijn: this would facilitate an invasion of Germany, and an assault crossing averted. The U.S. 82nd Airborne Division to the south was to capture the bridge over the River Maas at Grave and the road and railway bridges over the River Waal at Nijmegen and seize and hold the high ground to the south-east of the town: the U.S. 101st Airborne Division to seize the canal crossings at Eindhoven, Zon and Veghel and capture and hold the road from Eindhoven to Grave, laying down an aerial carpet for an attack by the British Second Army – Operation Garden.

Dempsey's plan for the land operation was a breakout from the De Groot Bridgehead on the Meuse-Escaut canals by armour and infantry in support of the airborne troops, pass over the captured bridges and then a rapid thrust to the Zuider Zee to secure the area from Arnhem to Nunspeet; XXX Corps would form the spearhead of the attack with VIII Corps (Lieut.-General Sir Richard O'Connor) on the right and XII Corps (Lieut.-General Sir Neil Ritchie) on the left to widen the axis and give flank protection.

Troops allotted to XXX Corps were:

Guards Armoured Division
50th (Northumbrian) Division
43rd (Wessex) Division
8th Armoured Brigade
A Dutch Brigade

The Guards Armoured Division was to lead the Corps with the 43rd (Wessex) Division; the 50th Division following up to hold the ground taken and guard the flanks, sending part of the force to secure a crossing over the River Ijssel at Duesberg, about twelve miles north-east of Arnhem; then secure the high ground north of Arnhem.

At 1330 hours on Sunday, 17th September, the airborne armada passed over the bridgehead on the Meuse-Escaut Canals; beneath an 'umbrella' of fighters, transport 'planes, and aircraft towing gliders, and flew northwards. North of Eindhoven, U.S. 101st Airborne Division began to lay its carpet of paratroops.

Zero Hour for XXX Corps was set for 1435 hours. Half-an-hour earlier a barrage from 350 guns signalled the advance into Holland. The Guards Armoured Division, led by the 2nd Irish Guards, moved up to the start line, and out of the Escaut bridgehead.

It was not long before they met heavy resistance, nine of the tanks being knocked out by German anti-tank guns. A furious battle broke out just short of the frontier, and the 231st Brigade, who with the 151st Brigade were holding bridgehead positions on the Escaut canal, was called upon to move up and clear woods on the left of the main road from where the Irish Guards were being strongly opposed. The Germans were driven off but a counter-attack was repulsed by the troops from the 231st Brigade. By evening the town of Valkenswaard, just across the Dutch border and six miles south of Eindhoven had been reached. A halt was called by Brigadier Gwatkin commanding the 5th Guards Brigade, a message having been received that the bridge crossing the canal at Zon had been blown by the enemy. A halt would give time for repairs to be made to the bridge, and provide an opportunity to maintain the tanks and give rest to the troops who had been fighting hard all day.

The next morning the Guards Armoured Division advanced and by mid-day had passed through Eindhoven where contact was established with the U.S. 101st Airborne Division, which had taken the town. The Guards Armoured Division pushed north through the American bridgehead at Zon and Veghel to Grave which had fallen to the U.S. 82nd Airborne Division, and came into contact with the enemy at the southern ends of the bridges at Nijmegen and between the Rivers Maas and Waal just west of the Reichswald. The bridge over the River Maas had been captured intact.

Nijmegen was reached on the 19th. There it was found that the town was being held by the Germans together with the road bridge on the east, and the railway bridge on the west, crossing the River Waal The capture of the road bridge, a modern 5-span structure of concrete and steel some 6,000 feet in length, was essential; otherwise it would be necessary for a hazardous crossing by assault boats. The southern ends of both road and railway bridges were held by a formidable force of tough German SS troops, strongly entrenched in pre-war concrete emplacements.

The Guards Armoured Division, supported by the U.S. 505th Parachute Regiment of the U.S. 82nd Airborne Division, launched an attack to capture the bridges. One battalion of the 505th Regiment and the Grenadier Guards were detailed to capture the road bridge, while the remainder were directed on to the rail bridge. An attempt by armour to get through met with heavy fire from anti-tank guns sited in houses near the approaches. The determination of the Germans to hold the bridges, in the hope that they might be used for a counter attack, resulted in a decision to cross the river in assault boats upstream from the bridges, and attack the northern approaches, held by the enemy in strength, while pressure continued from the southern end.

At 1500 on the 20th, the Irish Guards and the U.S. 504th Parachute Regiment, having cleared the western suburbs of the town, began the crossing in flimsy British assault boats with which they were completely unfamiliar. Covered by fire from tanks of the Irish Guards and some 100 guns, they met with opposition, only half of the first wave reaching the far bank. Nevertheless a small bridgehead was established and during the remainder of the afternoon other troops were ferried across. By evening both bridges had been cut off from the rear. The attack from the south was successful, the demolition charges removed, and both bridges captured intact.

At Arnhem the important bridge over the Neder Rijn was still in German hands. The 1st British Airborne Division and 1st Polish

Parachute Brigade (Major-General Sosabovsky) were fighting desperately to hold their bridgehead against ferocious counter attacks. They had been dropped too far away from their vital objective – the bridge – and before they had time to secure their positions they were pinned down by the 2nd S.S. Panzer Corps refitting in the Arnhem area after demolition in Normandy. Thick mists shrouded the ground forces, hampering air drops of supplies as well as personnel to reinforce the fighting troops. XXX Corps was still ten miles off. Attempts by the Guards Armoured Division to get through were held up on 22nd September when the route was blocked five and a half miles from the Arnhem bridge.

The area between Nijmegen and Arnhem was low-lying and boggy, intersected by numerous ditches and water-channels; the roads running along the top of high embankments restricting use to a one-tank front and exposing tanks and other vehicles to fire from well-sited anti-tank guns in the many surrounding orchards; any vehicle knocked out could cause a road blockage and consequent hold-up.

The country, being more suitable to infantry tactics, on the 22nd the 43rd (Wessex) Division was called to strike out across country, force a way to the north bank of the Neder Rijn and reach the perimeter of the 1st Airborne Division where the 2nd Parachute Regiment had been overrun on the Arnhem bridge the previous day. The attempt failed.

That day, in an endeavour to prevent XXX Corps relieving the airborne forces at Arnhem, a German formation operating on either side of the road launched attacks with tanks and infantry cutting the road at several places, penetrating St. Oedenrode, and stopping all vehicles on the road for some time.

On the 23rd September the G.O.C-in-C Second Army gave the commander XXX Corps permission to withdraw the division if things did not improve, and finally on 25th September Major-General Urquart was ordered to withdraw to the south bank: that night all that were left were across the Lower Rhine. Casualties had been heavy, the Division losing 7,000 in missing, killed and wounded; 2163 got away.

Operation *Market Garden,* Montgomery's bid to end the war in 1944, had failed. Although crossings had been established over four of the major water obstacles on the Maas and Waal rivers, the prime objective, the crossing at the Neder Rijn, remained in German hands.

* * * * *

We must now return to the 50th (Northumbrian) Division, particularly to the 69th Brigade, which we left holding positions in the Beeringen bridgehead over the Escaut Canal.

The fall of Nijmegen and the capture of the bridges across the River Waal now called for an advance by the 69th Brigade, to widen the bridgehead there and then go on to Arnhem. It was placed under command of the Guards Armoured Division. The road to Eindhoven was

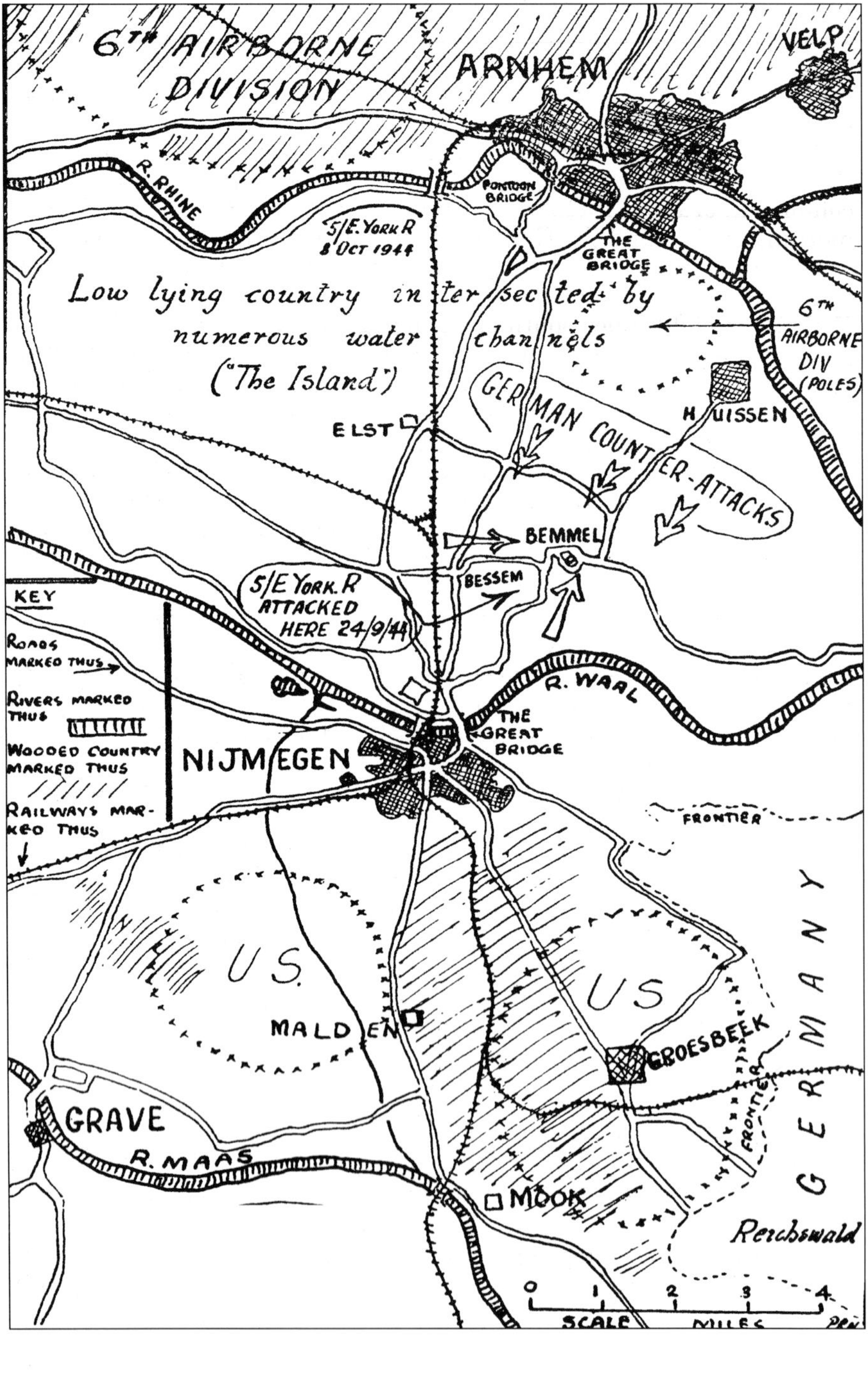

6TH AIRBORNE DIVISION
ARNHEM
VELP
R. RHINE
PONTOON BRIDGE
5/E. York R 8 Oct 1944
THE GREAT BRIDGE
Low lying country inter sected by numerous water channels ("The Island")
6TH AIRBORNE DIV (POLES)
GERMAN COUNTER-ATTACKS
HUISSEN
ELST
BEMMEL
BESSEM
5/E York. R ATTACKED HERE 24/9/44
KEY
ROADS MARKED THUS
RIVERS MARKED THUS
WOODED COUNTRY MARKED THUS
RAILWAYS MARKED THUS
R. WAAL
THE GREAT BRIDGE
NIJMEGEN
FRONTIER
U.S.
US
MALDEN
GROESBEEK
GERMANY
FRONTIER
GRAVE
R. MAAS
MOOK
Reichswald
0 1 2 3 4
SCALE MILES

congested with traffic and it was not until 1000 hours on the morning of 21st September that priority was given to the 69th Brigade to move off; the infantry in Troop Carrying vehicles. Progress was slow: the first Dutch town of Valkenswaard was reached at 0800 hours on the 22nd, and, at midday, Eindhoven.

As the Brigade moved forward to Nijmegen the Brigade Commander, Brigadier Knox, summoned the battalion commanders to the head of the column. In order to further increase their hold on the road, in the early morning of the 22nd the Germans launched an attack with two infantry battalions and a regiment of tanks to cut the road which XXX Corps was using as its main line of advance. Crossing the road near Uden, north of Veghel and eight miles south of the bridge at Grave, they split the 69th Brigade; the Brigade Commander and the battalion commanders together with the 5th East Yorkshires were to the north of the crossing and the 6th and 7th Green Howards to the south. The next day, in an attempt to strengthen their positions, the Germans put in an attack at Veghel further south. Driven off with heavy losses by British artillery and troops of the U.S. 101st Airborne Division holding the crossing near St. Oedenrode, the road was temporarily reopened and by 1600 hours the battalion commanders had returned to their units and the 69th Brigade unified.

The Commander XXX Corps, General Horrocks, had also been stranded by the cutting of the road. When a despatch rider from the 9th D.L.I. got through he was asked how he had managed it. He explained that he had made the journey by going across country to avoid the enemy positions across the road. Asked by the General if he could get him back, he gave his assurance. The General got into his jeep escorted by a platoon of carriers, followed the despatch rider and successfully returned to his Headquarters.

The advance was resumed at 0300 hours on the 24th; Veghel, Uden and Grave were passed without any trouble, and at 0800 hours Nijmegen was reached, the 69th Brigade taking its place alongside the defenders of the bridgehead over the River Waal from those who had been defending it. Soon they were in action against German S.S. troops, and were subjected to dive-bombing by the new German jet aircraft, but there were no casualties. This was their first sighting of jet aircraft.

* * * * *

There was now to be a change of priority in operations, probably brought about by Admiral Sir Bertram Ramsey, Eisenhower's Naval C-in-C., who on the 3rd September had sent a telegram to SHAEF and H.Q. Twenty-first Army Group warning that Antwerp and Rotterdam were vulnerable to mining and blocking, which if successful would cause considerable delay in operations to clear them. This was followed on the 16th September by a firm note to Eisenhower from the Combined Chiefs of

Staff meeting in Quebec, instructing him to undertake the opening of Antwerp as a matter of the first priority. Whilst ordering Montgomery to 'open the port of Antwerp as a matter of urgency', Eisenhower stressed that equally important were 'operations culminating in a strong attack on the Ruhr from the north'. With insufficient resources to accomplish both simultaneously, Montgomery would have preferred to go for the Ruhr. He was now instructed to concentrate on Antwerp. This operation was placed in the hands of General Crerar commanding the Canadian Army, together with the clearance of South Beveland, the capture of Walcheren and control of the Scheldt estuary.

General Dempsey's Second British Army was to clear the area east of the Canadian Army and to the west of the River Maas.

* * * * *

With the withdrawal of the airborne division to the south bank of the Neder Rijn, the Second Army was charged to advance through the corridor to Arnhem and cross the Neder Rijn. The Germans holding the line to north of Nijmegen had been reinforced by tanks and infantry freed from action against the airborne troops at Arnhem. Soon they would be attacking the bridgehead over the Waal in strength.

The 50th Division was now to be employed in widening the bridgehead around Nijmegen by clearing the enemy from between the Rivers Waal and Neder Rijn. The country was low-lying and marshy, with orchards of apples and pears, criss-crossed with dykes and water channels. A road running from Nijmegen to Arnhem divided the area into two halves. The 50th Division was to give it the name 'The Island'. During the months of October and November spent there it was surrounded by water.

Early in the afternoon of the 24th September, the 69th Brigade crossed the River Waal and took up positions near Ressen. On its earlier arrival at Nijmegen it had come under command of the Guards Armoured Division.

The 5th East Yorkshires were given the task of attacking the village of Bemmel about five miles north-east of the Nijmegen-Arnhem road. With co-operation from some tanks of the Guards Armoured Division, and with artillery support, aided by the Battalions 3-inch mortars, the attack went in at 1630 hours on the 25th the artillery putting down a heavy bombardment. The terrain was difficult for tanks, made worse by the shelling; the infantry found the going hard. By dusk 'B' and 'D' Companies, having overcome the enemy's outpost lines, were held up south of the village, and 'A' Company which had been sent to attack from the left flank had not been able to break through the defences surrounding the village.

During the night, plans were made for an attack the next morning. At dawn, following five minutes intensive artillery fire, 'C' Company, led by Major K. C. Harrison, with tanks in support, attacked, broke through the defensive position, clearing the determined enemy SS from house to house and entered the village. By 0200 hours on the 25th, Bemmel had been captured, 40 enemy were killed, 80 prisoners taken, and a number of guns captured. Later it was found that Bemmel had been held, not by two enemy companies as had been supposed, but by 700 SS men supported by anti-tank guns.

* * * * *

Early in the afternoon of the 24th, the 6th and 7th Green Howards crossed the Waal, the 7th to Merm and the 6th to Ressen, west of the 5th East Yorkshires at Bemmel.

Orders were received by the 69th Brigade to attack Heuval. The 5th East Yorkshires moved up from Bemmel to join the 7th Green Howards at Merm. These two battalions were to advance eastward on Heuval, the 6th Green Howards on the right flank to attack Baal and then turn north on Heuval.

At midday on the 26th the attack from Merm went in. The leading companies soon ran into opposition, and it was not until 1630 hours when tanks were brought up in support that they were able to enter the village. During the fighting Major N. S. (Paddy) Atley, a Territorial Officer of the 4th East Yorkshires attached to the 7th Green Howards, was wounded.

Throughout the 27th and 28th there was irregular enemy artillery and mortar fire, which continued at intervals throughout the next day. During the 27th, 'A' Company of the 5th East Yorkshires, was called upon to make a short advance without tanks to improve the position. They were supported by a barrage from the 55th Field Regiment, R.A., their usual attached gunner regiment, the 124th Field Regiment, R.A., being in support of the Green Howards. The objective was successful and nine prisoners taken. With the withdrawal of the airborne troops at Arnhem the Germans had tanks and infantry available to set about eliminating the bridgehead at Nijmegen by the destruction of the bridges across the Waal.

On the 29th the Luftwaffe dropped a parachute bomb on the railway bridge; a 40-foot section was demolished making it temporarily unusable. On the same day several German 'human torpedoes' swam down to the road bridge carrying explosives to attach to the supports, causing serious damage. Had the British front been broken through, those to the north of the Waal might well have been destroyed, it being impossible to get back over the river. The 69th Brigade and the 5th Guards Brigade, now came under command of the 43rd (Wessex) Division, the only complete division north of the Waal.

On the 30th September, after heavy shelling, an enemy counter-attack was directed on that part of the front held by the 5th East Yorkshires, the enemy being repulsed by light machine-gun and artillery fire. The Battalion was then relieved and moved two miles to the south-west to a rest area in some orchards. There was to be little rest, the area was very wet and during the night there was torrential rain. At 2200 hours the movement of tracked vehicles was heard beyond the Canal de Ligne as the Germans collected a force, equivalent of an infantry division and some 70 tanks, to begin a determined assault on a broad front with the intention of eliminating the Nijmegen bridgehead.

At 0300 hours on 1st October heavy small arms fire broke out near the bridge. 'B' Company of the 5th East Yorkshires was detailed to give support to a Royal Engineer unit in close protection of the road bridge, The company 'stood to' and fired on what appeared to be a patrol working its way down to the bridge, but the results were indecisive.

As dawn approached on 1st October, the Germans laid down a heavy bombardment with artillery and mortar fire on the fronts of the 69th Brigade, and 5th Guards Brigade. At 0500 hours, riflemen and Spandau teams were seen coming through the mist from across the Canal de Ligne north-east of Heuval and were soon within 50 yards of the forward companies of the 7th Green Howards. Heavy shelling and mortar fire was followed at 0515 by a counter-attack with twelve tanks, and although two were knocked out, the remainder succeeded in infiltrating between the positions of 'B' and 'C' Companies. This forced 'C' Company to give ground, and exposed 'A' Company, who were soon isolated.

At 0630 hours artillery support was called for and a barrage was laid down around the whole of the enemy lines, putting out of action a number of tanks and causing many casualties. By 0645 the enemy attack had been halted, but not long afterwards flared up again with waves of tanks and infantry, supported by self-propelled guns. The attack went on throughout the day and evening. The 7th Green Howards tenaciously held on.

At 1800 hours, the 5th East Yorkshires, supported by tanks of a squadron of the 13th/18th Hussars and 124th Field Regiment, R.A., were called on to relieve the 7th Green Howards. This was carried out under severe enemy shelling. By the time the relief force arrived at 2300 hours the enemy attack had failed. The 69th Brigade was now relieved, the 6th and 7th Green Howards moved back to Nijmegen, their positions being taken over by the 151st and 231st Brigades. The 5th East Yorkshires remained in their positions, coming under command of the 231st Infantry Brigade.

The actions between the 17th and 27th September were recognised by the Battle Honour **Nederrijn**, and gained by the East Yorkshire Regiment.

Early on 2nd October the Germans put in a major attack on the village of Aam to the north-west of Bemmel held by the 1st Dorsetshires and a machine gun platoon of the 2nd Cheshires of the 231st Brigade who were heavily engaged. The 5th East Yorkshires and the 2nd Irish Guards Armoured Regiment were called upon to give support and placed under command of the 231st Brigade.

During the night 'C' Company with some tanks and anti-tank guns suffered from enemy shell fire, losing Major K. C. Harrison (attached from the West Yorkshire Regt.), Lieutenant Scarr (also attached), the C.S.M., C.Q.M.S., and others of Company Headquarters. Captain Robinson was sent by Battalion HQ to take command.

At 0530 hours on 3rd October, after a further artillery bombardment, enemy infantry advanced, and despite defensive gun fire occupied parts of 'C' Company's position. Battalion H.Q. sent R.S.M. F. Gibson with the Battalions snipers to reinforce the company. As they moved forward with supporting tanks, houses in which the enemy had taken up defensive positions were cleared. The area was shelled throughout the day and by 1500 hours only Lieutenant Kemp and some 20 men were left holding the position. Of nine tanks only five were serviceable. The rest of the Battalion had also been subjected to shell fire, and a minor infantry attack repulsed. On the night of 3rd/4th October the Battalion was relieved, and by midnight had moved back over the bridge to billets at Nijmegen.

Casualties between the 1st and 4th October were 24 O.Rs. killed: 2 Officers and 62 O.Rs. wounded and 5 O.Rs. missing.

The East Yorkshire Regiment together with the Irish Guards, the Cheshires and the Dorsetshire Regiment were awarded the Battle Honour **Aam.** (1st-4th October).

The 5th East Yorkshires spent the 4th-7th October at rest in Nijmegen, enjoying entertainment whilst carrying out some training. There was a little shelling and occasional bombing raids.

The 50th Division, having been ordered to take over the eastern sector of the bridgehead on 4th October, the 151st and 231st Brigades took up positions to improve the line. An attack was launched on Halderen, south-east of Bemmel, a small town where the high chimneys of a number of factories were being used as enemy observation posts. The country there is flat and enclosed and intersected with wide and deep ditches: difficult country in which to operate. The attack was supported by machine guns and mortars of 'B' Company the 2nd Cheshire Regiment. The enemy strongly resisted but by the 6th October the objectives had been taken.

On 8th October the 69th Brigade re-crossed the Waal to relieve units of the U.S. 101st Airborne Division. The 5th East Yorkshires moved to the north of the salient near to the railway bridge over the River Nederrijn, and along the embankment on the south of the river across which the British 1st Airborne Division had withdrawn on 25th September.

The Battalion was in contact with the Germans, who confined their activities to intermittent shelling and mortaring, with some sniping. The Battalion's snipers replied, recording several successes, while others lobbed bombs over the embankment. At night patrols went out to harass the forward enemy troops in an attempt to take prisoners and identify opposing units.

The weather was wet, cold and extremely unpleasant resembling the winter trench warfare conditions of World War I. On two occasions the dykes rose; once as much as three feet in one hour, ascribed to heavy rain. On 15th November the Battalion returned to the comfort of billets in Nijmegen for a period of rest. The G.O.C. XXX Corps, Lieutenant-General Sir Brian Horrocks, visited the Battalion and addressed all officers and N.C.O.s.

There was a move on 19th November for a further period of defensive duties in the bridgehead. The weather continued as before, and duck-boards and corrugated iron sheets were supplied to make the conditions more bearable for the companies who were in close contact with the enemy. Conditions were so bad that the men had to remain almost immobile during daylight, and the minimum numbers were kept there, being relieved every two days. In order to make conditions more amenable, waterproof barrels with straw inside were sunk in the ground for sentries to stand in; behind revetted emplacements, lean-to sheds were provided. Patrolling went on by day and night, it being thought that the Germans might breach the dykes at the eastern end and flood 'The Island'.

To save manpower, extensive minefields were laid. Whole platoons were given a day in Nijmegen every third day, and 48-hour leave passes to Brussels and Antwerp were issued.

After some nine weeks in the bridgehead during which the 69th Brigade experienced some heavy fighting, shelling and mortaring, and spells of exhausting patrolling, warning was received of an impending move back into Belgium, the 6th and 7th Green Howards to Roulers; the 5th East Yorkshires to the small town of Iseghem, near Ypres,

An advance party of the 5th East Yorkshires left on 21st November, and, on the 27th, the Battalion having been relieved, was withdrawn; Iseghem was reached on the 29th November. Here, personnel were accommodated in civilian billets.

CHAPTER XVI

THE BREAK-UP OF THE 50th (NORTHUMBRIAN) DIVISION

The 21st Army Group was suffering limitations in its strength. The Manpower Committee of the Ministry of Labour had for some time been finding it difficult to make more men available to the services. Casualties had reduced the strength of battalions, and it was found necessary to break up one division. The 50th (Northumbrian) Division was selected.

In a letter to Major-General Lyne, who was temporarily commanding the Division in the absence of Major-General Graham through a leg injury, Field Marshal Montgomery explained the situation. The 50th Division had given long and distinguished service throughout the war: France and Belgium in 1939/40; Egypt; Cyprus; Palestine; TransJordania; Iraq; Northern Syria; El Alamein to Tunisia; Sicily: and as one of the first divisions to land in Normandy on 'D' Day had been in the forefront of battle continuously. The Field Marshal said it was unthinkable that a division with so fine a record should lose its identity. The authorities back in England then confirmed that the identity should be retained and the Division would return to England to be used as a training formation.

This did not mean that all would be going back to England; personnel were to be categorised for future service. Men of higher medical category to be sent to reinforce other fighting units; specialists to Northern Ireland to be trained as riflemen; cadres to return to England to form battalions to train the many anti-aircraft gunners for whom in England there was no longer an operational role.

On 1st December, the C.O., Lieutenant-Colonel Charles informed the 5th East Yorkshires of the breaking up of the 50th Division. The battalions of the 69th Brigade held their last church parade on the 3rd December 1944 in the cathedral of Notre Dame at Roulers, and on 5th December, Major-General D. A. H. Graham, C.B.E., D.S.O., M.C., G.O.C. 50th Division, accompanied by the Brigade Commander, Brigadier F. Y. C. Knox, D.S.O., addressed all ranks warmly thanking them for their valuable services. General Sir Brian Horrocks, G.O.C. XXX Corps, sent a special message of good wishes for the future. ending with the words, 'The T.T. boys will be much missed by everyone.'

That day an advance party of the 5th East Yorkshires left for England. On 8th December, Field-Marshal Sir Bernard Montgomery presented decorations to officers and men of 50th Division. Those of the 5th East Yorkshires receiving awards were R.S.M. F. Gibson, M.M., who received the Military Cross, and Private F. Miller who received the Military Medal. Transport having been handed in, the Battalion cadre left Iseghem by train on the 13th December for Ostend, where they embarked on *H.M.T.*

Lady of Man destined for Southampton from where they had left on 5th June, 1944, for the Normandy landings.

On the 15th December the cadres from the 69th Brigade, each of 100 men, boarded trains for Malton in Yorkshire where billets were occupied, the 5th East Yorkshires at Malton, the 6th Green Howards at Pickering and the 7th Green Howards at Scampston. The battalions were now organised on a six-company basis, HQ 5th East Yorkshires being at Malton, the companies in villages around. An intake of instructors arrived from the School of Infantry for the new role, after which personnel left for Christmas leave.

The first trainee course began at the beginning of January, 1945. It was of eight weeks' duration, after which the former gunners passed out as infantrymen, and were sent on Embarkation Leave, the staff having a break prior to starting with the next batch of trainees.

Lieut.-Colonel Charles relinquished command of the Battalion on the 17th January for a War Office appointment, being succeeded by Major R. E. H. Ward, who shortly afterwards gave over command to Lieut.-Colonel Hugh Manford Vaux, M.C., a Regular officer of the Durham Light Infantry. The second batch of trainees assembled at Malton on the 22nd March and the course was recommenced.

The war in Europe came to an end on the 8th May, 1945. There were victory celebrations in Malton on the 13th May. The 5th Battalion paraded and marched through the town, the salute being taken by Colonel The Lord Middleton, M.C., T.D., Lord Lieutenant of the East Riding of Yorkshire, who had been instrumental in raising the Battalion, and had been its first Commanding Officer. Only a few would have heard the Regimental Quick March – 'A Yorkshire Lass', Regimental Bands having been kept out of war zones after Dunkirk until autumn 1944.

CHAPTER XVII

PEACE-TIME SOLDIERING

With the ending of the war in Europe the need for infantry reinforcements lessened, but the Battalion carried on its courses of training, mostly of men from the Pioneer Corps, who like those from Anti-Aircraft Command were no longer required in their original role.

Japan capitulated on the 14th August, 1945, after the dropping of atomic bombs on the 6th and 9th August, allowing part of the Battalion to be released to take part in agricultural work around Malton, mainly getting in the harvests. The intakes that followed were of ex-Prisoners of War who had more than six months to serve before being due for release from the army.

The aftermath of World War Two found the British Army providing troops for the Army of Occupation in Western Germany, Austria and the disputed areas around Trieste, claimed by Italy and Yugoslavia. Egypt, Cyprus, and the colonies had to be garrisoned. There was also the mandated territory of Palestine, where pre-war terrorism had restarted with the Jews endeavouring to establish a Zionist state.

There was no longer the necessity to train as many infantrymen, and the role of the Battalion had come to an end. The 5th East Yorkshires were too good to be disbanded as were many other battalions of the Territorial Army. Lieut.-Colonel J. G. Morrogh Bernard, M.B.E., who in March, 1945, had been commanding the 1st Battalion in India, took command on 13th October from Lieut.-Colonel Vaux, M.C., and soon after, the Battalion was re-formed as a normal infantry battalion.

On 31st December, 1945, the unit left England for Egypt where it was stationed at Fayid in the Canal Zone. From here in February, 1946, a party of Officers, W.O.s and Sergeants went to Port Said to meet Lieut.-Colonel R. J. Springhall and the 1st Battalion on its way back from the Burma Theatre of War. In the party was Lieut.-Colonel Morrogh Bernard, who in March, 1945, was in command of the 1st Battalion, Majors A. L. R. H. Thresher, A. B. Whitehead and J. D. G. Walker Brash, Capt. (Q.M.) Finch, C.S.M.s Carr, Darley, Coaster and Sgt. Dooley

With unrest in Cairo, and an anti-British attitude by the Egyptians, it was necessary to protect the British Embassy and Headquarters of the G.O.C.-in-C. British Troops in Egypt, and two companies of the 5th East Yorkshires were sent as guards.

In May, 1946, orders were received for the 5th Battalion to disband and what was left after demobilisation to proceed to Austria to amalgamate with the 1st Battalion.

When the two guard companies were withdrawn from Cairo, the G.O.C. (Lieut.-General C. W. Allfrey, C.B., D.S.O., M.C.) wrote a personal letter to Lieut.-Colonel Morrogh Bernard, part of which read:

'I want to thank you for the way they have looked after me here . . . I am so glad the battalion is happy about its future. It is very sad for you that the battalion is being broken up, but I do want to congratulate you on the fine show you and they have put up. You have got them right on their toes and you can be really proud of the way they have responded to your lead in the training. You have a splendid battalion of men and you have done the job really well . . . All good luck to you and well done.

Yours sincerely,'

On 23rd June, 1946, the Battalion left Egypt for Austria where amalgamation with the 1st Battalion would take place.

The following letter was sent to Lieut.-Colonel Morrogh Bernard by Lieut.-General J. S. Steele, C.B., D.S.O., M.C., Commander-in-Chief, British Troops in Austria.

'Headquarters
British Troops in Austria
1125/1 G
23rd August 1946

Lt.Col. J.G. Morrogh Bernard, M.B.E.,
Commanding 5th Battalion, The East Yorkshire Regiment.

Now that the time has come to place the 5th Battn. The East Yorkshire Regiment in suspended animation I would like to express to all ranks my warm appreciation for your magnificent services.

Few Battalions can have seen longer or more gruelling active service in this war. In 1940 you fought in France. Early in 1942 you were once more in action at Gazala. You were at Alamein and the Mareth Line. You fought with great distinction at the Wadi Akarit, and won a Victoria Cross. In the invasion of Sicily and Normandy you filled the role of first assault troops with outstanding valour, and played a stout part in the Battles in North-West Europe.

Since the war you have carried out security duties in Egypt and Austria with your usual efficiency and success, finishing your career under the Oak Tree of the 46th Division. Your allegiance must ever be to the twin T's of the 50th Northumbrian Division, but I have been proud to have you under my command.

(Signed) J. S. Steele,
Lt.General, Commander-in-Chief.'

Thus ended the life of a battalion raised in 1939, which had been sent, only partly trained, to the British Expeditionary Force to carry out pioneer and construction work, drawn into the fighting and acquitting itself with credit. In North Africa, Sicily and north-west Europe it had fought with distinction, and won more Battle Honours for the Regiment than any other battalion.

The Words of the Song to the Music of the Regimental March

The Yorkshire Lass

1. Kind friends I come before you now,
   My happy tale to tell;
   I sing in praise of a charming girl
   With whom in love I fell,
   She came from out of Yorkshire,
   Her name was Emily;
   About as nice a buxom lass,
   As ever you did see.

Chorus
   Her eyes are like the little stars
   That shine so bright above,
   Her cheeks are like the red rose blush,
   And her I fondly love,
   She's pearly teeth and golden hair,
   A fairy she'd surpass;
   The pride of all the country is
   My bonny Yorkshire Lass.

2. Her father keeps a little farm,
   Not many miles from here,
   Amongst the flowers and in the dells.
   I roam with Em'ly dear;
   Her father, mother, sister,
   Are happy as can be,
   But the pride of all the country is,
   My own sweet Emily

Chorus

3. To see her in the dairy
   To me seems quite a treat;
   Her milking pails, and pots, and pans,
   They are so trim and neat;
   But best of all among them,
   And sweetest far to me,
   Is my bonnie little Yorkshire lass,
   My own sweet Emily.

Chorus

OFFICERS OF THE 5TH BATTALION
23rd APRIL 1940

Lieut.-Colonel	Daniel James Keating, M.C.		Regular Army
Major	Cyril Cameron Rice	2 i/c Bn	Regular Army
Major	J. R. H. Ellery	O.C.Coy	
Major	T. E. Anderson		Attached 23rd Division Signals
Captain	Roland F.Bilton	O.C.Coy	from the 4th Battalion
Captain	R. T. Percival	O.C.Coy	
Lieutenant	Andrew William Edgar	O.C.Coy	Regular Army
2nd Lieutenant	G. A. Mainprize.		
2nd Lieutenant	J. E. Cooke		
2nd Lieutenant	R. M. L. Baxter		
2nd Lieutenant	F. A. W. Durrant	Signals Officer	
2nd Lieutenant	J. F. Fillingham		
2nd Lieutenant	G. W Taylor		
2nd Lieutenant	J. H. F. Dixon		Killed in action. N.W.Europe 11.6.44 (Major)
2nd Lieutenant	D. Carnley		Died Persia 17.1.42
2nd Lieutenant	H. L. Birtles	M.T.O.	
2nd Lieutenant	G. Gardner		
2nd Lieutenant	Alexander Somerled Angus Bosville, Bart. Macdonald of the Isles		
2nd Lieutenant	G. Stockdale	Intelligence Officer	
2nd Lieutenant	A. R. Collingwood	Adjutant	
2nd Lieutenant	R. A. Berriff		
2nd Lieutenant	C. J. Carle		
2nd Lieutenant	J. Ormiston	O.C.Coy	
2nd Lieutenant	G. D. Wood		Killed in action. Middle East 6.4.43 (Captain)
2nd Lieutenant	J. R. Y. Wilson		
2nd Lieutenant	W. A. Alexander		
2nd Lieutenant	J. B. S. Davis		
2nd Lieutenant	T. H. Holdsworth		
2nd Lieutenant	H. R. D. Oldham		
2nd Lieutenant	C. Aske		
2nd Lieutenant	A. R. A. Wilson		
Lieutenant	J. W. Scott	Quartermaster	
Captain	F. E. Deacon, RAMC.	Medical Officer	
Captain	R. Mort, R.A. Ch.D.	Chaplain	
2nd Lieut.	Thomas L. Ward		Posted to the 69th Infantry Brigade as Intelligence Officer, October1939 Later Major, (M.B.E.) and Senior Liaison Officer Eighth Army/ Desert Air Force North Africa/Italy

OFFICERS OF THE 5TH BATTALION
28th MARCH 1942

Rank	Name	Appointment	Remarks
T/Lieutenant-Colonel	James Thornhill Thornhill		Regular Army
T/Major	A.C. Scott	2 i/c	Green Howards
T/Major	Frederick Reginald Yorke	O.C. Coy	Regular Army
T/Major	Roland F. Bilton	O.C. Coy	Territorial Army
Captain	Andrew William Edgar	Adjutant	Regular Army
T/Captain	Herbert Noel Wallace,	O.C. Coy	Regular Army Killed in action Middle East 6.4.43 (Major M.C.)
T/Captain	A. R. Collingwood	O C. Coy	Territorial Army
T/Captain	H. R. D. Oldham	O.C. Coy	
T/Captain	H. L. Birtles		Tpt.Offcr
T/Captain	F. F. Robins		Killed in action Middle East. 42 (Major M.C.)
T/Captain	D. J. Penwill	S.O.	
A/Captain	J. F Fillingham	Liaison Officer	
Lieutenant	R. M. L. Baxter		
Lieutenant	F. A. W. Durrant		
Lieutenant	J. J .H. Thompson		
Lieutenant	G. D. Wood		Killed in action Middle East 6.4.43 (Captain)
Lieutenant	A. Carter		
Lieutenant	C. Aske		
Lieutenant	G. R. Aspin		
Lieutenant	R. Thornback		
Lieutenant	E. J. Crews		Died of wounds N.W. Europe 11.9.44 (Captain)
Lieutenant	W. Sugarman		
2nd Lieutenant	B. Anderson		
2nd Lieutenant	W. B. Day		
2nd Lieutenant	F. R. Jackman		
2nd Lieutenant	R. G. Towers		
2nd Lieutenant	J. E. Hoy		
Lieutenant	C. H. Brashaw, M.M.	Quartermaster	
Captain	T. C. MacInnes R.A.M.C.	Medical Officer	
Captain	R. Mort, R.A.Ch.D.	Chaplain	

OFFICERS OF THE 5TH BATTALION
27th JUNE 1942

This was the position on the day when the Battalion, in the retirement after the Gazala Battle, held off the Germans surrounding the 69th Brigade at Mersa Matruh.

Rank	Name	Appointment	Remarks
A/Lieut.-Colonel	Thomas Wolryche Guy Stansfield Appointed C.O. 13.5.42		Regular Army Green Howards
T/Major	Roland F. Bilton Appointed 2 i/c 1.6.42		Territorial Army
T/Major	Frederick Richard Yorke	O.C. Coy	Regular Army
Captain	Andrew William Edgar	Adjutant	Regular Army
T/Captain	Herbert Noel Wallace	O.C. Coy	Regular Officer Killed in action Middle East 6.4.43 Major M.C.
T/Captain	A.R. Collingwood	O.C. Coy	Territorial Army
T/Captain	H. R. D. Oldham		Carrier Platoon Officer
T/Captain	F. F. Robins	O.C. Coy	Killed in action Middle East .-42 Major M.C.
T/Captain	D. J. Penwill	O.C. Coy	
T/Captain	R. M. L. Baxter		
A/Captain	J. J. M. Thompson		
Lieutenant	T. L. Ward		Territorial Army
Lieutenant	F. A. W. Durrant	S.O.	
Lieutenant	G. D. Wood		Killed in action Middle East 6.4.43 Captain
Lieutenant	A. Carter		Presumed killed Middle East Approx 25.7.42
Lieutenant	A. R. A. Wilson		Joined 10.6.42
Lieutenant	R. Thornback		
Lieutenant	E. J. Crews		Died of wounds N.W. Europe 11.9.44 Captain
Lieutenant	W. Sugarman		
Lieutenant	B. Anderson		
Lieutenant	W. B. Day		
2nd Lieutenant	R. G Towers		
2nd Lieutenant	J. E. Hoy		
2nd Lieutenant	H. F. Owen		Joined 10.6.42
2nd Lieutenant	A. B. S. Gibson		Border Regiment
2nd Lieutenant	C. G. Hervey-Murray		Border Regiment
2nd Lieutenant	C. J. Young		Border Regiment
Lieutenant	G. H. Brashaw, M.M.	Quartermaster	
Captain	T. C. MacInnes, R.A.M.C.	Medical Officer	
Captain	T. Russel, R.A. Ch.D.	Chaplain Joined 18.6.42	

All the above, except those noted, joined the Battalion and assumed their appointments on or before the 1st June, 1942.

OFFICERS OF THE 5TH BATTALION
3rd JULY 1943

T/Lieut-Colonel	Robert Brian James, D.S.O. & Bar	C.O.	Essex Regiment Regular Army Killed in action N.W.Europe 3.8.44
T/Major	Andrew William Edgar	2 i/c	Regular Army
T/Major	J. H. F. Dixon		
T/Major	A. R. A. Wilson, M.C.		
T/Captain	D. J. Penwill, D.S.O.		
T/Captain	W. Sugarman		
T/Captain	H. C. Cocking		Killed in action N.W.Europe 11.6.44 (Major)
T/Captain	F. Holtby		
T/Captain	L. E. L. Steele	Adjutant	Royal Berkshire Regiment
Captain	J. R. H Owen		Manchester Regiment
T/Captain	A. M. N. Rice		Northamptonshire Regiment
T/Captain	F. E. Donkersley		Duke of Wellington's Regt.
T/Captain	T. A. J. Hill	M.T.O.	Royal Berkshire Regt. T/
Captain	W. Watney		Royal Fusiliers
Lieutenant	T. G. Fenwick		
Lieutenant	E. J. Boyce		
Lieutenant	H. A. Lewisohn		Bedfordshire & Hertfordshire Regt
Lieutenant	T. F. Lowe		Suffolk Regiment
Lieutenant	J. H. White		South Lancashire Regiment
Lieutenant	W. J. Soaft		East Surrey Regiment
Lieutenant	A. L. Davis		West Yorkshire Regt.
Lieutenant	K. C. Harrison		West Yorkshire Regt.
Lieutenant	E. Smith		Bedfordshire & Hertfordshire Regiment
Lieutenant	A.B. Oram		Leicestershire Regt.
Lieutenant	R. Clifford		Gloucestershire Regt.
Lieutenant	G.R. Earle-Welby		Devonshire Regiment
Lieutenant	H. Morgan		Welch Regiment
Lieutenant	E. C. Johnson		East Lancashire Regt.
2nd Lieutenant	J. R. May		
2nd Lieutenant	D. G. Stanley		Killed in action Sicily. 15th July, 43.
2nd Lieutenant	T.A. Watts		
Lieutenant	G. Petre	Quartermaster	
Captain	R. F. Clarke, R.A.M.C.	Medical Officer	
Captain	K. Baker, R.A.Ch.D.	Chaplain	

OFFICERS OF THE 5TH BATTALION ON THE 31st MAY, 1944

Rank	Name	Appointment	Remarks
T/Lieut.-Colonel	Gilbert William White, M.B.E.		King's Royal Rifle Corps Regular Army
T/Major	J. H. F. Dixon	2 i/c	Killed in actionN.W Europe 11.6.44
T/Major	C. W. S. Belas		
T/Major	A. N. Rice		Northamptonshire Regiment.
A/Major	H. C. Cocking		Killed in action. N.W.Europe 11.6.44
A/Major	K. C. Harrison		West Yorkshire Regt.
T/Captain	W. Sugarman		
T/Captain	T. A. J. Hill	M.T.O.	Royal Berkshire Regt.
T/Captain	F. E. Donkersley	Carriers	Duke of Wellington's
T/Captain	W. Watney, M.C.	Anti-tank	Royal Fusiliers
T/Captain	T. G. Fenwick	Adjutant	
T/Captain	W. J. Soaft		East Surrey Regt.
A/Captain	J. H. White		South Lancashire Regt.
A/Captain	A. Consitt		
A/Captain	E. J. Crews		Died of wounds. N.W.Europe. 11.9.44
Lieutenant	J. M. Danby		
Lieutenant	T. F. Lowe, M.C.		Suffolk Regiment
Lieutenant	A. L. Davis		West Yorkshire Regt.
Lieutenant	R. Clifford		Gloucestershire Regt.
Lieutenant	H. Morgan		Welch Regiment
Lieutenant	T. A. Watts		
Lieutenant	P. B. Branson		
Lieutenant	D. F. Mundy		
Lieutenant	R. Cheney		Killed in action. N.W.Europe 16.6.44
Lieutenant	M. P. Piers		King's Regiment (Rhodesia)
Lieutenant	F. A. G. Dean		Royal Fusiliers
Lieutenant	J. R. Welch		
Lieutenant	J. L. Sykes		Killed in action. N.W.Europe 11.6.44
Lieutenant	R. Appleton		Died of Wounds. N.W.Europe 6.6.44
Lieutenant	N. B. Cook		
2nd Lieutenant	W. H. J. McIlroy		Killed in action. N.W.Europe. 6.6.40
2nd Lieutenant	D. J. Smith		
2nd Lieutenant	J. Grieve		
2nd Lieutenant	N. W. J. White		
Lieutenant	?, Petre	Quartermaster	
Captain	W. R. Lamb, R.A.M.C.	Medical Officer	
Captain	K. Baker, R.A.Ch.D.	Chaplain	

Lieutenant M. P. Piers was one of several officers of the Dominion Forces who volunteered for service with the British Army in the campaign in Normandy.

AWARD OF THE VICTORIA CROSS PRIVATE ERIC ANDERSON

5th Battalion, East Yorkshire Regiment, T.A. Won at Wadi Akarit, Tunisia, 6th April 1943.

Private Eric Anderson was a stretcher bearer in "A" Company. When the advance was stalled and the company pulled back, leaving behind on the crest of a hill, some wounded men who were pinned down by enemy fire on the crest of a hill and unable to crawl to safety.

The citation reads:

'Private Anderson seeing these men lying wounded in No-Man's-Land, quite regardless of his own safety, went forward alone through intense fire and single-handed carried back a wounded soldier to a place of safety where medical attention could be given.

Knowing that more men were lying wounded in the open, located a second wounded man and carried him to safety. Pte Anderson went forward once again and safely rescued a third casualty.

Without any hesitation or consideration for himself, he went out a fourth time, but now he was the only target the enemy had to shoot at and when he reached the fourth wounded man, and was administering first-aid so he could prepare for the return journey, he himself was hit and mortally wounded.

Private Anderson, by his valour, complete disregard for his own safety. and courage under fire, probably saved the lives of three of his comrades, and his example was an inspiration to all who witnessed his gallant acts.'

Pte. Anderson was 27 years of age. He joined the Army in June, 1940, was married for only a few days when he was posted abroad and killed on the day of his first wedding anniversary. He was an only son and his mother died of shock soon after. Before the war he sang in the Choir at Eccleshill Parish Church, Bradford. The Victoria Cross was presented to his widow Irene by King George VI in October, 1943.

Born at Fagley, Eccleshill, Bradford, Yorkshire, 15th September 1915. Memorials at Sfax War Cemetery, Tunisia, Thornbury Boys' School, Bradford, Beverley Minster, and St. John's United Reformed Church, Bradford.

A photograph along with details of his life appears in Bradford City Hall. Newspaper cuttings, other photographs and material are on view in glass cabinets to visitors to City Hall

His Victoria Cross in now in the Regimental Museum at 3 Tower Street, York.

BATTLE HONOURS GAINED BY THE 5th BATTALION

Defence of Arras	19th-24th May, 1940	Shared with 4th Battalion
North-West Europe 1940-42*	19th May,1940- 31st May, 1940	Shared with 2nd & 4th
Gazala	26th May-21st June, 1942	Shared with the 4th
Mersa Matruh	26th-30th June, 1942	
Defence of the Alamein Line	1st-27th June, 1942	
El Alamein	23rd October-4th Nov.1942	
Mareth	16th-23rd March, 1943	
Wadi Zigzaou	20th-23rd March, 1943	
Akarit	6th-7th April, 1943	
North Africa 1942-43	12th June, 1940- 12th May, 1943	Shared with 4th Battalion
Primosole Bridge	13th-18th July, 1943	
Sicily 1943	9th July-17th August, 1943	
Normandy Landing	6th June, 1944	Shared with 2nd Battalion
Tilly sur Seulles	14th-19th June, 1944	
Mont Pincon	30th July-9th August, 1944	
St. Pierre La Valle	9th-16th August, 1944	
Gheel	8th-11th September, 1944	
Nederrijn	17th-27th September, 1944	
Aam	1st-4th October, 1944	
North West Europe 1944-45	6th June, 1944- 5th May, 1945	Shared with 2nd Battalion

*This Battle Honour covers the period 19th May, 1940-18th June, 1940. It was extended to the 19th August, 1942, to cover the raid at Dieppe by forces of the Canadian Army on the 19th August, 1942 and to include the raid by a detachment of the 2nd Parachute Regiment on the night of the 27th-28th February, 1942 on the radiolocation site at Bruneval on the French coast when equipment was brought back to England; and the raid by Canadian forces on the 27th-28th March, 1942 on the harbour installations at St. Nazaire.

The dates given for the 5th Battalion are from the commencement of the battle until evacuation from Dunkirk on the 31st May. The 2nd and 4th Battalions embarked at Dunkirk on the 2nd June, 1940.

A Battle Honour **Dunkirk 1940** covering the period 26th May-3rd June, 1940, was awarded to those units taking part in the defence of Dunkirk but not to those passing through. It was gained for the Regiment by the 2nd and 4th Battalions. One company of the 5th Battalion was co-opted by the 4th Battalion on the 29th May and played a part in that Battalion's defence of Houtem on the night of the 29th-30th May and the next day, but the numbers involved did not qualify the Battalion for the award of the Honour.

GLOSSARY - SECOND WORLD WAR

ADGB	Air Defence of Great Britain
AVRE	Armoured Vehicle Royal Engineers
Battalion	Basic Infantry Unit of 600 – 1000 men, subdivided into four rifle companies and a support company of 100 men, each with anti-tank guns, heavy machine guns and mortars. Rifle companies divided into platoons of three or four rifle squads.
BEF	British Expeditionary Force.
BGS	Brigadier General Staff
Bren	0.303 British light machine-gun
Brigade	British name for a formation normally composed of three or four infantry or tank battalions.
CIGS	Chief of the Imperial General Staff
Corps	A group of divisions under command of a lieutenant-general, the number and identity varying according to the task for which the corps was employed.
CP	Command Post
CQMS.	Company Quarter-Master-Sergeant
CSM	Company Sergeant-Major
DD	Duplex-Drive amphibious Sherman tank
DF	Defensive fire
Division	A formation command by a major-general comprising 12 – 18,000 men. An armoured division normally comprised two tank brigades and one infantry.
DCM	Distinguished Conduct Medal
DSO	Distinguished Service Order
DUKW	Duplex-Drive amphibious truck
Flail	A tank fitted with heavy chains on a revolving drum that beat the ground in front of the vehicle for clearing mines. Initially fitted to Matilda, Crusader and Grant tanks (Balron, Scorpion I and II). The system was latterly fitted to Sherman tanks, the rotor being powered by a take off from the main engine.
GHQ	General Headquarters
GOC	General Officer Commanding
GOC-in-C	General Officer Commanding in Chief
GSO	General Staff Officer.
HE	High Explosive
LCA	Landing Craft Assault
LCT	Landing Craft Tank
LCVP	Landing Craft Vehicle and personnel
LST	Landing Ship Tank
LMG	Light Machine Gun – Sten
MM	Military Medal
MC	Military Cross
MMG	Medium Machine Gun
NCO	Non-commissioned officer
ODs	American army combat clothing.
OKW	Oberkommando der Wehrmacht – German Armed Forces High Command
OP	Observation Post.
Petard	Short-range tank-mounted mortar with high explosives,
PIAT	Projector Infantry Anti-tank – British hand-hel platoon anti-tank weapon.
Priest	British self-propelled 25-pdr guns mounted on tank chassis..
SHAEF	Supreme Headquarters Allied Expeditionary Force.
Spandau	Allied name for the rapid firing German 7.92 Mauser MG34 machine-gun and its successor, the MG42 machine-gun.
TD	Territorial Decoration
Vickers	British 0.303 water-cooled heavy machine-gun used by infantry battalions.

BIBLIOGRAPHY

Baker, A., *Battle Honours of the British and Commonwealth Armies* (London, Ian Allan, 1986).

Barker, A. J., *The East Yorkshire Regiment* (London, Leo Cooper, 1971).

Barnes, B.S., *The Sign of the Double 'T': the 50th Northumbrian Division, July 1943 to December 1944* (Hull, Sentinel Press, 1999).

Barnett, Corelli, *The Desert Generals* (London, Kimber, 1960).

Belchem, D., *Victory in Normandy* (London, Chatto & Windus, 1981).

Bredin, A. E. C., *Three Assault Landings: the Story of the 1st Battalion, The Dorsetshire Regiment in Sicily, Italy and N.W. Europe* (Aldershot, Gale & Polden, 1946).

Churchill, Winston S., *The Second World War* (London, Cassell, 1959).

Clay, E. W., *The Path of the 50th: the Story of the 50th Northumbrian Division in the Second World War 1939-45* (Aldershot, Gale & Polden, 1950).

Colville, J. R., *Man of Valour: Field Marshal Lord Gort* (London, Collins, 1972).

Crookenden, Arthur, *History of the Cheshire Regiment in the Second World War* (Chester, Evans, n.d.).

D'Este, Carlo, *Decision in Normandy* (London, Collins, 1983).

The 8th Battalion, Durham Light Infantry 1939-45 (London, London Stamp Exchange, 1990).

Ellis, L. F., *War in France and Flanders 1939-40* (London, H.M.S.O., 1953).

Hamilton, Nigel, *Monty: the Making of a General* (London, Hodder & Stoughton, 1981).

Hamilton, Nigel, *Monty: Master of the Battlefield 1942-44* (London, Hodder & Stoughton, 1983).

Hamilton, Nigel, *Monty: the Field Marshal 1944-76* (London, Hodder & Stoughton, 1986).

Hamilton, Nigel, *Monty: the Battles of Field Marshal Bernard Law Montgomery* (London, Hodder & Stoughton, 1994).

Hart, B. L., *The Second World War* (London, Cassell, 1970).

Hastings, Max, *Overlord: D-Day and the Battle for Normandy 1944* (London, Joseph, 1984).

How, J. J., *Normandy: the British breakout* (London, Kimber, 1981).

Laffin, John, *British V.C.s of World War 2: a Study in Heroism* (Stroud, Sutton, 1997).

Lewis, P. J. & English, I. R., *Into battle with the Durhams: the 8th Battalion Durham Light Infantry 1939-45* (Newcastle-on-Tyne, Bealls, 1949).

Montgomery, Field Marshal Viscount, of Alamein, *Memoirs* (London, Collins, 1958).

Mullaly, B. R., *The South Lancashire Regiment (Prince of Wales's Volunteers)* (Bristol, White Swan Press, 1955).

Nicholson, N., *Alex* (London, Weidenfeld, 1973).

Nicholson, W. N., *The Suffolk Regiment 1928 to 1946* (Ipswich, East Anglian Magazine, 1948).

Nightingale, P. R., *History of the East Yorkshire Regiment (Duke of York's Own) in the War 1939/45* (York, the Regiment, 1952).

Norfolk, R. W. S., *Militia, Yeomanry and Volunteer Forces of the East Riding 1689-1908* (York, East Yorkshire Local History Society, 1965).

Reeves, Valerie & Showan, Valerie, *Dan Billany: Hull's Lost Hero* (Hull, Kingston Press, 1991).

Rissik, D., *The D.L.I. at War 1939 to 1945* (Brancepeth Castle, the Regiment, 1953).

Ryan, Cornelius, *The Longest Day* (London, Gollancz, 1959).

Stacey, C. P., *The Canadian Army in the Second World War, Volume 3: the Victory Campaign* (Ottawa, Queen's Printer, 1960).

Synge, W. A. T., *The Story of the Green Howards 1939-45* (Richmond, the Regiment, 1952).

Ward, Major T. L., transcripts of tapes held at the Imperial War Museum.

Warner, J. K., *History of the 3rd Reconnaissance Regiment (Northumberland Fusiliers)* (unpublished manuscript).

Whiting, Charles & Taylor, Eric, *Fighting Tykes: the Yorkshire Regiments in WWII* (London, Leo Cooper, 1993).

Wilmot, Chester, *The Struggle for Europe* (London, Collins, 1952).

Wilson, R. & Collinson, G. A., *East Yorkshire Volunteer Infantry 1859-1908* (Hull, Fineprint, 1982).

Wyatt, W., *Confessions of an Optimist* (London, Collins, 1985).

INDEX